AI and Sustainability for Global Security

Amal Jmaii
https://orcid.org/0000-0002-6918-9839
University of Tunis el Manar, Tunisia

IGI Global
Scientific Publishing
Publishing Tomorrow's Research Today

Vice President of Editorial Melissa Wagner
Director of Acquisitions Mikaela Felty
Director of Book Development Jocelynn Hessler
Production Manager Mike Brehm
Cover Design Jose Rosado

Published in the United States of America by
IGI Global Scientific Publishing
701 East Chocolate Avenue
Hershey, PA, 17033, USA
Tel: 717-533-8845 | Fax: 717-533-7115
Website: https://www.igi-global.com E-mail: cust@igi-global.com

Library of Congress Cataloging-in-Publication Data

Names: Jmaii, Amal, 1984- editor
Title: AI and sustainability for global security / edited by Amal Jmaii.
Other titles: Artificial intelligence and sustainability for global security
Description: Hershey, PA : IGI Global Scientific Publishing, [2026] | Includes bibliographical references and index. | Summary: "This book aims to explore the multifaceted role that artificial intelligence (AI) can play in advancing sustainability while addressing critical global security challenges"-- Provided by publisher.
Identifiers: LCCN 2025011873 (print) | LCCN 2025011874 (ebook) | ISBN 9798337310770 h/c | ISBN 9798337310787 s/c | ISBN 9798337310794 ebook
Subjects: LCSH: Artificial intelligence--Environmental applications | Sustainability http://id.loc.gov/authorities/subjects/sh2009000375 | Artificial intelligence--Security measures--Government policy--International cooperation
Classification: LCC GE45.D37 A523 2026 (print) | LCC GE45.D37 (ebook) | DDC 304.20285/63--dc23/eng/20250612
LC record available at https://lccn.loc.gov/2025011873
LC ebook record available at https://lccn.loc.gov/2025011874

British Cataloguing in Publication Data
A Cataloguing in Publication record for this book is available from the British Library.

Table of Contents

Preface ix

Chapter 1
AI Approaches to Diversity and Inclusion in Hospitality 1
Mohammad Badruddoza Talukder, International University of Business Agriculture and Technology, Bangladesh
Sanjeev Kumar, Lovely Professional University, India
Kuldeep Singh, Amity University, Gurugram, India

Chapter 2
AI for Environmental Sustainability 29
G. R. Manjunathareddy, Bangalore University, India

Chapter 3
Dynamic Interactions Between Economic Growth, Renewable Energy, and CO_2 Emissions in Norway Using a Fourier-Augmented ARDL Model 73
Nerimene Gzara, University of Tunis el Manar, Tunisia
Amal Jmaii, University of Tunis El Manar, Tunisia

Chapter 4
Future of AI in Global Sustainability 113
Satya Subrahmanyam, Holy Spirit University of Kaslik, Lebanon

Chapter 5
Hydrogen Supply Chain Effectiveness: Conceptualizing Uncertainties Through Genetic Simulations 155
Nishtha Chhabra, M.S. Ramaiah University of Applied Sciences, India
Rudrodip Majumdar, National Institute of Advanced Studies, Bengaluru, India
Tapasi Ghosh, M.S. Ramaiah University of Applied Sciences, India
T. Subramanyam, M.S. Ramaiah University of Applied Sciences, India

Chapter 6
Sustainable AI Technologies: Challenges and Opportunities 197
Mohammad A. Al Khaldy, Department of Business Intelligence and Data Analytics, University of Petra, Jordan
Amjad Aldweesh, College of Computing and Information Technology, Shaqra University, Shaqra, Saudi Arabia
Ahmad Al-Qerem, Computer Science Department, Faculty of Information Technology, Zarqa University, Zarqa, Jordan
Mohammad Alauthman, Department of Information Security, University of Petra, Amman, Jordan
Ammar Almomani, Department of Computer Information Science, Higher Colleges of Technology, Sharjah, UAE
Mouhammd Alkasassbeh, Princess Sumaya University for Technology, Jordan

Chapter 7
The Green Finance: AI's Contribution to Environmental Sustainability 225
Chedlia Farhat, Faculty of Economic Sciences and Management of Tunis, Tunisia
Mouna Mouelhi, Faculty of Economic Sciences and Management of Tunis, Tunisia

Compilation of References 251

About the Contributors 293

Index 301

Detailed Table of Contents

Preface ix

Chapter 1
AI Approaches to Diversity and Inclusion in Hospitality 1
Mohammad Badruddoza Talukder, International University of Business Agriculture and Technology, Bangladesh
Sanjeev Kumar, Lovely Professional University, India
Kuldeep Singh, Amity University, Gurugram, India

Incorporating Artificial Intelligence in the hotel business has also presented new opportunities for promoting diversity and inclusion. This chapter analyzes the role of AI-based tools and techniques in making the workforce more diverse, improving the experience of inclusive hospitality, and promoting fair treatment in hospitality functions. AI helps promote personnel knowledge about inclusiveness and cultural sentiments by offering virtual and tailor-made learning opportunities. The chapter discusses the pitfalls and ethical issues of applying AI for diversity and inclusiveness purposes, including concerns over the algorithms' reliability and problems regarding the privacy of information used. Instances of confirmed cases where the AI-driven inclusivity strategies worked successfully among different hospitality businesses are discussed in detail. On conscious cross-pollination of ideas, this chapter demonstrates how hospitality leadership can and should take advantage of AI as instrumental in enabling employee and guest diversity and inclusion.

Chapter 2
AI for Environmental Sustainability 29
G. R. Manjunathareddy, Bangalore University, India

The accelerating pace of global environmental degradation—from climate change to biodiversity loss—demands bold and innovative solutions. This chapter explores how artificial intelligence (AI) is emerging as a transformative force in tackling these challenges. By harnessing technologies such as machine learning, computer vision, and natural language processing, AI offers unprecedented capabilities for monitoring ecosystems, forecasting climate impacts, managing resources efficiently, and guiding sustainable development. AI with complementary technologies like IoT, GIS, and cloud computing enhances data-driven decision-making across agriculture, urban planning, energy, water, and biodiversity conservation. However, the application of AI also raises ethical, social, and environmental concerns that must be addressed to ensure responsible and inclusive deployment. Through a multidisciplinary lens, this chapter examines AI's potential, limitations, and implications in advancing environmental sustainability, aiming to inform policy and practice for a resilient and equitable future.

Chapter 3
Dynamic Interactions Between Economic Growth, Renewable Energy, and CO_2 Emissions in Norway Using a Fourier-Augmented ARDL Model 73
Nerimene Gzara, University of Tunis el Manar, Tunisia
Amal Jmaii, University of Tunis El Manar, Tunisia

This study investigates the relationship between renewable energy consumption, technological innovation, economic growth, and CO_2 emissions in Norway from 1990 to 2021 using the Fourier-Augmented ARDL model. The long-run results show that GDP growth increases emissions, while renewable energy and patent activity contribute to emissions reduction. In the short run, GDP significantly impacts emissions, whereas the effects of renewable energy and innovation are limited. These findings highlight the importance of sustained investments in green technologies and energy transition policies. The study provides new empirical evidence for the role of innovation and renewables in decarbonizing high-income economies

Chapter 4
Future of AI in Global Sustainability 113
Satya Subrahmanyam, Holy Spirit University of Kaslik, Lebanon

The integration of artificial intelligence (AI) into global sustainability presents a transformative opportunity to address critical challenges such as climate change, resource depletion, and social inequities. This chapter explores AI's role in achieving the United Nations Sustainable Development Goals (SDGs) through innovative applications in environmental conservation, resource efficiency, and social impact. It examines AI-driven advancements in climate modeling, renewable energy optimization, and equitable economic development. Additionally, the chapter highlights challenges including ethical concerns, technological limitations, and policy gaps. Future trends, such as AI-IoT convergence and international collaborations, are discussed as key drivers of sustainable innovation. Through case studies and policy recommendations, this chapter provides a roadmap for leveraging AI to build a more sustainable and equitable world.

Chapter 5
Hydrogen Supply Chain Effectiveness: Conceptualizing Uncertainties Through Genetic Simulations 155
Nishtha Chhabra, M.S. Ramaiah University of Applied Sciences, India
Rudrodip Majumdar, National Institute of Advanced Studies, Bengaluru, India
Tapasi Ghosh, M.S. Ramaiah University of Applied Sciences, India
T. Subramanyam, M.S. Ramaiah University of Applied Sciences, India

The shift from carbonaceous sources to cleaner alternatives necessitates reorienting and optimizing energy supply chains. Despite technological advancements, energy security remains susceptible to disruptions caused by geopolitical tensions, resource constraints, and market fluctuations. This chapter explores how genetic simulations, leveraging metaheuristic optimization techniques, facilitate a trade-off between the resilience and cost-effectiveness of green hydrogen supply chains. A data-driven case study examines the first-level viability of the envisaged green hydrogen system, covering prominent pathways for production, storage, and transportation and distribution (T&D). Scenarios are ranked based on cost per tonne for production, storage, and T&D. Prima facie viable cases are further discussed considering supply chain vulnerability under geopolitical and logistical constraints. Such studies help strategize long-term energy security for developing economies like India.

Chapter 6
Sustainable AI Technologies: Challenges and Opportunities 197
Mohammad A. Al Khaldy, Department of Business Intelligence and Data Analytics, University of Petra, Jordan
Amjad Aldweesh, College of Computing and Information Technology, Shaqra University, Shaqra, Saudi Arabia
Ahmad Al-Qerem, Computer Science Department, Faculty of Information Technology, Zarqa University, Zarqa, Jordan
Mohammad Alauthman, Department of Information Security, University of Petra, Amman, Jordan
Ammar Almomani, Department of Computer Information Science, Higher Colleges of Technology, Sharjah, UAE
Mouhammd Alkasassbeh, Princess Sumaya University for Technology, Jordan

Sustainable AI merges artificial intelligence (AI) development with ecological, social, and economic resilience. It addresses energy consumption, resource management, ethical implications, and policy integration. This chapter explores current practices, identifies challenges, and uncovers opportunities for developing systems that align with sustainable goals. It reviews existing research on carbon footprints, data governance, ethical frameworks, public policy, and cross-sector collaboration. It also analyzes potential methods to measure and mitigate AI's environmental impact, with illustrative tables and diagrams spread throughout. Finally, the chapter offers an outlook on integrating these findings into a cohesive vision for sustainable AI, bridging academic and industry efforts, and enhancing practical governance frameworks.

Chapter 7
The Green Finance: AI's Contribution to Environmental Sustainability 225
Chedlia Farhat, Faculty of Economic Sciences and Management of Tunis, Tunisia
Mouna Mouelhi, Faculty of Economic Sciences and Management of Tunis, Tunisia

This study examines the interplay between artificial intelligence, sustainable finance, and environmental sustainability in four OECD countries from 2007 to 2023. Using the panel ARDL method, our analysis shows that AI reduces carbon emissions, particularly in the long run. Initially, AI investments lead to a temporary rise in emissions due to implementation costs, but this trend reverses over time, aiding carbon neutrality and supporting SDGs, especially SDG 7 and SDG 13. The findings stress the need for short-term fiscal incentives and long-term regulatory frameworks integrating AI into sustainable finance. This research enriches the literature by addressing AI's overlooked role in sustainability and providing policy insights. Future studies could expand the geographic scope and examine AI's specific contributions to sustainable finance.

Compilation of References 251

About the Contributors 293

Index 301

Preface

INTRODUCTION

As the Editor of *AI and Sustainability for Global Security*, it is my privilege to introduce a volume that engages with one of the most consequential intersections of our time: the convergence of artificial intelligence, sustainability, and global security. We are living in an era marked by accelerating technological change alongside escalating global challenges—climate disruption, resource depletion, public health emergencies, and persistent geopolitical tensions. These forces are deeply interconnected, and addressing them in isolation is no longer sufficient.

Artificial intelligence has emerged as a powerful catalyst with the potential to reshape how societies understand, anticipate, and respond to these challenges. From optimizing energy systems and strengthening climate resilience to enhancing healthcare delivery and informing security strategies, AI offers unprecedented tools for innovation and problem-solving. Yet, alongside these opportunities lie profound risks. Ethical concerns, governance gaps, unequal access, and the potential misuse of AI—particularly in military, surveillance, or coercive contexts—raise urgent questions about how these technologies should be developed, deployed, and regulated.

This edited volume was conceived in response to these tensions. Its objective is not merely to celebrate technological progress, but to critically examine the conditions under which AI can contribute meaningfully to sustainability and global security. The chapters collected here explore both promise and peril, emphasizing that responsible AI development must be grounded in ethical frameworks, inclusive governance, and international cooperation. Contributors from diverse disciplinary and professional backgrounds offer insights into how AI can be leveraged to address climate change, resource scarcity, public health crises, and geopolitical instability, while also safeguarding human rights, equity, and global stability.

The book is intended for a broad yet interconnected audience. Policymakers, researchers, and professionals working at the nexus of technology, sustainability, and security will find rigorous analyses and forward-looking perspectives. Scholars and students in artificial intelligence, environmental science, international relations, and security studies will benefit from the interdisciplinary approach and critical reflections presented throughout. Business leaders and innovators in sectors such as energy, agriculture, healthcare, and technology will gain valuable insights into how AI-driven solutions can align economic progress with sustainable and secure outcomes. Equally, government officials and regulators engaged in shaping technology policy and international cooperation will find the discussions of governance and geopolitical implications particularly relevant.

Ultimately, *AI and Sustainability for Global Security* seeks to contribute to a larger conversation about the kind of future we wish to build. It argues that AI, when guided by shared values and collective responsibility, can be a powerful force for advancing sustainability, strengthening peace, and promoting global well-being. It is my hope that this volume will inform, challenge, and inspire readers to engage thoughtfully with AI—not only as a technological tool, but as a socio-political force capable of shaping a more secure, equitable, and sustainable world.

ORGANIZATION OF THE BOOK

Chapter 1: AI Approaches to Diversity and Inclusion in Hospitality

The opening chapter situates artificial intelligence within the human-centered domain of hospitality, demonstrating how technological innovation can advance diversity, equity, and inclusion in service-oriented industries. It examines AI-driven tools for recruitment, training, and guest engagement, showing how personalized learning systems and data-informed decision-making can enhance cultural sensitivity and fair treatment. At the same time, the chapter does not shy away from critical concerns, addressing ethical pitfalls such as algorithmic bias, data privacy, and the reliability of automated systems. By grounding its discussion in real-world hospitality cases, this chapter underscores how responsible AI adoption can support inclusive leadership practices and enrich both employee and guest experiences.

Chapter 2: AI for Environmental Sustainability

This chapter broadens the discussion to the planetary scale, exploring AI as a transformative enabler of environmental sustainability. Through a multidisciplinary lens, it illustrates how machine learning, computer vision, and natural language processing—often combined with IoT, GIS, and cloud technologies—are reshaping environmental monitoring, climate forecasting, and resource management. Applications across agriculture, energy, water systems, urban planning, and biodiversity conservation are critically examined. Importantly, the chapter balances optimism with caution, engaging ethical, social, and environmental concerns surrounding AI deployment and emphasizing the need for inclusive and responsible governance to ensure that sustainability gains are equitably distributed.

Chapter 3: Dynamic Interactions Between Economic Growth, Renewable Energy, and CO_2 Emissions in Norway

Focusing on empirical evidence from a high-income economy, this chapter investigates the long- and short-run relationships among economic growth, renewable energy use, technological innovation, and carbon emissions in Norway. Employing a Fourier-Augmented ARDL model and data spanning three decades, the study reveals the complex trade-offs between growth and environmental impact. While GDP growth is shown to increase emissions, renewable energy adoption and innovation—captured through patent activity—contribute to long-term emissions reduction. This chapter offers valuable insights for policymakers by reinforcing the importance of sustained investment in green technologies and innovation-led energy transitions.

Chapter 4: Future of AI in Global Sustainability

Looking ahead, this chapter explores AI's evolving role in advancing global sustainability agendas, particularly the United Nations Sustainable Development Goals. It surveys emerging applications in climate modeling, renewable energy optimization, and socially inclusive economic development, while also addressing persistent challenges such as ethical risks, technological constraints, and policy fragmentation. By highlighting future trends—including AI–IoT convergence and international collaboration—the chapter presents a forward-looking roadmap for harnessing AI as a driver of sustainable innovation. Case studies and policy recommendations reinforce its central argument: that strategic, well-governed AI adoption can accelerate progress toward a more equitable and resilient global future.

Chapter 5: Hydrogen Supply Chain Effectiveness: Conceptualizing Uncertainties Through Genetic Simulations

This chapter addresses energy security through the lens of green hydrogen supply chains, a critical component of the global transition away from fossil fuels. Using genetic simulations and metaheuristic optimization techniques, it examines how resilience and cost-effectiveness can be balanced amid geopolitical, logistical, and market uncertainties. A data-driven case study evaluates production, storage, and transportation pathways, ranking scenarios by cost and vulnerability. With a particular focus on developing economies such as India, the chapter demonstrates how advanced modeling approaches can inform long-term energy planning and strengthen strategic decision-making under uncertainty.

Chapter 6: Sustainable AI Technologies: Challenges and Opportunities

This chapter turns the analytical lens inward, critically examining the sustainability of AI itself. It explores how AI development intersects with ecological, social, and economic resilience, addressing issues such as energy consumption, carbon footprints, data governance, ethical frameworks, and public policy. Drawing on current research and illustrative analyses, the chapter identifies both challenges and opportunities in aligning AI systems with sustainability goals. Its forward-looking outlook emphasizes cross-sector collaboration and the integration of academic and industry efforts, proposing pathways toward more coherent governance frameworks for sustainable AI technologies.

Chapter 7: The Green Finance: AI's Contribution to Environmental Sustainability

The final chapter bridges technology, finance, and environmental policy by examining AI's role in advancing green finance across selected OECD countries. Using panel ARDL analysis, it demonstrates that while AI investments may initially increase emissions due to implementation costs, their long-term impact is decisively beneficial, contributing to emissions reduction and progress toward carbon neutrality. The chapter highlights AI's alignment with key Sustainable Development Goals, particularly SDG 7 and SDG 13, and offers policy insights that balance short-term fiscal incentives with long-term regulatory strategies. By foregrounding AI's often-overlooked role in sustainable finance, this chapter closes the volume with a compelling case for integrated, data-driven approaches to environmental sustainability and global security.

CONCLUSION

As Editor, I conclude this volume with a renewed appreciation for both the promise and the responsibility embedded in the rapid advancement of artificial intelligence. *AI and Sustainability for Global Security* has brought together diverse perspectives that collectively demonstrate how AI is no longer a peripheral tool, but a central force shaping environmental stewardship, economic resilience, social inclusion, and global security architectures. Across sectors and regions, the chapters in this book illustrate that AI's true value lies not only in its technical capabilities, but in how thoughtfully and ethically those capabilities are aligned with broader societal goals.

The contributions underscore a recurring theme: sustainability and security are deeply interdependent, and AI sits at the nexus of this relationship. Whether applied to inclusive workforce practices, environmental monitoring, clean energy transitions, cyber-physical security, or sustainable finance, AI has the capacity to enhance decision-making, optimize complex systems, and anticipate emerging risks. At the same time, the volume makes clear that these benefits are neither automatic nor evenly distributed. Without robust governance, ethical oversight, and international cooperation, AI risks reinforcing inequalities, exacerbating environmental burdens, or introducing new forms of insecurity.

This book also highlights the importance of interdisciplinary and cross-sector collaboration. The challenges addressed herein—climate change, energy security, geopolitical instability, and social inequity—cannot be solved by technology alone. They demand coordinated efforts among policymakers, researchers, industry leaders, and civil society, supported by transparent data practices and inclusive policy frameworks. Several chapters point toward the need for long-term investment in innovation, capacity building, and regulatory systems that can evolve alongside technological change.

Ultimately, this volume is intended not as a definitive endpoint, but as a foundation for ongoing dialogue and action. We hope it encourages readers to think critically about how AI is designed, governed, and deployed, and to recognize their role in shaping its trajectory. If guided by shared values of sustainability, equity, and peace, artificial intelligence can become a powerful instrument for global good—helping to secure not only technological progress, but a more resilient, just, and sustainable future for generations to come.

Chapter 1
AI Approaches to Diversity and Inclusion in Hospitality

Mohammad Badruddoza Talukder
https://orcid.org/0009-0008-1662-9221
International University of Business Agriculture and Technology, Bangladesh

Sanjeev Kumar
https://orcid.org/0000-0002-7375-7341
Lovely Professional University, India

Kuldeep Singh
https://orcid.org/0000-0002-7999-1585
Amity University, Gurugram, India

ABSTRACT

Incorporating Artificial Intelligence in the hotel business has also presented new opportunities for promoting diversity and inclusion. This chapter analyzes the role of AI-based tools and techniques in making the workforce more diverse, improving the experience of inclusive hospitality, and promoting fair treatment in hospitality functions. AI helps promote personnel knowledge about inclusiveness and cultural sentiments by offering virtual and tailor-made learning opportunities. The chapter discusses the pitfalls

DOI: 10.4018/979-8-3373-1077-0.ch001

and ethical issues of applying AI for diversity and inclusiveness purposes, including concerns over the algorithms' reliability and problems regarding the privacy of information used. Instances of confirmed cases where the AI-driven inclusivity strategies worked successfully among different hospitality businesses are discussed in detail. On conscious cross-pollination of ideas, this chapter demonstrates how hospitality leadership can and should take advantage of AI as instrumental in enabling employee and guest diversity and inclusion.

INTRODUCTION

However, the issue is that several industries have now recognised AI as a disruptive force in their respective areas of work. The travel industry is among those promoting diversity and inclusion efforts. The hotel industry can utilise AI as a powerful mechanism for addressing a multitude of broad social and operational challenges, as it can handle large datasets of information and generate real-time insights. AI has been identified as one of the key valuable enablers to serve initiatives addressing bias removal, visitor experience enrichment, and accessibility improvement. This is significant because companies in this industry are shifting their focus from creating a homogeneous environment to one that is more diverse. This also corresponds with the broader trend towards a more diverse and equitable industry, which acknowledges that diversity can contribute. The fact that the business and guest experience impact sustainability is why businesses in the hotel sector have become successful in embracing diversity and inclusion around the world. From this standpoint, in accordance with the United Nations World Tourism Organisation (UNWTO), tourism and hospitality are fundamental in respecting the characteristics of community involvement, mitigating economic disparities, and promoting cultural enrichment. In the past few years, AI-based tools and solutions have become one of the assets that hospitality companies can utilise to enhance their effectiveness in these efforts. Well-established evidence to tackle unconscious biases, for instance, during the recruitment and selection of staff, such as personalised services made to fit individuals and populations with a diverse array of needs, including people with disabilities (Ivanov & Webster, 2019). The D&I strategies are varied, but AI in hospitality emerges to address the current struggles and facilitate sustainable growth of diverse, equal opportunities.

But despite all that has been said, there are challenges in using artificial intelligence when it comes to diversity and inclusion in the industry. Now, there is evidence of algorithmic bias; data privacy remains a significant problem; and third, organisations can only implement AI effectively with the right employee resources in place to control the use and deployment of AI tools. All of these questions underscore the importance of an ethical approach to the application of artificial intelligence. This ensures that AI success is achieved and provides, as noted by the relevant authorities, that ethical AI in services for diversity and inclusion should support industry players, governments, and research to be present and enforce laws, as well as set good governance for AI.

Therefore, this chapter focuses on understanding the impact of AI on diversity and inclusion in hospitality. It will also explore the advantages of AI and examine the debate and real-world considerations of this technology. This paper provides information on current approaches in AI for diversity and inclusion, as well as guidance on creating welcoming and fair environments in the long term. These are all ideas compiled from existing literature and case studies. The study presented in this paper aims to contribute to the ongoing discussion on how artificial intelligence can help shape a fairer and more efficient hospitality industry that meets the needs of all its stakeholders.

OBJECTIVES

1. To explore how AI technologies can enhance diversity and inclusion in the hospitality industry.
2. To examine the impact of AI on recruitment, guest services, and accessibility.
3. To analyse potential ethical concerns and the role of AI in maintaining inclusivity.
4. To propose recommendations for integrating AI into diversity and inclusion strategies in hospitality.

LITERATURE REVIEW

The concept of D&I emphasises the need for an inclusive environment where individuals can thrive, regardless of their background. Social Identity Theory and Unconscious Bias Theory explain how AI will help mitigate human biases. Such theories explain how people naturally relate to and favour those with similarities to themselves, hence the in-group bias that often leads to exclusionary behaviour. AI is entirely objective in data processing and creates opportunities to counteract biases, particularly in recruitment and offering personalised experiences to guests (Mohammad, 2020).

A transformational and complicated dynamic is revealed in the literature surrounding the application of artificial intelligence (AI) to improve diversity and inclusion in the hospitality sector. Traditional service forms have been rethought in response to the growing demand for inclusive and personalised guest experiences, driven by the expansion of hospitality enterprises into global markets. According to Ivanov and Webster (2019), artificial intelligence can provide data-driven insights and decision-making, which may help overcome human biases, increase operational efficiency, and promote inclusive experiences. Both capabilities support this change. The studies highlight obstacles, notably algorithmic biases, data privacy concerns, and ethical issues, that must be addressed to fully realise the potential of artificial intelligence in the hospitality industry. However, although AI technologies promise to encourage inclusion and diversity in this context, the studies also emphasise challenges.

By utilising machine learning algorithms that prioritise credentials and abilities over demographic characteristics, the application of artificial intelligence (AI) in recruiting for the hospitality industry has demonstrated the potential to mitigate bias (Li et al., 2021). Several studies have shown that artificial intelligence-driven recruiting technologies, such as applicant tracking systems (ATS), have the potential to streamline the hiring process by automating the screening of resumes and identifying candidates based solely on their merit. A more general industry aim is to establish a diverse team indicative of a worldwide client base, which aligns with that goal. On the other hand, scholars warn that biases entrenched in training datasets may unwittingly perpetuate or intensify prejudice (Raghavan et al., 2021).

Such biases in applicant selection may be replicated by AI algorithms trained on historical hiring practices, for example, if these methods have been shown to demonstrate bias in the past. Furthermore, this highlights the importance of algorithmic transparency and regular audits to mitigate the risk of potential harm.

Extensive studies have also been conducted on the role that artificial intelligence plays in enhancing the individualised experiences of guests. According to Wang et al. (2022), academics emphasise the potential of artificial intelligence to analyse vast quantities of visitor data and personalise services based on individual preferences. These preferences might include language preferences, dietary restrictions, and demands for accessibility from guests. According to Mohammad (2021), personalisation of this kind is especially beneficial in the hotel industry, where guests' satisfaction depends significantly on attentive and culturally sensitive interactions. The employment of chatbots powered by Natural Language Processing (NLP), for example, is becoming increasingly widespread to provide multilingual assistance and enable staff members to bridge language barriers efficiently.

Nevertheless, issues over privacy are a significant obstacle in this area, as AI-driven customisation necessitates the collection and processing of a substantial amount of data. The ethical balance between providing tailored services and preserving guests' privacy remains a topic of continuous debate in the literature. Recommendations often focus on establishing transparent data practices and obtaining explicit guest consent (Floridi et al., 2018).

Much emphasis has also been placed on the function of artificial intelligence, facilitating accessibility within hospitality environments. In the literature, numerous artificial intelligence-powered solutions are highlighted. These tools include voice-activated room controls and real-time captioning systems, which enable guests with impairments to access services more autonomously (Chen & Hu, 2020). Mohammad (2024) highlighted the fact that these innovations not only comply with accessibility criteria but also enhance the inclusiveness of the guest experience and increase guest satisfaction. Despite these advancements, many argue that artificial intelligence should not replace human connection, as the personal touch of hospitality remains quite significant. It is believed that striking a balance between the effectiveness of artificial intelligence and human connection is essential to ensure inclusion in hospitality settings that are enabled by AI (Saxena & Khandelwal, 2020).

When deploying artificial intelligence, ethical AI frameworks in the hospitality industry highlight the importance of justice, transparency, and responsibility. Because artificial intelligence systems have the potential to influence employment decisions, customer interactions, and the services provided, hospitality firms must establish policies and procedures that uphold ethical standards. Moral norms are essential for preventing misuse, protecting visitor data, and fostering trust among staff and guests. According to Florida et al. (2018), academics advocate for stringent rules for data storage, human oversight in decision-making processes, and transparent information regarding the role of artificial intelligence in hospitality services. In an industry that relies on trust and connections with customers, addressing these ethical concerns is crucial to ensure the sustainable adoption of artificial intelligence.

According to a study conducted, artificial intelligence (AI) offers significant prospects for enhancing diversity and inclusion in the hotel sector; however, several obstacles remain to be overcome. Addressing algorithmic biases, ensuring ethical data practices, and striking a balance between AI-enabled efficiency and individualised, human-centred service are among the challenges that need to be addressed. Future studies are necessary to further develop the application of artificial intelligence in the hotel industry, with a particular emphasis on inclusive design principles, ethical considerations, and culturally sensitive AI systems. By bridging these gaps, the hotel sector has the potential to employ artificial intelligence not just as a tool for operational efficiency but also as a method to create an atmosphere that is more welcoming and inclusive for visitors worldwide.

AI in Recruitment and Unbiased Hiring

One of the uses of artificial intelligence that has received the most significant attention for diversity and inclusion is the use of AI in recruiting. According to Miller and Smith (2019), artificial intelligence techniques, such as applicant tracking systems (ATS) and resume screening algorithms, have the potential to help reduce human biases. These tools concentrate entirely on applicants' credentials, abilities, and experiences rather than on demographic criteria such as gender, age, or race. According to the McKinsey & Company (2020) study, businesses that used AI-driven hiring tools experienced increased workforce diversity, particularly in leadership positions. Artificial intelligence can evaluate massive datasets to determine the characteristics of high-performing individuals. This provides objective insights that may be used to steer the recruiting process.

On the other hand, academics have expressed concerns over the possibility that artificial intelligence systems might perpetuate bias if they are trained on historical data that reflects current inequities (Dastin, 2018). One example is that if an artificial intelligence system is trained on data from a workforce predominantly comprised of men, it may inadvertently prefer male applicants. The design and training of these systems must be carefully monitored to ensure that they are fair. This is because artificial intelligence has the potential to minimise prejudice.

Personalised Guest Experiences and Inclusivity

An additional area of study in literature is the capacity of artificial intelligence to improve guests' experiences through customisation. According to Kumar et al. (2022), machine learning algorithms can assess client preferences and behaviours to provide individualised services that cater to a wide range of diversity in terms of cultural origins, dietary requirements, and accessibility needs. Artificial intelligence systems, for instance, can offer activities suitable for a particular culture or eating alternatives ideal for visitors with nutritional constraints, such as halal or kosher meals (Mohammad, 2025). The visitors are given the impression that their specific requirements are being considered and respected, which contributes to the development of a sense of inclusion. Artificial intelligence was utilised in a case study conducted by Marriott International to analyse customers' comments and preferences across various areas and provide individualised experiences to guests from diverse cultural backgrounds. According to Kuschel and Sanders' 2020 study, this resulted in increased levels of customer satisfaction and loyalty among a larger number of foreign tourists.

On the other hand, whereas there are obvious advantages to be gained from AI-driven customisation, there are also ethical considerations around data privacy. With improper management, the collection of massive volumes of data to personalise guests' experiences can potentially compromise the confidentiality of these guests. To protect guests' personal information, hotels must guarantee that they have adequate data protection procedures in place.

Artificial Intelligence (AI) in Hospitality

Several technologies that utilise machine learning, deep learning, and natural language processing are integral to the hospitality industry's artificial intelligence (AI) landscape. These technologies automate processes, optimise decision-making, and improve guest services. Artificial intelligence applications include chatbots, automated booking systems, and data analytics platforms that can anticipate guests' preferences and needs. Predictive analytics is a notable trend that enables hotels to forecast high-demand seasons, optimise room pricing, and tailor their marketing activities. This is a highly advantageous situation for hotels. Additionally, artificial intelligence plays a significant role in resource allocation by providing managers with real-time data that enables them to adjust personnel levels and manage inventories effectively (Lu et al., 2020; Ivanov & Webster, 2019).

On the other hand, deploying AI in the hotel industry is a complex process. There are several concerns regarding the privacy and security of data, particularly when handling sensitive information about guests. When artificial intelligence is used for decision-making, ethical concerns also arise because biases in algorithms might unwittingly impact how customers are treated and the quality of the service they get.

Diversity and Inclusion (D&I) in Hospitality

When it comes to creating a welcoming environment for visitors from diverse backgrounds, diversity and inclusion (D&I) are crucial. By fostering an inclusive culture in the workplace, diversity and inclusion tactics in the hotel industry enable the organisation to cater to a global clientele, enhance employee satisfaction, and improve retention rates (Talukder, 2025). Studies have shown that hospitality firms with diverse teams enjoy greater productivity and creativity. This is because varied views contribute to the successful resolution of complex customer service challenges (Saxena & Khandelwal, 2020; Singh et al., 2021). Providing tools that assist in monitoring diversity metrics, promoting fair recruitment practices, and supporting multicultural engagement initiatives are all examples of how artificial intelligence plays a crucial role in enhancing diversity and inclusion. AI has the potential to assist in personalising services that respect cultural and personal sensitivities, thereby establishing an inclusive atmosphere. This can be achieved by analysing data on visitor demographics and preferences.

Unbiased Hiring through AI

Using AI techniques in recruiting helps eliminate the possibility of prejudice in hiring decisions, thereby fostering equality through the objective evaluation of candidates. Resumés and profiles can be evaluated by algorithms, which concentrate on skill sets rather than personal identifiers (such as name, gender, or ethnicity), which might inadvertently affect human recruiters. This allows algorithms to make more informed hiring decisions. Applicant tracking systems (ATS) driven by artificial intelligence, for example, can screen enormous quantities of applications and determine the most qualified individuals based on their abilities and experience, without considering any irrelevant aspects (Raghavan et al., 2021; Li et al., 2021). Artificial intelligence may also identify biased wording in job descriptions, which helps hospitality organisations recruit a more diverse pool of applicants. However, there are certain drawbacks to using AI for recruiting, such as biased data, which might cause algorithmic evaluations to be inaccurate. To ensure fairness, continuous monitoring and modification of these algorithms are necessary.

Personalised Guest Experience

According to Talukder and Kumar (2024), artificial intelligence enables hyper-personalisation in the hospitality industry by analysing the preferences and behaviours of individual guests. This allows hotels to personalise their offerings to each unique client. To offer personalised suggestions, room settings, and experiences, machine learning algorithms analyse previous booking habits, feedback, and interactions to examine historical data, enabling the provision of tailored recommendations. For example, artificial intelligence can provide recommendations for activities, lodging amenities, or dining alternatives that align with a visitor's preferences, which increases the guest's level of satisfaction and loyalty (Wang et al., 2022; Tussyadiah, 2020). The potential for customisation offered by artificial intelligence also has implications for inclusion, as it enables hospitality organisations to cater to the specific needs of visitors from diverse backgrounds. On the other hand, preserving data privacy and protecting sensitive visitor information is a considerable concern. Artificial intelligence systems need access to substantial personal data to deliver a seamless experience.

Ethical AI

Regarding artificial intelligence applications, the ethical use of AI in the hospitality industry underscores the importance of justice, transparency, and accountability. The principles of ethical artificial intelligence ensure that judgments produced by AI are free from prejudice and that these systems protect the security of user data (Floridi et al., 2018). In the hotel industry, ethical artificial intelligence helps eliminate bias in visitor encounters, employment practices, and service customisation by developing algorithms that adhere to moral principles. The ethical deployment of artificial intelligence also includes openness, which means that consumers and staff are informed about AI applications that impact them. This transparency helps to cultivate confidence and facilitates the responsible deployment of AI. To ensure compliance and fairness, it is necessary to conduct regular reviews and external audits to guarantee ethical AI practices in the hotel industry.

Data-Driven Decision-Making in Hospitality

A decision-making process in the hospitality industry driven by data utilises artificial intelligence and big data analytics to analyse patterns in customer behaviour, operational efficiency, and market trends. By utilising predictive analytics, hotels can anticipate their guests' needs, optimise their resources, and enhance their service delivery. Using historical data, for example, artificial intelligence systems may assist in predicting peak seasons, adjusting personnel levels, and providing tailored marketing (Gretzel et al., 2021; Kim et al., 2019).

With the use of real-time data, hotels can make educated decisions that directly influence the enjoyment of their guests and their profitability. On the other hand, implementing data-driven decision-making requires a solid data architecture and a comprehensive understanding of privacy standards to secure visitor information effectively.

Language Accessibility Tools in Hospitality

Guests' pleasure can be negatively impacted by language barriers in the hospitality industry, particularly for international guests. To break down these boundaries, it is necessary to have translation tools powered by artificial intelligence, such as real-time translators and multilingual chatbots. These solutions utilise natural language processing (NLP) to accurately and instantly interpret and answer guests' requests, thereby enhancing accessibility and inclusivity (Chen & Hu, 2020; Fan et al., 2020).

For example, a multilingual artificial intelligence chatbot can respond to queries in various languages, making the experience more pleasant for guests. Because artificial intelligence may misread context-specific subtleties, it can be challenging to ensure high-quality translations and culturally sensitive responses, even though language accessibility tools are beneficial.

Employee Diversity Training With AI

Building cultural awareness among hospitality personnel is accomplished via simulations, virtual reality, and adaptive learning in employee diversity training driven by artificial intelligence. According to Huang and Back (2020) and Verma et al. (2021), these training programs utilise realistic scenarios that enable employees to practice their responses in high-stress circumstances or culturally diverse contexts. This helps employees develop more empathy and flexibility.

Artificial intelligence-based training systems enable the customisation of training modules to each employee's individual development through adaptive learning. This ensures that employees are well-prepared to handle a diverse range of customers. On the other hand, the dependence on AI-based training necessitates an initial investment and ongoing upgrades to meet the requirements of contemporary social norms and cultural trends.

Inclusive Customer Experience Through AI

Guest experience techniques in the hotel industry, powered by artificial intelligence, attempt to accommodate visitors from various backgrounds by anticipating their preferences and modifying services accordingly. According to Zheng et al. (2019), artificial intelligence systems may, for instance, provide insights into how specific visitor segments, such as those related to facilities or experiences, interact. This knowledge enables hotels to create a more inclusive service. Additionally, AI can monitor accessibility requirements, ensuring that services and accommodations are tailored to fit the needs of hotel customers with impairments (Talukder et al., 2023).

It is becoming widely acknowledged that providing an inclusive customer experience through AI enhances visitor loyalty, as it makes customers feel respected and understood. Nevertheless, the problem lies in ensuring that artificial intelligence models are trained on varied datasets to prevent the unintentional exclusion of minority groups.

AI-Driven Customer Personalisation

Artificial intelligence in hospitality enables the delivery of personalised suggestions and services to customers. Artificial intelligence systems can anticipate the demands of visitors and tailor their experience from check-in to check-out (Mao & Zhang, 2021; Talukder et al., 2024). This is accomplished by evaluating data such as previous preferences, booking patterns, and social media interactions. The targeted approach provided by this personality not only increases the level of happiness that guests feel but also motivates them to return for further business.

For instance, if a visitor routinely schedules spa services or purchases specific items, artificial intelligence might advise the staff to provide similar alternatives during their subsequent visit. However, a significant drawback is the difficulty of balancing personalisation and privacy, as excessive dependence on personal data may cause guests to be concerned about their privacy.

Challenges and Ethical Considerations in AI Deployment

Furthermore, literature emphasises the need to resolve the ethical concerns of using AI, even though AI has significant potential to promote diversity and inclusion in the hospitality industry. Several vital issues include algorithmic unfairness, data privacy, and the possibility that AI systems could exacerbate existing disparities (Talukder et al., 2025). There is a growing need for ethical rules to guarantee that AI-driven decision-making processes are transparent, fair, and responsible (Siau & Wang, 2020). This is because artificial intelligence is becoming increasingly integrated into hospitality operations. Ethics guidelines are necessary. As the literature notes, the teams responsible for developing AI also have a dearth of diversity. Artificial intelligence (AI) systems developed and tested by groups like these may inadvertently reflect the biases of the people who created them. As a result, ensuring fairness requires essential actions, such as incorporating diverse teams in the development of artificial intelligence and performing regular audits of AI systems to detect bias.

Findings from the Literature

The literature indicates that Artificial Intelligence (AI) is transforming Diversity and Inclusion (D&I) initiatives in the hotel sector by delivering crucial interventions in areas such as workforce equity, guest inclusiveness, and organisational transparency. Hiring & Transformative Tech By and large, Recruiters and Transformative Tech Scholars concur that talent and hiring are where AI is most often employed in service of the change we need. For instance, studies show that AI-driven hiring platforms can strip applications of demographic details such as gender, age, and ethnic background – meaning unconscious bias can be reduced and a more level playing field can be created for underrepresented communities. Nowhere is this philosophy more acutely applied than in hospitality, where a multicultural staff is essential to meeting the needs of international travellers.

The effect of AI on employee training and development is also a recurrent theme in the literature. Adaptive learning based on AI encourages learning programs in cultural sensitivity, gender inclusivity and disability awareness that cater to you. Using VR-based AI simulations, the inclusion of immersive technologies in work-integrated learning programs can enhance the development of empathy and intercultural capability through the virtual simulation of real-life scenarios, such as when an international guest speaks to an employee. These strategies not only enhance inclusivity within a workforce but also collectively improve service levels, as employees are empowered to cater to a broader range of guests.

With respect to guest service, the literature demonstrates that AI has the potential for increased accessibility and greater inclusivity. AI chatbots, live translation services, VA or voice bots are overcoming these limitations to engage guests intelligently from all four corners of the world and optimise cross-language communication. Similarly, accessibility-focused AI features, such as predictive directions for blind travellers or hotel rooms designed for wheelchair accessibility, have been hailed for expanding the reach of hospitality offerings. Hospitality companies that utilise such systems are not only compliant with international accessibility codes, but also able to service a larger, more diverse portion of the market, one that includes disabled travellers.

Similarly, relevant work includes data-driven monitoring of inclusivity. A.I.-driven sentiment analysis tools that track guest reviews, employee surveys and social media to help them identify more nuanced forms of exclusion or bias in their workplaces and in the guest experience. Such perspectives and real-time surveillance tools provide managers with an early warning system to adjust policies and interventions that may help save lives and mitigate the socioeconomic impact. AI-powered workforce analytics have also been purported to assist managers in monitoring diversity statistics, pay parity and promotion rates, thereby codifying responsibility for inclusion throughout an entire company.

BUT, this literature also highlights the adverse effects and limitations. One of the primary concerns is that AI, which is designed to prevent bias, may actually magnify it if the training data reflects longstanding biases. And biased recruitment data sets, for instance, tilt the selection process against minority candidates even when the algorithms for doing so are fair. In addition, the ethical concerns of hospitality research also underscore the importance of transparency, interpretability, and auditability in AI systems to prevent biased results. Human contact with visitors is another warning that goes hand in hand with the loss of this item. And although AI holds the promise of efficiency and customised service, experts warn that too much automation risks stripping the soul out of hospitality — warmth, empathy, and personal connections that still rank among guests' favourite qualities.

The literature converges on the perception that AI is the potential solution of choice for advancing diversity and inclusion (D&I) within the hospitality industry. Its uses include hiring, training, guest service skills and oversight of the business. However, such promising outcomes require responsible conduct, ongoing human oversight, and a sound ethical framework. The review, however, highlights potential future research directions, including hybrid AI efficiency and real human interaction (vs. inclusivity), the inclusivity and cross-cultural adaptability of AI inclusivity tools, and the long-term organisational effects of AI-enabled initiatives toward inclusivity.

FINDINGS AND DISCUSSIONS

The paper, titled "Artificial Intelligence and Diversity and Inclusion in the Hospitality Industry," underscores that AI is increasingly becoming a change agent for diversity and inclusion (D&I) in the hospitality industry, which relies on multicultural labour forces and global guest profiles and requires problems to be addressed equitably. The results show that AI-based hiring systems remove biases by not revealing a user's personal information from their application, instead focusing on their skills and proficiency, resulting in a fairer and more transparent recruitment process. Adaptive AI-based training platforms demonstrate inclusivity by presenting personalised training modules on cultural awareness, gender sensitivity, and accessibility, ultimately promoting employees' intercultural competence and their ability to service diverse guests. On the customer side, AI-driven chatbots and voice assistants provide multilingual support, enhance communication with travellers from overseas, and offer accessibility functionality for guests with disabilities. Based on sentiment analysis, hospitality organisations can also detect exclusion and discrimination experiences from guest reviews and feedback, as well as employee surveys, providing data-driven guidance to address these issues proactively.

The conversation highlights that while AI can serve as an opportunity to promote equality, fairness, and diversity, it also presents essential ethical and operational challenges. Algorithms, although they can operate fairly, may inadvertently perpetuate systemic inequalities if trained on biased datasets. For instance, AI-based hiring platforms risk encoding hidden bias if the historical data sets used for new hires are prejudiced. Furthermore, too much reliance on automation in the guest experience may actually lead to a decrease in the genuineness of the personalised human touch that is key to guest satisfaction. Accordingly, the AI-enabled efficiency should be balanced with human oversight, i.e., ensuring the three parts of the model effectively play their roles and counterbalance each other while auditing algorithms in real-time, maintaining transparent data management, and implementing ethical accountability schemes. Ultimately, AI can serve not only as a technical enabler but also as a cultural agent of change, focusing on inclusivity in staff practices and the guest experience. Here are a few key elements that organisations need to adopt to fulfil the promise of AI for the hospitality industry. These elements include a proactive plan that responsibly incorporates AI, makes inclusivity metrics a feature of how employees are evaluated, and emphasises diversity and inclusion in all technological and managerial decision-making.

Practical Implications

The implications of these results are beneficial for practitioners in hospitality management, HR managers, technologists, and policymakers seeking to promote diversity and inclusion through AI. AI-driven recruitment technologies, first of all, can be used as direct aids to make hiring processes more fair. By removing identifying information from resumes and focusing on relevant skills, companies can expand their candidate pool and ultimately position themselves to have a workforce that is more reflective of the many differences across social, cultural, and gender lines. This not only satisfies equal employment laws but also fosters creativity and innovation by promoting diverse perspectives in the workplace.

Second, adaptive AI training and development systems enable managers to provide employees with personalised learning tracks. Intercultural awareness, unconscious bias reduction, gender inclusiveness and disability sensitivity modules can be integrated in regular training, ensuring that inclusivity is an ongoing and quantifiable component of working life. These efforts don't just prepare workers to provide equitable guest experiences, but they can also help forge a greater sense of belonging among employees from underrepresented groups.

Lastly, guest services can be revolutionised through AI-powered personalisation and enhanced accessibility. Some other multilingual chatbots, voice recognition solutions, and even real-time translation software can help bridge the language gap, and assistive technologies, powered by AI, including screen readers, automated navigation, and speech-to-text capabilities, ensure that differently abled guests are also taken care of in the case of accessibility. Not only does this comply with global accessibility standards, but it also allows us to tap into new markets by targeting previously unaddressed guest segments.

Fourth, the application of AI in analysing guest reviews, employee surveys and social media posts offers management tangible feedback on how inclusive it is perceived. Such instruments help notice patterns of discrimination, exclusion, or inequality which might otherwise remain hidden. Early-action interventions, powered by AI analytics, can enhance both the loyalty of guests and the satisfaction of employees.

Finally, at the organisational level, AI-based workforce analytics can be used to monitor pay equity, advancement opportunities and representation on management floors. Don't forget –make your analytics a part of performance reviews and executive dashboards, connecting them back to decision-making. This way, you hold the organisation accountable and keep goals around inclusivity top of mind. These practices also enhance brand image, attract environmentally conscious consumers, and establish businesses in alignment with sustainability and corporate social responsibility directives, such as the United Nations' Sustainable Development Goals (SDGs).

Ultimately, AI is not just a tech innovation; it's an operational tool that facilitates the permeation of inclusivity throughout the entire guest experience. When addressed ethically, these strategies can make the hospitality sector more equitable and offer a better experience for guests while providing long-term competitive advantages for hospitality businesses in a diverse and globalising industry.

SOLUTIONS AND RECOMMENDATIONS

1. To limit the likelihood of algorithmic bias, ensure that AI development teams are diverse.
2. Regular audits of artificial intelligence systems should be conducted to check for bias and fairness.
3. Implement stringent data protection procedures to safeguard guests' privacy.
4. Artificial intelligence can be used to develop comprehensive recruiting procedures by eliminating demographic information from the recruitment process.
5. Utilise customisation technologies powered by artificial intelligence to cater to guests' varied tastes.
6. Invest in accessibility solutions led by artificial intelligence to serve visitors with impairments.
7. Provide hospitality professionals with training on the ethics of artificial intelligence.
8. To develop AI systems that are both fair and transparent, it is essential to encourage collaboration between AI engineers, ethicists, and hospitality industry executives.

CONCEPTUAL FRAMEWORK

This chapter's conceptual framework integrates AI technologies with diversity and inclusion (D&I) strategies in the hospitality industry. It emphasises the interplay between AI's objective decision-making capabilities and the subjective nature of human diversity. The framework suggests that AI can enhance inclusivity, provided it is designed and implemented with due consideration for ethical principles.

Figure 1. Conceptual framework

(Author's compilation)

FUTURE STUDY DIRECTIONS

The development of artificial intelligence technologies specifically designed to promote justice and inclusion in the hospitality industry should be the primary focus of future studies. Further research is necessary to investigate the influence of artificial intelligence on workforce diversity and visitor satisfaction. Additionally, there is a need for additional studies on how artificial intelligence can effectively handle intersectionality in diversity and inclusion initiatives. This is because various aspects of identity impact experiences in the hotel industry.

CONCLUSION

Artificial intelligence (AI) has the potential to significantly revolutionise diversity and inclusion (D&I) in the hotel industry – which is currently almost non-existent in many respects. Artificial intelligence can create more fair recruiting practices, leading to candidates from all different backgrounds enjoying the same level playing field when it comes to the hiring process, by automating processes and reducing human bias. Moreover, personalising visitor services using artificial intelligence by sifting through data to gain insights about personal preferences, cultural nuances, and special needs remains a significant boost to the guest experience. People with disabilities could, for example, be catered to through technology, with AI-enabled offerings of personalised services - whether in the form of voice-activated room controls or real-time translation services for those whose spoken language is not their native tongue. This adds to the inclusiveness and comfort of everyone.

On the other hand, the application of AI in diversity and inclusion initiatives presents some specific ethical concerns. Evening out disparities may not happen by accident to begin with: algorithmic bias — often the result of training data that doesn't reflect the population — may actually exacerbate existing disparities. Likewise, the adoption of AI raises privacy and data security concerns, as the technology relies on the use of personal data and its analysis. These are some of the challenges that underscore the urgency of deploying artificial intelligence responsibly, with a focus on transparency, accountability, and fairness.

Assuming it's implemented thoughtfully and responsibly. In such cases, AI could serve as a powerful aid to the hospitality industry in helping create environments more conducive to people of all sorts, both employees and patrons. AI could disrupt the status quo of equity and inclusion in an industry that actively welcomes people of all backgrounds. This can be achieved by increasing workplace diversity and providing customised, accessible services.

REFERENCES

Chen, W., & Hu, M. (2020). The impact of AI-driven technologies on accessibility in the hospitality industry. *Journal of Hospitality and Tourism Technology*, *11*(3), 397–415. DOI: 10.1108/JHTT-08-2019-0105

Chen, X., & Hu, Y. (2020). The Role of AI-Driven Translation Tools in Hospitality. *Tourism and Hospitality Study*, *21*(2), 190–204. DOI: 10.1177/1467358420974316

Dastin, J. (2018). "Amazon Scraps Secret AI Recruiting Tool That Showed Bias Against Women." Reuters, Retrieved from https://www.reuters.com

Fan, Y.. (2020). Multilingual Chatbots in Hospitality: Addressing Language Accessibility. *Service Industries Journal*, *40*(7-8), 620–634. DOI: 10.1080/02642069.2020.1718845

Floridi, L., Cowls, J., Beltrametti, M., Chatila, R., Chazerand, P., Dignum, V., Luetge, C., Madelin, R., Pagallo, U., Rossi, F., Schafer, B., Valcke, P., & Vayena, E. (2018). AI4People—An ethical framework for a good AI society: Opportunities, risks, principles, and recommendations. *Minds and Machines*, *28*(4), 689–707. DOI: 10.1007/s11023-018-9482-5 PMID: 30930541

Floridi, L., Cowls, J., Beltrametti, M., Chatila, R., Chazerand, P., Dignum, V., Luetge, C., Madelin, R., Pagallo, U., Rossi, F., Schafer, B., Valcke, P., & Vayena, E. (2018). AI4People—An Ethical Framework for a Good AI Society. *Minds and Machines*, *28*(4), 689–707. DOI: 10.1007/s11023-018-9482-5 PMID: 30930541

Gretzel, U.. (2021). Big Data and Artificial Intelligence in Tourism and Hospitality. *Journal of Hospitality Marketing & Management*, *30*(3), 289–309. DOI: 10.1080/19368623.2021.1841100

Huang, A., & Back, K. (2020). Using AI for Diversity Training in Hospitality. *Journal of Hospitality & Tourism Study*, *45*(5), 1062–1079. DOI: 10.1177/1096348020965701

Ivanov, S., & Webster, C. (2019). Adoption of robots, artificial intelligence, and service automation by travel, tourism, and hospitality companies – A cost-benefit analysis. *International Journal of Contemporary Hospitality Management, 31*(9), 3875–3896. DOI: 10.1108/IJCHM-07-2018-0580

Ivanov, S., & Webster, C. (2019). *Robots, Artificial Intelligence, and Service Automation in Travel, Tourism, and Hospitality*. Emerald Publishing., DOI: 10.1108/9781787566873

Kumar, R., Singh, P., & Sharma, L. (2022). AI-driven Personalization in Hospitality: A Cultural Sensitivity Perspective. *Journal of Service Study, 29*(2), 145–160.

Kuschel, K., & Sanders, M. (2020). AI Personalization Strategies in Hospitality: Enhancing Guest Experience while Maintaining Privacy. *Journal of Hospitality Marketing & Management, 31*(3), 210–223.

Li, J., Chen, W., & Wu, L. (2021). Reducing bias in AI-powered recruitment processes: A study in the hospitality industry. *Tourism Management Perspectives, 40*, 100873. DOI: 10.1016/j.tmp.2021.100873

Lu, Y.. (2020). Artificial Intelligence in Hospitality: The Innovative Role of Chatbots. *Journal of Hospitality and Tourism Management, 45*, 89–98. DOI: 10.1016/j.jhtm.2020.08.008

Mao, Z., & Zhang, L. (2021). The Role of AI in Personalized Guest Experiences. *Tourism Review, 76*(4), 827–839. DOI: 10.1108/TR-03-2021-0135

Miller, J., & Smith, T. (2019). AI in Hiring: An End to Bias? *Technology in Human Resources, 34*(2), 77–89.

Mohammad, B. T. (2020). The Future of Culinary Tourism: An Emerging Dimension for the Tourism Industry of Bangladesh. I-Manager's. *Journal of Marketing, 15*(1), 27. DOI: 10.26634/jmgt.15.1.17181

Mohammad, B. T. (2021). An assessment of the roles of the social network in developing the Tourism Industry in Bangladesh. *International Journal of Business, Law, and Education, 2*(3), 85–93. DOI: 10.56442/ijble.v2i3.21

Mohammad, B. T. (2024). Implementing Artificial Intelligence and Virtual Experiences in Hospitality. In Manohar, S., Mittal, A., Raju, S., & Nair, A. J. (Eds.), *Advances in Hospitality, Tourism, and the Services Industry* (pp. 145–160). IGI Global., DOI: 10.4018/979-8-3693-2019-8.ch009

Mohammad, B. T. (2025). Maximizing Impact: The Role of Influencer Marketing in Contemporary Tourism Marketing. In Özsungur, F. (Ed.), *Navigating Organizational Behavior in the Digital Age with AI* (pp. 277–304). IGI Global Scientific Publishing., DOI: 10.4018/979-8-3693-8442-8.ch011

Raghavan, M., Barocas, S., Kleinberg, J., & Levy, K. (2021). Mitigating bias in algorithmic hiring: Evaluating claims and practices. *Proceedings of the 2021 ACM Conference on Fairness, Accountability, and Transparency*, 469-481. DOI: 10.1145/3442188.3445923

Saxena, S., & Khandelwal, P. (2020). AI-enabled personalized service and human touch in hospitality: A study of guest experiences. *Tourism and Hospitality Study*, *20*(3), 300–315. DOI: 10.1177/1467358419869432

Saxena, S., & Khandelwal, P. (2020). Diversity and Inclusion in Hospitality: A Comprehensive Overview. *Hospitality & Society*, *10*(2), 153–170. DOI: 10.1386/hosp_00023_7

Siau, K., & Wang, W. (2020). Ethical and Legal Implications of AI: Ensuring Fairness and Accountability in AI Systems. *Journal of Artificial Intelligence Study*, *69*(1), 229–248.

Singh, R.. (2021). The Role of Inclusive Culture in Enhancing Employee and Customer Experience in the Hospitality Industry. *International Journal of Hospitality Management*, *95*, 102887. DOI: 10.1016/j.ijhm.2021.102887

Talukder, M. B. (2025). Revolutionizing Hospitality: Leveraging Mobile Apps and Cutting-Edge Room Technologies in the Hotel Industry. In B. Varghese & S. H. (Eds.), *Advancing Smart Tourism Through Analytics* (pp. 315-332). IGI Global Scientific Publishing. DOI: 10.4018/979-8-3693-3715-8.ch017

Talukder, M. B., Kabir, F., Kaiser, F., & Hoque, M. (2025). Perspectives for the Potential and Future of Marine Tourism in Bangladesh. In Alkier, R., Catenazzo, G., Milojica, V., & Zając, A. (Eds.), *Cases on Effective Destination Management* (pp. 83–104). IGI Global Scientific Publishing., DOI: 10.4018/979-8-3693-1548-4.ch004

Talukder, M. B., & Kumar, S. (2024). The Development of ChatGPT and Its Implications for the Future of Customer Service in the Hospitality Industry. In Derbali, A. M. S. (Ed.), (pp. 100–126). Advances in Information Security, Privacy, and Ethics. IGI Global., DOI: 10.4018/979-8-3693-1511-8.ch005

Talukder, M. B., Kumar, S., & Das Tonny, O. (2025). Innovative Solutions for Employee Well-Being in the Digital Hospitality Era. In Ahmad, B., Abrar, M., & Saeed, M. (Eds.), *Marketing Technology-Infused Hospitality: Upskilling Frontline Employees for Competitiveness* (pp. 231–258). IGI Global Scientific Publishing., DOI: 10.4018/979-8-3693-7127-5.ch009

Talukder, M. B., Kumar, S., Sood, K., & Grima, S. (2023). Information Technology, Food Service Quality, and Restaurant Revisit Intention. *International Journal of Sustainable Development and Planning*, *18*(1), 295–303. DOI: 10.18280/ijsdp.180131

Talukder, M. B., Kumar, S., & Tyagi, P. K. (Eds.). (2024). *Impact of AI and Tech-Driven Solutions in Hospitality and Tourism*. IGI Global., DOI: 10.4018/979-8-3693-6755-1

Talukder, M. B., Swarna, D. A., & Kabir, F. (2025). Innovative Tech Strategies for Employee Wellness in Hospitality. In Ahmad, B., Abrar, M., & Saeed, M. (Eds.), *Marketing Technology-Infused Hospitality: Upskilling Frontline Employees for Competitiveness* (pp. 259–290). IGI Global Scientific Publishing., DOI: 10.4018/979-8-3693-7127-5.ch010

United Nations World Tourism Organization (UNWTO). (2019). Inclusive growth and the future of tourism: A United Nations perspective. Retrieved from https://www.unwto.org

Wang, Y., Li, C., & Zhang, H. (2022). AI-driven personalization in hospitality: Balancing efficiency and guest privacy. *Journal of Hospitality Marketing & Management*, *31*(6), 671–690.

KEY TERMS AND DEFINITIONS

AI-Powered Recruitment: The utilization of artificial intelligence to automate and optimize various aspects of the recruiting process. These aspects include the screening of resumes, the evaluation of candidates, and the scheduling of interviews. By utilizing artificial intelligence, hospitality organizations can swiftly discover the most qualified individuals and reduce the impact of human biases throughout the recruitment process. A more effective and equitable recruiting process may be achieved by utilizing artificial intelligence systems that scan job descriptions, match talents with jobs, and even employ natural language processing to evaluate candidates' potential. Inclusive Hospitality Practices: Inclusive hospitality practices relate to tactics and actions meant to guarantee that hospitality services are friendly and accessible to all people, regardless of their background, identity, or ability. A few examples of these practices include the provision of wheelchair-accessible rooms, the accommodation of dietary needs, the provision of bilingual personnel or materials, and the promotion of cultural awareness in the provision of services. Practises that are inclusive contribute to the creation of an atmosphere that is inviting, celebrates diversity, and maximizes the happiness of guests.

Artificial Intelligence: Artificial intelligence is the replication of human intellect in computers that have been designed to execute activities such as learning, reasoning, problem-solving, and decision-making for themselves. Artificial intelligence enables systems to evaluate enormous amounts of data, detect patterns, and make predictions or judgments with minimum human assistance. Chatbots, recommendation engines, innovative room systems, and customer support tools are all powered by artificial intelligence in the hotel sector. This is helping to improve operational efficiency and overall visitor experience.

Cultural Sensitivity: Cultural sensitivity is the knowledge and comprehension of cultural differences and the capacity to appreciate and adapt to such variations in interactions and activities. To provide individualized services that cater to the specific tastes and expectations of visitors from various cultural backgrounds, it is vital for those working in the hospitality industry to demonstrate cultural sensitivity. This involves ensuring that staff members are taught to engage effectively with a varied clientele while respecting community members' traditions, languages, and customs. Not only can cultural awareness enhance the experiences of guests, but it also helps to boost the reputation of a company on a worldwide scale.

Diversity and Inclusion (D&I): Diversity is the presence of distinctions within a group. These differences might include variances in color, gender, age, ethnicity, talents, and other factors. What we mean when we talk about inclusion is establishing an atmosphere in which people from various backgrounds feel appreciated, respected, and empowered to participate. In the hospitality industry, diversity and inclusion ensure businesses welcome diverse customers and staff, promoting equality and a sense of belonging. To do this, it is necessary to develop equitable employment processes, provide culturally inclusive services, and cater to the specific requirements of visitors from various backgrounds.

Hospitality: Hospitality is the business of providing services, including accommodation, food, drinks, and entertainment, to visitors to guarantee their comfort, contentment, and memorable experiences. In the hospitality sector, which is centered on the satisfaction of customers, establishments such as hotels, restaurants, resorts, and other service-oriented enterprises are included. As a result of its emphasis on providing individualized experiences and cultivating cultural ties, it recognizes the importance of diversity and creativity as essential components of success.

NOTE

When it comes to the role of artificial intelligence in diversity and inclusion in the hotel sector, more insights can be found in the writings of professionals such as Brynjolfsson and McAfee (2017). These authors examine the more significant social consequences of AI technology. The study conducted by academics such as Siau and Wang (2020) offers valuable insights into the ethical challenges that need to be addressed to ensure that artificial intelligence systems will positively contribute to efforts to promote inclusion. McKinsey & Company and Deloitte have published industry papers that provide insightful viewpoints on implementing artificial intelligence in real-world business contexts, including the hotel industry.

Chapter 2
AI for Environmental Sustainability

G. R. Manjunathareddy
https://orcid.org/0009-0002-4476-5710
Bangalore University, India

ABSTRACT

The accelerating pace of global environmental degradation—from climate change to biodiversity loss—demands bold and innovative solutions. This chapter explores how artificial intelligence (AI) is emerging as a transformative force in tackling these challenges. By harnessing technologies such as machine learning, computer vision, and natural language processing, AI offers unprecedented capabilities for monitoring ecosystems, forecasting climate impacts, managing resources efficiently, and guiding sustainable development. AI with complementary technologies like IoT, GIS, and cloud computing enhances data-driven decision-making across agriculture, urban planning, energy, water, and biodiversity conservation. However, the application of AI also raises ethical, social, and environmental concerns that must be addressed to ensure responsible and inclusive deployment. Through a multidisciplinary lens, this chapter examines AI's potential, limitations, and implications in advancing environmental sustainability, aiming to inform policy and practice for a resilient and equitable future.

DOI: 10.4018/979-8-3373-1077-0.ch002

1. INTRODUCTION

Humanity is pivotal in its relationship with the planet, facing urgent environmental crises such as climate change, deforestation, biodiversity loss, pollution, and unsustainable consumption (Shivanna, 2022). While policy reforms, international agreements, and grassroots efforts remain essential, AI offers a transformative tool for environmental sustainability (van Wynsberghe, 2021).

AI enables machines to mimic human intelligence, which is increasingly integral to advancing sustainability goals (Collins et al., 2021). It enhances real-time data analysis, improves climate and disaster prediction, and empowers decision-makers with efficient, scalable solutions. The synergy of AI with technologies such as the Internet of Things (IoT), cloud computing, and geospatial systems opens up new avenues for optimizing resources, automating sustainable practices, and enhancing ecological resilience (Miller et al., 2025).

This chapter examines the diverse contributions of AI to environmental sustainability, focusing on its applications, limitations, and impacts across agriculture, energy, water management, urban planning, and biodiversity conservation. It highlights how AI can align with ecological values and sustainability objectives through technical insights, case studies, and ethical considerations.

The discussion begins by outlining key environmental challenges and the need for integrated solutions. It then explores the emergence of AI in sustainability, detailing innovations in monitoring, resource use, smart cities, and climate action. Ultimately, it provides ethical perspectives and policy recommendations for the responsible integration of AI into environmental governance.

2. OVERVIEW OF ENVIRONMENTAL CHALLENGES

The 21st century faces interconnected environmental crises exacerbated by industrialization, population growth, and unsustainable consumption. Despite global efforts, climate change, deforestation, biodiversity loss, and pollution continue to escalate, placing immense pressure on ecosystems (Orssatto, 2001). Climate change, driven by greenhouse gas emissions, contributes to extreme weather events, rising sea levels, and disruptions to ecosystems. Air, water, and soil degradation impact ecosystems, harm human health, and exacerbate environmental challenges (Shetty et al., 2023). Furthermore, unsustainable agricultural practices exacerbate soil depletion and water contamination, while industrialization and urbanization lead to resource depletion and habitat destruction (Yu et al., 2024).

Addressing these challenges requires innovative solutions, with AI offering significant potential through data analysis, predictive modeling, and automation to monitor, manage, and mitigate environmental impacts (Bibri et al., 2024b). However, a deeper understanding of these environmental issues is essential to leverage AI for sustainable solutions (Olawade et al., 2024a).

2.1 Climate Change

Climate change, primarily caused by greenhouse gas emissions, has severe consequences. Rising global temperatures are causing the melting of polar ice, resulting in higher sea levels and more extreme weather events, including heatwaves, storms, and heavy rainfall (Das & Swain, 2024). These changes impact agricultural productivity, disrupt ecosystems, and pose a threat to food security (Furtak & Wolińska, 2023). Moreover, biodiversity loss compromises essential ecosystem services, including pollination and soil health (Wang et al., 2024). Addressing climate change requires reducing emissions, enhancing resilience, and utilizing technologies like AI to mitigate and adapt to its effects (Lawrence et al., 2022).

2.2 Biodiversity Loss

Biodiversity underpins healthy ecosystems, providing essential services such as pollination, climate regulation, and soil fertility (Weiskopf et al., 2020). However, biodiversity is declining rapidly due to habitat destruction, pollution, and overexploitation (Sharma & Birman, 2024). Nearly one million species are at risk of extinction, a trend exacerbated by climate change, which hinders their ability to adapt (Abbass et al., 2022). Loss of biodiversity poses a threat to food security, medicinal resources, and indigenous cultures (Van der Sluijs & Vaage, 2016). AI can help monitor ecosystems and support conservation efforts by predicting trends and identifying threats (Salmi et al., 2023).

2.3 Pollution and Resource Depletion

Air, water, and soil have reached alarming levels due to industrial, agricultural, and urban activities, posing a significant threat to human health and ecosystems (Zhou & Gu, 2024). Air pollution, caused by the burning of fossil fuels, leads to respiratory issues, while water pollution from agricultural runoff and industrial waste affects aquatic ecosystems (Shetty et al., 2023). Over-extraction of resources, including freshwater and fossil fuels, compounds environmental stress and threatens long-term sustainability (Rockström et al., 2009). AI can optimize resource use, monitor pollution levels, and support sustainable practices (Bolón-Canedo et al., 2024b).

2.4 Urbanization and Land Use Change

Urbanization leads to deforestation, increased carbon emissions, and pollution. As cities expand, they replace natural habitats with built environments, reducing carbon sinks and biodiversity (Choudhary et al., 2024). Urban areas also face significant waste management challenges, which strain resources and exacerbate environmental degradation (Aminzadegan et al., 2022). Sustainable urban planning, which integrates green spaces and renewable energy, is crucial for mitigating these effects. AI can optimize urban growth, resource management, and infrastructure efficiency to reduce environmental footprints (Regona et al., 2024).

2.5 Agricultural Challenges and Food Security

Agriculture significantly contributes to environmental degradation, with practices such as deforestation, excessive water use, and the use of chemical inputs driving climate change and soil depletion (Futa et al., 2024). Climate change impacts crop yields, soil fertility, and water availability, threatening food security (Shah et al., 2021). Shifting to sustainable agricultural practices, such as agroecology and precision farming, can minimize environmental damage while improving food security (Javaid et al., 2022). AI can help optimize farming practices by predicting crop yields, managing irrigation, and detecting pests early, promoting sustainability (Mana et al., 2024).

2.6 Water Scarcity and Management

Water scarcity affects billions globally, exacerbated by climate change, pollution, and over-extraction (Bolan et al., 2024). Shifting precipitation patterns and pollution of freshwater resources make water increasingly scarce, threatening public health and ecosystems (Jakhar et al., 2023). Over-extraction of water for agriculture and industry depletes vital freshwater systems (Ingrao et al., 2023). AI-driven solutions for monitoring water quality and optimizing usage are crucial to effective water management and addressing these challenges (Pérez-Beltrán et al., 2024).

These challenges are interconnected and require a holistic approach to environmental stewardship. Leveraging AI for monitoring, predictive analysis, and sustainable practices can help mitigate environmental risks and promote a sustainable future.

3. EMERGENCE OF AI IN SUSTAINABILITY

As environmental challenges grow increasingly complex, traditional approaches are often scale and intricate. Conventional methods, such as limited data availability and reactive management, struggle to adapt to rapidly changing conditions. AI has emerged as a transformative force, offering innovative solutions that enhance human decision-making and tackle environmental challenges (Javanmardi et al., 2023).

3.1 Defining AI

AI simulates human intelligence in machines capable of thinking, learning, and solving problems autonomously. It encompasses technologies like machine learning (ML), deep learning (DL), natural language processing (NLP), computer vision, and robotics. Unlike traditional computational models that follow predefined rules, AI systems can adapt and improve by processing vast datasets, identifying patterns, making predictions, and optimizing processes, making them invaluable for addressing complex environmental issues (Rashid & Kausik, 2024).

3.2 The Data-Driven Shift in Environmental Management

AI excels in processing large, complex datasets—known as "big data"—sourced from satellites, sensors, mobile devices, and citizen science initiatives. AI detects patterns and correlations in this data, offering insights that would otherwise be difficult or time-consuming to extract manually (Xu et al., 2021).

In environmental management, where timely, location-specific data is crucial, AI's ability to combine climate models, satellite imagery, and ground-level observations enhances the understanding of hazards such as droughts, wildfires, or floods (Olawade et al., 2024c). AI can also monitor illegal activities, such as deforestation or poaching, by analyzing real-time data, thereby boosting enforcement efforts.

3.3 Integration with Emerging Technologies

AI's potential is amplified when integrated with other technologies, creating a digital convergence to address environmental challenges (Bibri et al., 2024a). The Internet of Things (IoT) enables continuous environmental monitoring via sensor networks, while cloud computing provides the infrastructure for handling large data volumes (Kumar et al., 2019).

Geographic Information Systems (GIS) add spatial context, enabling the visualization of environmental trends and patterns.

Blockchain also provides transparency in environmental transactions, such as verifying carbon credits or tracking sustainable supply chains (Friedman & Ormiston, 2022). AI, combined with IoT, cloud computing, GIS, and blockchain, enables the development of adaptive and innovative systems, such as AI-powered drones for wildlife monitoring or intelligent irrigation systems that optimize water use in agriculture.

3.4 AI's Role in Accelerating Sustainable Development Goals (SDGs)

AI in achieving the United Nations' 2030 Agenda for Sustainable Development, particularly in environmental sustainability. Key contributions of AI to the SDGs include:

- Enhancing early warning systems for natural disasters (Goal 13: Climate Action) by predicting extreme weather events, such as hurricanes, floods, and droughts (Figure 3).
- Supporting conservation and sustainable land use (Goal 15: Life on Land) by monitoring biodiversity, detecting illegal activities, and optimizing land management.
- Promoting efficient energy use and renewable energy (Goal 7: Affordable and Clean Energy) by optimizing energy systems and integrating renewable sources.
- Improving water quality and access (Goal 6: Clean Water and Sanitation) through AI-driven water resource monitoring and real-time contaminant detection (Figure 3).
- Enabling sustainable cities (Goal 11) by supporting smart city infrastructure and reducing waste through data-driven urban planning.

As research evolves, AI is increasingly recognized as a key enabler of transformative, system-wide changes that align economic, social, and environmental priorities.

3.5 The Shift Toward Proactive Environmental Governance

AI is shifting environmental governance from reactive to proactive strategies. Traditional approaches often address environmental degradation after it occurs, while AI enables anticipatory actions by identifying early warning signs, predicting risks, and recommending preventive measures (Zhao et al., 2024).

This proactive approach is crucial for achieving sustainability goals, such as transitioning to a circular economy, implementing ecosystem-based management, and enhancing climate resilience. AI facilitates real-time monitoring, predictive analytics, and data-driven decision-making, enabling stakeholders to act before problems escalate, thereby promoting sustainable and resilient ecosystems (Hariyani et al., 2024).

The role of AI in sustainability continues to expand, offering transformative tools for addressing complex environmental challenges. Integrating AI into environmental management paves the way for adaptive, efficient, and forward-thinking approaches to sustainability.

4. THEORETICAL FRAMEWORK AND BACKGROUND

To harness AI for environmental sustainability, its applications must align with the core principles of sustainability. This section explores the foundational concepts, the evolution of AI technologies, and interdisciplinary perspectives that inform the integration of AI in environmental management (Alzoubi & Mishra, 2024).

4.1 Defining Sustainability in the Context of AI

Sustainability, as defined by the Brundtland Commission (1987), refers to meeting present needs without compromising the ability of future generations to meet their own. It involves balancing three pillars: environmental health, economic viability, and social equity (Purvis et al., 2019).

When applied to AI, sustainability focuses on utilizing AI to achieve outcomes such as reducing carbon emissions, conserving biodiversity, and optimizing resource use while ensuring that the development, deployment, and maintenance of AI systems are sustainable. This includes minimizing AI's environmental impacts, such as energy consumption, and addressing biases in data to prevent inequitable outcomes (Olawade et al., 2024b; Greif et al., 2024).

Thus, AI for sustainability represents both a tool and a paradigm that ensures AI development aligns with ecological balance, social justice, and responsible governance.

4.2 Evolution of AI Technologies Relevant to Environmental Sustainability

AI has undergone a significant transformation in recent years, evolving from experimental tools to powerful technologies capable of addressing complex environmental issues. The convergence of AI with big data, remote sensing, and the Internet of Things (IoT) has opened new avenues for understanding, managing, and preserving the environment. A range of AI methodologies is now being applied across various domains to support sustainability initiatives and ecological conservation (Shobanke et al., 2025). Below is an overview of some of the most impactful AI technologies and how they are contributing to environmental progress:

4.2.1. Machine Learning (ML)

Machine Learning, one of the foundational pillars of AI, involves training algorithms to identify patterns and make data-driven predictions without being explicitly programmed. Its adaptive nature makes it highly suitable for modeling complex environmental systems. For instance, ML is widely employed in climate prediction models, air and water quality forecasting, and species distribution modeling. By analyzing vast datasets collected from sensors, satellites, and climate stations, ML facilitates more informed environmental decision-making and early warning systems for natural disasters (Alotaibi & Nassif, 2024).

4.2.2 Deep Learning (DL)

Deep Learning, a sophisticated subset of machine learning, utilizes artificial neural networks with multiple layers to analyze large volumes of unstructured data, particularly visual and audio inputs. In the environmental sector, DL has proven highly effective in analyzing satellite imagery to detect land-use changes, such as urban expansion, deforestation, and crop pattern shifts. These insights are crucial for monitoring ecosystem changes over time, assessing biodiversity loss, and evaluating the impact of human activities on natural resources (Dritsas & Trigka, 2025).

4.2.3. Natural Language Processing (NLP)

Natural Language Processing enables AI systems to comprehend, interpret, and generate human language. In the realm of environmental science and policy, NLP is instrumental in scanning and analyzing textual data from scientific literature, policy documents, social media, and public comments. This allows researchers and policymakers to detect emerging trends, measure public sentiment on environmental policies, and assess the effectiveness of regulations. For example, NLP can highlight public concerns related to climate change or pollution, guiding responsive policymaking (Supriyono et al., 2024).

4.2.4. Computer Vision

Computer Vision focuses on enabling machines to interpret and make sense of visual information. When applied to environmental monitoring, it enhances the analysis of images captured by drones, satellites, and camera traps. This technology plays a vital role in wildlife surveillance, enabling automated identification of species and tracking of animal movements. It also supports pollution detection by recognizing patterns of waste in water bodies or illegal dumping sites, used in land cover classification to distinguish between forests, water bodies, and built environments (Reynolds et al., 2025).

4.2.5. Reinforcement Learning (RL)

Reinforcement Learning is a type of AI where agents learn to make decisions by interacting with their environment and receiving feedback in the form of rewards or penalties. This approach is efficient for managing dynamic systems that require adaptive control strategies. In environmental contexts, RL has been applied to optimize energy consumption in smart grids, regulate traffic flow to reduce emissions in urban areas, and manage resource allocation in water distribution networks. Its trial-and-error learning mechanism allows for continuous improvement in system efficiency and sustainability outcomes (Rajasekhar et al., 2025).

4.2.6 Integrative Potential of AI in Environmental Monitoring

The real strength of AI lies not only in the capabilities of individual technologies but also in their integration with traditional environmental data sources. By combining AI tools with remote sensing data, geographic information systems (GIS), and IoT-based sensor networks, researchers and environmental managers can create robust frameworks for monitoring, prediction, and intervention. This integrated approach supports a wide range of sustainability goals, including reducing greenhouse gas emissions, improving waste management, protecting endangered species, and enhancing natural resource governance.

As AI technologies continue to evolve, their role in shaping a more sustainable and resilient planet will become even more critical. By harnessing these tools responsibly and ethically, we can advance environmental stewardship and drive meaningful action toward global sustainability targets.

4.3 Interdisciplinary Perspectives

AI applications for environmental sustainability require an interdisciplinary approach, incorporating ecological, social, economic, and ethical perspectives. Key perspectives include:

- **Ecological Science:** Understanding natural systems is essential for collecting relevant data and monitoring ecosystem health, ensuring AI aligns with ecological principles.
- **Social Science:** Social science offers valuable insights into human behavior, community engagement, and policy, thereby helping to ensure that AI interventions are socially equitable and effective.
- **Systems Thinking:** Systems thinking fosters a holistic perspective, recognizing the complexities and interdependencies of environmental challenges. It helps AI consider long-term impacts and interconnected systems.
- **Ethics and Philosophy:** Ethical perspectives address moral questions, such as species protection priorities and the potential surveillance risks of AI, ensuring the responsible use of AI in environmental contexts.

An interdisciplinary approach ensures that AI systems are both practical and responsible, striking a balance between human and ecological needs.

4.4 Human-Centered and Ecosystem-Centered AI

AI for sustainability should adopt both human-centered and ecosystem-centered perspectives:

- **Human-centered design** ensures AI systems are accessible, understandable, and aligned with users' needs, especially for marginalized communities, prioritizing inclusivity and equity (Schmager et al., 2025).
- **Ecosystem-Centered Design:** This design extends beyond human needs, incorporating ecosystem services and planetary boundaries,

thereby helping to preserve biodiversity and maintain ecological balance (Buckton et al., 2023).

This dual approach ensures that AI systems contribute to human well-being and environmental preservation, supporting the planet's long-term sustainability.

5. AI APPLICATIONS IN ENVIRONMENTAL MONITORING

Environmental monitoring is critical for understanding ecosystem health, detecting changes over time, and guiding policy and management decisions. While traditional monitoring approaches have been instrumental, they often face challenges related to spatial and temporal constraints, data gaps, and resource-intensive processes. AI revolutionizes environmental monitoring by enabling faster, more precise, and scalable assessments across diverse environmental parameters (Ramadan et al., 2024).

5.1 Remote Sensing and Satellite Imagery Analysis

AI technologies, particularly machine intelligence (MI) and deep learning (DL), have significantly enhanced remote sensing data processing. Satellites collect vast amounts of Earth observation data daily, producing terabytes of information that would be overwhelming to process manually. AI's ability to analyze this data efficiently and effectively has led to significant advancements in environmental monitoring (Janga, 2023).

- **Land Use and Land Cover (LULC) Change Detection:** AI algorithms classify land cover types—such as forests, urban areas, and water bodies—and detect changes over time. This application is crucial for tracking deforestation, urban expansion, and land degradation, enabling policymakers to manage land resources effectively and plan for conservation or urban development (Pushpalatha et al., 2025).
- **Disaster Monitoring:** AI-powered satellite imagery analysis allows for near real-time detection of natural disasters, including floods,

wildfires, and hurricanes. AI can identify affected areas and monitor the progression of these events, supporting more effective emergency response and recovery efforts (Akhyar et al., 2024).

- **Climate Impact Analysis:** Long-term satellite data, when processed with AI, provides insights into slow-moving environmental changes, such as glacial retreat, sea-level rise, and desertification. AI's ability to analyze historical data trends aids in understanding the long-term impacts of climate change and predicting future environmental shifts.

For instance, Google's Earth Engine combines satellite data with AI tools, enabling global monitoring of environmental changes and supporting conservation efforts and scientific research.

5.2 Biodiversity and Wildlife Monitoring

Traditional biodiversity monitoring methods—such as manual surveys, camera traps, and field studies—are often time-consuming and geographically limited. AI is transforming these efforts by automating data collection and analysis, enabling the effective and real-time monitoring of ecosystems (Davison et al., 2025).

- **Species Identification:** AI-powered computer vision models, trained on large datasets of images, can identify plant and animal species from photos, camera traps, and drone footage. Platforms like iNaturalist use AI to assist citizen scientists in identifying species and democratizing biodiversity data collection (Islam et al., 2023).
- **Acoustic Monitoring:** AI-driven analysis of bioacoustics data, such as bird calls, frog croaks, and whale songs, enables researchers to detect and track the presence and abundance of species over time (Figure 2). This method is especially useful in remote or difficult-to-access areas where traditional surveys may not be feasible (Jeantet et al., 2023).
- **Poaching and Illegal Trade Detection:** AI detects suspicious activities in protected areas through surveillance data, helping combat poaching and wildlife trafficking (Figure 2). By analyzing video

feeds and sensor data, AI can identify unusual patterns or behaviors indicative of illegal activity, enabling quicker response times and more targeted conservation efforts (Kamminga et al., 2018).

These AI applications provide conservationists with real-time, cost-effective tools to protect endangered species, monitor biodiversity hotspots, and mitigate ecosystem threats.

5.3 Pollution Detection and Air Quality Forecasting

Air and water pollution are significant threats to human health and the environment. AI technologies monitor, predict, and mitigate pollution through advanced sensing, modeling, and forecasting (Popescu et al., 2024).

- **Air Quality Prediction:** AI models analyze various data sources, including meteorological conditions, traffic patterns, and industrial emissions, to predict air pollution levels. These predictions enable local governments to issue public health warnings, inform urban planning, and implement policies that improve air quality (Natarajan et al., 2024).
- **Water Quality Monitoring:** AI to real-time sensor data parameters like pH, temperature, turbidity, and chemical concentrations to detect water contamination. By providing early detection, AI helps prevent widespread water pollution, ensuring cleaner and safer water sources for communities and ecosystems (Durgun, 2024).
- **Plastic Waste Detection:** AI, intensive learning, is used to identify plastic waste in oceans and rivers by analyzing drone or satellite imagery. This technology helps locate and assess the scale of plastic pollution, enabling more targeted cleanup efforts and supporting initiatives to prevent plastic waste from entering aquatic environments (Nivedita et al., 2024).

By providing timely, actionable insights, AI enables governments and communities to reduce exposure to harmful pollutants, improve air and water quality, and ensure compliance with environmental regulations.

These capabilities are crucial for protecting public health and safeguarding ecosystems.

AI significantly enhances environmental monitoring by automating data analysis, providing real-time insights, and enabling scalable solutions. From satellite imagery analysis to biodiversity monitoring and pollution detection, AI enables more efficient, accurate, and proactive environmental management. The following section will explore how AI is applied to environmental management and decision-making, further advancing sustainability efforts (Olawade et al., 2024c).

6. CLIMATE CHANGE MITIGATION AND ADAPTATION

Climate change presents one of the most complex and urgent challenges of our time. It requires both mitigation—reducing greenhouse gas (GHG) emissions—and adaptation—adjusting societal systems to cope with the impacts of climate change. AI is playing a growing role in supporting both strategies by enhancing our understanding of climate dynamics and informing effective responses (Chen et al., 2023).

6.1 Predictive Climate Modeling

Climate modeling involves simulating the Earth's climate system to understand how it responds to various forces, including greenhouse gas (GHG) emissions, land-use changes, and natural variability. Traditional climate models, although robust, often require substantial computational resources and lengthy simulation times (Andersson-Sköld et al., 2015).

- **AI-Enhanced Forecasting:** AI can augment physical climate models by identifying hidden patterns in climate data, improving resolution, and reducing computational costs. For instance, AI models such as convolutional neural networks can emulate the specific outputs of global climate models (GCMs) at a fraction of the computational load (Waqas et al., 2024).
- **Localized Impact Assessments:** MI enables the downscaling of climate predictions to regional or city levels, making forecasts more

relevant for local planning and resilience strategies (Al-Falahi et al., 2024).

These innovations help policymakers and scientists prepare for various scenarios, including shifting rainfall patterns, increased heat waves, and rising sea levels.

6.2 Carbon Emission Tracking

Accurate monitoring and verification of emissions are crucial for implementing effective climate policies and international agreements, such as the Paris Accord.

- **Emission Source Identification:** AI algorithms analyze satellite imagery, sensor networks, and industrial data to detect and quantify sources of emissions, such as methane leaks or deforestation-related CO_2 output (Ding et al., 2025).
- **Carbon Footprint Estimation:** AI models can calculate the carbon footprint of individuals, organizations, or supply chains based on behavioral data, energy use, and transportation patterns (El Geneidy et al., 2021).
- **Carbon Market Optimization**: In carbon trading systems, AI can optimize pricing, track credits, and prevent fraud through blockchain integration and real-time monitoring (Boumaiza & Maher, 2024).

These tools promote transparency and accountability in climate governance, enabling businesses to comply with environmental regulations.

6.3 AI in Disaster Risk Reduction

The growing threat of climate change has led to a marked increase in the frequency, scale, and unpredictability of natural disasters, including floods, hurricanes, wildfires, and landslides. In this context, AI has emerged as a transformative tool in disaster risk reduction (DRR), offering innovative ways to enhance preparedness, response, and recovery efforts. By harnessing vast and complex datasets from meteorological stations, satellites, and sensors, AI technologies provide deeper insights and quicker responses to environmental hazards, thereby reducing both human and economic losses.

6.3.1 Early Warning Systems

AI-powered forecasting models have become a cornerstone of modern early warning systems. These models are trained on extensive meteorological, hydrological, and geological datasets to predict impending disasters with greater accuracy and lead time. For instance, AI can analyze real-time satellite and weather station data to forecast floods, cyclones, and forest fires with high precision. When integrated with communication platforms, these systems issue timely alerts to authorities and at-risk populations, enabling evacuations, resource mobilization, and contingency planning well in advance of the disaster (Albahri et al., 2024).

6.3.2 Post-Disaster Damage Assessment

In the immediate aftermath of a disaster, rapid assessment of the affected area is critical for directing aid and organizing rescue efforts. AI facilitates this process through the use of drones, remote sensing technologies, and satellite imagery analysis. Machine learning algorithms can automatically detect structural damage, identify inaccessible areas, and estimate the extent of destruction in a matter of hours, significantly faster than traditional ground surveys. This speed and accuracy help emergency responders prioritize areas most in need, streamline logistics, and allocate resources more effectively (Soleimani et al., 2024).

6.3.3 Risk Mapping and Vulnerability Analysis

AI tools are also instrumental in creating detailed risk and vulnerability maps. By integrating diverse datasets—such as land topography, vegetation cover, population density, infrastructure layout, and historical disaster patterns—machine learning models can identify regions at high risk of specific hazards. These maps are invaluable for urban planning, informing decisions about where to build critical infrastructure like hospitals, schools, and roads, and how to reinforce them against potential disasters. Moreover, risk mapping supports policy formulation and community-based disaster preparedness strategies by highlighting local vulnerabilities (Ghaffarian et al., 2023).

7. AI IN SUSTAINABLE RESOURCE MANAGEMENT

Sustainable resource management is crucial for the health of our ecosystems, economies, and future generations. It involves responsibly managing natural resources such as land, water, and energy, ensuring they are used efficiently and preserved for future use. AI has a significant impact on this area by enabling smarter, data-driven decision-making, optimizing resource utilization, and enhancing operational efficiency. AI plays a crucial role in promoting more sustainable practices across various sectors (Feng et al., 2023).

7.1 Smart Agriculture and Precision Farming

Agriculture is a key contributor to global resource consumption, accounting for a substantial portion of land use, water consumption, and greenhouse gas emissions. As the demand for food continues to grow, it becomes critical to enhance agricultural productivity while minimizing environmental impact (Figure 1). AI is moving toward more sustainable farming methods (Sachithra & Subhashini, 2023).

- **Crop Monitoring and Yield Prediction:** AI systems analyze a combination of satellite imagery, drone footage, and ground-based sensor data to track crop health in real time. These systems detect early signs of stress from pests, diseases, or environmental factors, enabling farmers to respond promptly. AI also helps predict crop yields accurately, allowing farmers to plan their harvests more effectively and avoid overproduction or underproduction (Sharma & Shivandu, 2024).

- **Variable Rate Technology (VRT):** AI-driven VRT systems help optimize the use of fertilizers, pesticides, and water. By processing real-time data from soil moisture sensors, weather forecasts, and plant conditions, these AI models can determine the exact amount of resources needed at any given moment. This precision reduces waste and runoff, minimizing environmental impact and boosting crop productivity (Ravikumar et al., 2024).
- **Autonomous Machinery:** AI-powered autonomous machinery, including self-driving tractors and robotic harvesters, is revolutionizing the farming industry. Machines use computer vision and GPS technology to plant, weed, and harvest crops with minimal human input. This increases efficiency, reduces labor costs, and enables more precise and timely interventions, thereby enhancing overall productivity (Subeesh & Mehta, 2021).
- **Climate-Resilient Agriculture:** AI tools are also helping farmers adapt to changing climates. Through predictive modeling, AI can simulate how various crop varieties will perform under different climate conditions. This information enables farmers to select the most suitable crops for their regions, thereby enhancing their resilience to climate stresses such as droughts, floods, and temperature fluctuations (Sahoo et al., 2025).

7.2 Water Resource Optimization

As water scarcity becomes increasingly pressing due to overuse, contamination, and climate change, managing water resources has never been more critical. AI is helping to address these challenges by providing innovative solutions for monitoring, managing, and optimizing water use.

- **Smart Irrigation Systems:** Traditional irrigation practices often result in water wastage, particularly in regions where water is already scarce. AI-powered irrigation systems are more precise, using data from soil moisture sensors, weather forecasts, and crop water requirements to determine the optimal amount of water needed for each plant (Figure 1). This reduces water waste, ensuring crops receive the right amount of water without over-irrigation (Obaideen et al., 2022).

- **Leak Detection in Water Networks:** In urban areas, water distribution systems are prone to leaks, resulting in significant water loss. AI-powered sensors and analytics systems can detect anomalies in water pressure and flow patterns, pinpointing leaks early in development. This proactive approach allows for quicker repairs, reduces water waste, and minimizes the cost of lost resources (Mahdi et al., 2024).
- **Watershed Management:** AI is also helping to manage water resources on a larger scale. Ml models can forecast runoff patterns, manage reservoir water levels, and predict flood risks. These models assist water authorities in planning and implementing integrated water resource management (IWRM) strategies, balancing water supply with demand while minimizing environmental risks (Ahmed et al., 2024).

7.3 Energy Efficiency and Renewable Integration

Energy consumption is one of the most significant contributors to environmental degradation, and transitioning to cleaner, more efficient energy systems is essential for reducing our carbon footprint. AI is transformative in improving energy efficiency, integrating renewable energy sources, and reducing emissions across various sectors.

- **Smart Grids:** AI-powered smart grids transform how electricity is distributed and consumed. These systems use real-time data to balance electricity supply with demand, ensuring that energy is delivered where and when needed. AI also helps identify faults in the grid and facilitates the integration of renewable energy sources, such as solar and wind, which are often intermittent (Mahmood et al., 2024). By predicting demand patterns and optimizing energy flow, AI makes the grid more resilient and reliable while reducing dependence on fossil fuels.
- **Renewable Energy Forecasting:** Predicting the availability of renewable energy sources, such as solar and wind, is crucial for en-

suring efficient energy production and storage. AI models can accurately forecast solar irradiance and wind speeds, helping energy companies optimize the placement and operation of renewable energy assets. By improving the forecasting of these renewable sources, AI helps maximize their contribution to the energy mix, reducing reliance on non-renewable energy (Li et al., 2024).

- **Building Energy Management:** AI is also enhancing building energy efficiency. Through innovative building systems that adjust lighting, heating, and cooling based on occupancy and environmental conditions, AI can minimize energy consumption without compromising comfort (Alijoyo, 2024). These systems collect data from environmental sensors and occupancy detectors to dynamically adjust energy use, ensuring that buildings consume only the energy they need.
- **Battery Optimization:** Energy storage, primarily through batteries, is crucial for integrating renewable energy sources, such as solar and wind. AI enhances the efficiency and lifespan of batteries by optimizing charging and discharging cycles. This enhances the overall performance of energy storage systems, ensuring that renewable energy can be stored and utilized efficiently, even when the sun is not shining or the wind is not blowing (Bamisile et al., 2024).

By leveraging AI, we can create a more energy-efficient and sustainable future. These technologies enhance the efficiency of energy systems, mitigate environmental impacts, and facilitate the transition to a renewable energy-driven economy.

8. URBAN SUSTAINABILITY AND SMART CITIES

With more than half of the world's population residing in urban areas, which are responsible for over 70% of global greenhouse gas emissions (UN-Habitat, 2020), cities are at the forefront of both the climate challenge and the opportunity for change. As urbanization accelerates, so does the need for sustainable urban development that minimizes environmental impact while improving the quality of life for residents. AI plays a crucial role in creating smarter, more sustainable cities and driving innovation across various sectors of urban living (Das et al., 2024).

8.1 AI in Urban Planning and Infrastructure

Traditional urban planning processes often rely on static, historical data and long-term cycles, which may not be able to adapt quickly to rapidly changing urban dynamics. AI enables more agile, data-driven urban environments that are responsive to real-time trends and needs.

- **Urban Growth Prediction:** MI models can analyze a wide range of data, including population trends, economic indicators, land use patterns, and infrastructure needs, to predict future urban growth. These insights help urban planners make informed decisions about zoning, land allocation, and expanding essential services, such as schools and healthcare facilities (Korah et al., 2024). This allows for proactive planning rather than reactive measures.
- **Infrastructure Optimization:** AI aids in designing more efficient urban infrastructure by simulating various scenarios and determining the optimal placement of roads, utilities, and green spaces. AI models can consider factors like traffic flow, energy use, and environmental impact, ensuring that urban infrastructure is efficient and sustainable with minimal environmental impact (Huang et al., 2025).
- **Digital Twins:** A digital twin is a virtual representation of a city that integrates real-time data, providing a dynamic view of urban systems. Through AI, digital twins can simulate real-world conditions, including traffic, environmental changes, and the impact of new construction projects. This allows urban planners to test potential solutions (e.g., optimizing traffic flow or managing flood risks) before making costly and time-consuming changes in the physical world (Attaran & Celik, 2023). This approach enables better-informed decisions and smoother implementation.

8.2 Waste Management Solutions

Waste management is one of the biggest challenges growing cities face, with waste production constantly increasing. AI offers transformative solutions that enhance efficiency, reduce costs, and facilitate cities' transition to more sustainable waste management practices.

- **Smart Waste Collection:** Innovative waste management systems use sensors and AI algorithms to optimize the timing and routes for waste collection vehicles. Sensors in waste bins monitor fill levels, enabling the system to schedule pickups only when necessary. This reduces fuel consumption, operational costs, and unnecessary trips, contributing to environmental sustainability and economic savings (Hussain et al., 2024).
- **Waste Sorting and Recycling:** AI-powered computer vision systems are revolutionizing recycling by automatically sorting waste at recycling facilities. These systems can distinguish between different materials (such as plastics, metals, and paper) and evaluate their quality (Olawade et al., 2024a). By automating this process, AI increases recycling rates, reduces contamination, and improves resource recovery efficiency, supporting a circular economy where materials are reused and recycled rather than sent to landfills.
- **Illegal Dumping Detection:** AI-equipped surveillance systems detect illegal dumping in urban areas (Figure 3). These systems utilize ML algorithms to analyze images and video footage, identifying instances of unauthorized waste disposal. Once detected, the data will take enforcement actions, helping maintain cleaner and healthier urban spaces (Du et al., 2023).

8.3 Sustainable Transportation Systems

Transportation in urban areas is a significant source of pollution, congestion, and greenhouse gas emissions. AI is shifting its focus to making transportation systems more efficient, sustainable, and accessible.

- **Traffic Flow Optimization:** AI systems process real-time traffic data from sensors, cameras, and GPS devices to optimize traffic signals, manage congestion, and reduce waiting times at intersections. AI models can predict traffic patterns and adjust signal timing accordingly, ensuring smoother traffic flow and reduced emissions from idling vehicles.
- **Public Transit Management:** AI is also helping to optimize public transportation networks by predicting passenger demand, managing routes, and forecasting delays. For example, MI algorithms analyze historical transit data to predict peak times, allowing transit authorities to adjust service frequency and capacity in real time. This ensures that public transport remains efficient, reducing the need for car usage and lowering overall emissions (Grahn et al., 2021).
- **Autonomous Vehicles (AVs):** Self-driving cars, buses, and delivery robots rely on AI to navigate streets, avoid obstacles, and make real-time decisions based on traffic and road conditions. By optimizing routes and minimizing energy consumption, autonomous vehicles have the potential to enhance safety, reduce emissions, and increase transportation efficiency (Zhang et al., 2023).
- **Mobility-as-a-Service (MaaS):** AI is making urban mobility more flexible and sustainable through MaaS platforms that integrate multiple forms of transportation, such as public transit, bike-sharing, and ride-hailing, into a single digital service. This integration allows users to plan, book, and pay for their entire journey from start to finish, making sustainable transportation options more accessible and convenient for everyone (Narayanan & Antoniou, 2023).

By improving transportation efficiency, reducing emissions, and offering more sustainable mobility options, AI is helping cities meet their climate goals while enhancing the overall livability of urban environments.

AI is playing a critical role in shaping the future of urban sustainability. From transforming urban planning to optimizing waste management and revolutionizing transportation systems, AI enables cities to become smarter, more efficient, and more sustainable. These innovations not only help cities reduce their environmental impact but also enhance the quality of life for their residents, making urban living more sustainable for future generations.

9. ETHICAL AND SOCIETAL CONSIDERATIONS

AI has great potential for advancing environmental sustainability, and its use also raises ethical and societal concerns that must align with human rights and ecological values. Responsible deployment is essential to avoid unintended consequences and ensure fairness, transparency, and public trust.

9.1 Risks and Limitations of AI Deployment

AI is not without its challenges, and its effectiveness depends on factors such as data quality and model transparency. Key concerns include:

- Data Bias: AI models trained on incomplete or biased data can perpetuate inaccuracies, especially in under-monitored regions, exacerbating existing inequalities.
- Overdependence on Automation: Relying too much on AI can erode local knowledge and ignore cultural factors that influence environmental behavior.
- False Precision: AI systems can give the illusion of certainty, leading to overconfidence and potential harm if decisions are made without proper human oversight.

Recognizing these limitations encourages a cautious, context-aware approach to AI deployment.

9.2 Data Privacy and Surveillance Risks

The widespread use of AI for environmental monitoring, especially in urban areas, raises privacy concerns:

- Consent and Transparency: Individuals must be informed about how their data is collected and who is responsible for its control. Transparent governance models are key to maintaining trust.
- Surveillance Trade-offs: AI tools like drones can be misused for surveillance, infringing on privacy and civil liberties if not adequately regulated.
- Data Sovereignty: Global AI systems raise questions about data ownership and ethical oversight across borders, highlighting the need for international norms.

9.3 Ensuring Inclusivity and Global Equity

AI solutions often reflect the priorities of wealthier nations, potentially overlooking the needs of low-income or marginalized communities. To ensure global equity:

- Capacity Gaps: Low- and middle-income countries often lack the necessary infrastructure to leverage the benefits of AI fully. International cooperation and local training are necessary to bridge this gap.
- Cultural Context: Sustainability varies across regions, and AI models must be adaptable to local conditions.
- Participatory Design: Involving diverse stakeholders, including marginalized communities, ensures AI solutions are relevant and fair.

AI must reflect global diversity and empower marginalized voices to create equitable solutions.

9.4 Environmental Costs of AI

While AI supports sustainability, its environmental costs are significant, particularly in terms of energy consumption and infrastructure:

- Green AI: Advocates for energy-efficient AI models and transparency about their environmental footprint.

- Sustainable Computing: Reducing AI's ecological impact requires investment in renewable energy for data centers and optimizing code to minimize energy use.
- Lifecycle Assessment: To ensure AI supports sustainability goals, it must thoroughly assess its environmental impact, from resource extraction to end-of-life e-waste management.

For AI to be truly sustainable, it must minimize its environmental footprint while promoting global sustainability.

10. CONCLUSION

AI is a powerful ally in the global pursuit of environmental sustainability. By enabling more intelligent decision-making, real-time monitoring, and predictive capabilities, AI is reshaping how we understand and respond to pressing ecological challenges—from climate change and biodiversity loss to pollution and resource management. Its integration with other emerging technologies offers innovative solutions across agriculture, urban planning, energy, and water management. However, the path forward demands more than technological advancement—it calls for ethical responsibility, inclusivity, and a commitment to minimizing the environmental footprint of AI. With thoughtful application and governance, AI can play a transformative role in building a more sustainable and resilient future for all.

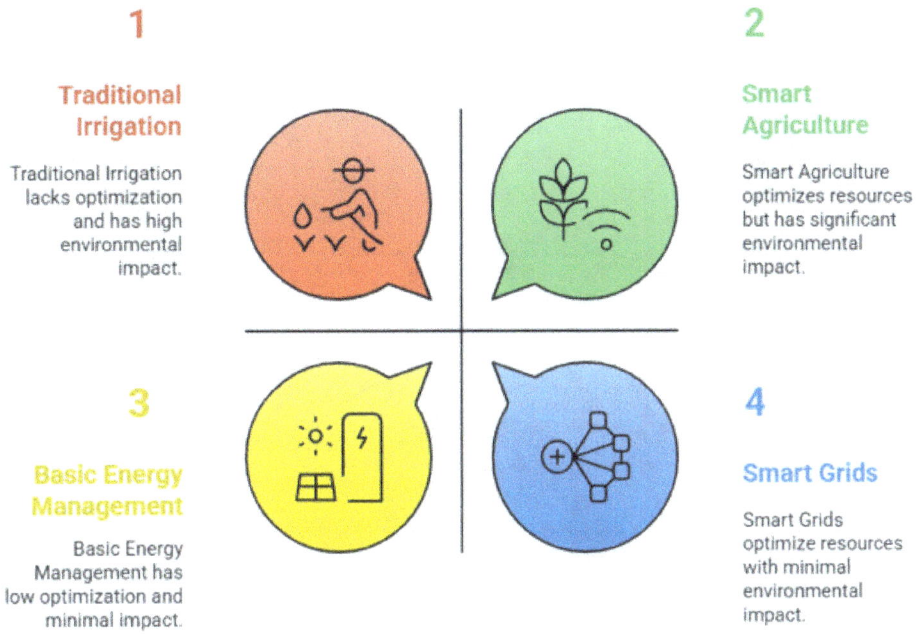
1
Traditional Irrigation
Traditional Irrigation lacks optimization and has high environmental impact.
2
Smart Agriculture
Smart Agriculture optimizes resources but has significant environmental impact.
3
Basic Energy Management
Basic Energy Management has low optimization and minimal impact.
4
Smart Grids
Smart Grids optimize resources with minimal environmental impact.

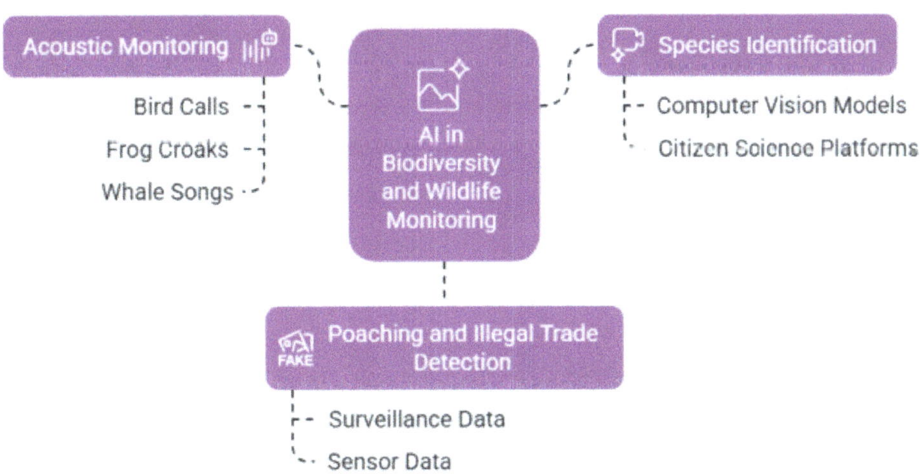
AI in Biodiversity and Wildlife Monitoring
Acoustic Monitoring
Bird Calls
Frog Croaks
Whale Songs
Species Identification
Computer Vision Models
Citizen Science Platforms
Poaching and Illegal Trade Detection
FAKE
Surveillance Data
Sensor Data

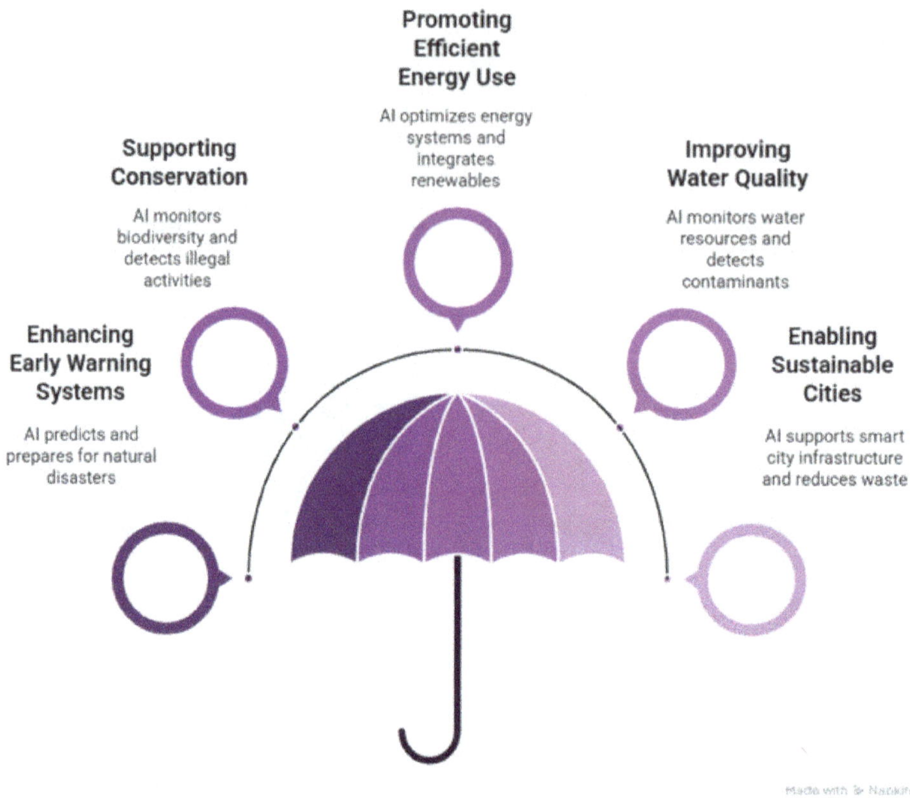
Promoting Efficient Energy Use
AI optimizes energy systems and integrates renewables
Supporting Conservation
AI monitors biodiversity and detects illegal activities
Improving Water Quality
AI monitors water resources and detects contaminants
Enhancing Early Warning Systems
AI predicts and prepares for natural disasters
Enabling Sustainable Cities
AI supports smart city infrastructure and reduces waste

REFERENCES

Abbass, K., Qasim, M. Z., Song, H., Murshed, M., Mahmood, H., & Younis, I. (2022). A review of the global climate change impacts, adaptation, and sustainable mitigation measures. *Environmental Science and Pollution Research International*, *29*(28), 42539–42559. DOI: 10.1007/s11356-022-19718-6

Ahmed, A. A., Sayed, S., Abdoulhalik, A., Moutari, S., & Oyedele, L. (2024). Applications of machine learning to water resources management: A review of present status and future opportunities. *Journal of Cleaner Production*, *441*, 140715. DOI: 10.1016/j.jclepro.2024.140715

Akhyar, A., Zulkifley, M. A., Lee, J., Song, T., Han, J., Cho, C., Hyun, S., Son, Y., & Hong, B.-W. (2024). Deep artificial intelligence applications for natural disaster management systems: *A methodological review. Ecological Indicators*, *163*, 112067. DOI: 10.1016/j.ecolind.2024.112067

Al-Falahi, A. H., Saddique, N., Spank, U., & Bernhofer, C. (2024). Building high-resolution projections of temperature potential changes using statistical downscaling for the future period 2026–2100 in the highland region of Yemen – A supportive approach for empowering environmental planning and decision-making. *Environmental and Sustainability Indicators*, *24*, 100490. DOI: 10.1016/j.indic.2024.100490

Albahri, A. S., Khaleel, Y. L., Habeeb, M. A., Ismael, R. D., Hameed, Q. A., Deveci, M., Homod, R. Z., Albahri, O. S., Alamoodi, A. H., & Alzubaidi, L. (2024). A systematic review of trustworthy artificial intelligence applications in natural disasters. *Computers and Electrical Engineering*, 118(Part B), 109409.DOI: 10.1016/j.compeleceng.2024.109409

Alijoyo, F. A. (2024). AI-powered deep learning for sustainable Industry 4.0 and Internet of Things: Enhancing energy management in smart buildings. *Alexandria Engineering Journal*, *104*, 409–422. DOI: 10.1016/j.aej.2024.07.110

Alotaibi, E., & Nassif, N. (2024). Artificial intelligence in environmental monitoring: In-depth analysis. *Discover Artificial Intelligence*, *4*(1), 84. DOI: 10.1007/s44163-024-00198-1

Alzoubi, Y. I., & Mishra, A. (2024). Green artificial intelligence initiatives: Potentials and challenges. *Journal of Cleaner Production*, *468*, 143090. DOI: 10.1016/j.jclepro.2024.143090

Aminzadegan, S., Shahriari, M., Mehranfar, F., & Abramović, B. (2022). Factors affecting the emission of pollutants in different types of transportation: *A literature review. Energy Reports*, *8*, 2508–2529. DOI: 10.1016/j.egyr.2022.01.161

Andersson-Sköld, Y., Thorsson, S., Rayner, D., Lindberg, F., Janhäll, S., Jonsson, A., Moback, U., Bergman, R., & Granberg, M. (2015). An integrated method for assessing climate-related risks and adaptation alternatives in urban areas. *Climate Risk Management*, *7*, 31–50. DOI: 10.1016/j.crm.2015.01.003

Attaran, M., & Celik, B. G. (2023). Digital Twin: Benefits, use cases, challenges, and opportunities. *Decision Analytics Journal*, *6*, 100165. DOI: 10.1016/j.dajour.2023.100165

Bamisile, O., Cai, D., Adun, H., Dagbasi, M., Ukwuoma, C. C., Huang, Q., Johnson, N., & Bamisile, O. (2024). Towards renewables development: Review optimization techniques for energy storage and hybrid renewable energy systems. *Heliyon*, *10*(19), e37482. DOI: 10.1016/j.heliyon.2024.e37482

Bibri, S. E., Huang, J., Jagatheesaperumal, S. K., & Krogstie, J. (2024a). The synergistic interplay of artificial intelligence and digital twin in environmentally planning sustainable smart cities: A comprehensive systematic review. *Environmental Science and Ecotechnology*, *20*, 100433. DOI: 10.1016/j.ese.2024.100433

Bibri, S. E., Krogstie, J., Kaboli, A., & Alahi, A. (2024b). Smarter eco-cities and their leading-edge artificial intelligence of things solutions for environmental sustainability: A comprehensive systematic review. *Environmental Science and Ecotechnology*, *19*, 100330. DOI: 10.1016/j.ese.2023.100330

Bolan, S., Padhye, L. P., Jasemizad, T., Govarthanan, M., Karmegam, N., Wijesekara, H., Amarasiri, D., Hou, D., Zhou, P., Biswal, B. K., Balasubramanian, R., Wang, H., Siddique, K. H. M., Rinklebe, J., Kirkham, M. B., & Bolan, N. (2024). Impacts of climate change on the fate of contaminants through extreme weather events. *The Science of the Total Environment, 909*, 168388. DOI: 10.1016/j.scitotenv.2023.168388

Bolón-Canedo, V., Morán-Fernández, L., Cancela, B., & Alonso-Betanzos, A. (2024b). A review of green artificial intelligence: Towards a more sustainable future. *Neurocomputing*, *599*, 128096. DOI: 10.1016/j.neucom.2024.128096

Boumaiza, A., & Maher, K. (2024). Leveraging blockchain technology to enhance transparency and efficiency in carbon trading markets. *International Journal of Electrical Power & Energy Systems, 162*, 110225. DOI: 10.1016/j.ijepes.2024.110225

Brundtland, G. H. (1987). Our Common Future: Report of the World Commission on Environment and Development (UN Document A/42/427). United Nations.

Buckton, S. J., Fazey, I., Sharpe, B., Om, E. S., Doherty, B., Ball, P., Denby, K., Bryant, M., Lait, R., Bridle, S., Cain, M., Carmen, E., Collins, L., Nixon, N., Yap, C., Connolly, A., Fletcher, B., Frankowska, A., Gardner, G., & Sinclair, M. (2023). The regenerative lens: A conceptual framework for regenerative social-ecological systems. *One Earth*, *6*(7), 824–842. DOI: 10.1016/j.oneear.2023.06.006

Chen, L., Chen, Z., Zhang, Y., Liu, Y., Osman, A. I., Farghali, M., Hua, J., Al-Fatesh, A., Ihara, I., Rooney, D. W., & Yap, P.-S. (2023). Artificial intelligence-based solutions for climate change: *A review. Environmental Chemistry Letters, 21*(5), 2525–2557. DOI: 10.1007/s10311-023-01617-y

Choudhary, B., Dhar, V., & Pawase, A. S. (2024). Blue carbon and the role of mangroves in carbon sequestration: Its mechanisms, estimation, human impacts, and conservation strategies for economic incentives. *Journal of Sea Research, 199*, 102504. DOI: 10.1016/j.seares.2024.102504

Collins, C., Dennehy, D., Conboy, K., & Mikalef, P. (2021). Artificial intelligence in information systems research: A systematic literature review and research agenda. *International Journal of Information Management, 60*, 102383. DOI: 10.1016/j.ijinfomgt.2021.102383

Das, A., & Swain, P. K. (2024). Navigating the sea level rise: Exploring the interplay of climate change, sea level rise, and coastal communities in India. *Environmental Monitoring and Assessment, 196*(11), 1010. DOI: 10.1007/s10661-024-13191-z

Das, S., Choudhury, M. R., Chatterjee, B., Das, P., Bagri, S., Paul, D., Bera, M., & Dutta, S. (2024). Unravelling the urban climate crisis: Exploring the nexus of urbanization, climate change, and their impacts on the environment and human wellbeing – *A global perspective. AIMS Public Health, 11*(3), 963–1001. DOI: 10.3934/publichealth.2024050

Davison, A. M., de Koning, K., Taubert, F., & Schakel, J.-K. (2025). Automated near real-time monitoring in ecology: Status quo and ways forward. *Ecological Informatics, 103157*, 103157. Advance online publication. DOI: 10.1016/j.ecoinf.2025.103157

Ding, N., Xi, Y., Jiang, W., Li, H., Su, J., Yang, S., & Lie, T. T. (2025). State-of-the-art carbon metering: Continuous emission monitoring systems for industrial applications. *Heliyon, 11*(3), e42308. DOI: 10.1016/j.heliyon.2025.e42308

Dritsas, E., & Trigka, M. (2025). Exploring the intersection of machine learning and big data: A survey. *Machine Learning and Knowledge Extraction, 7*(1), 13. DOI: 10.3390/make7010013

Du, L., Zuo, J., Vanzo, J., Chang, R., & Zillante, G. (2023). Assessing and predicting the risks of illegal dumping based on road characteristics. *Waste Management (New York, N.Y.), 169*, 332–341. DOI: 10.1016/j.wasman.2023.07.031

Durgun, Y. (2024). Real-time water quality monitoring using AI-enabled sensors: Detection of contaminants and UV disinfection analysis in smart urban water systems. *Journal of King Saud University. Science, 36*(9), 103409. DOI: 10.1016/j.jksus.2024.103409

El Geneidy, S., Baumeister, S., Marini Govigli, V., Orfanidou, T., & Wallius, V. (2021). The carbon footprint of a knowledge organization and emission scenarios for a post-COVID-19 world. *Environmental Impact Assessment Review, 91*, 106645. DOI: 10.1016/j.eiar.2021.106645

Feng, T., Xiong, R., & Huan, P. (2023). Productive use of natural resources in agriculture: The main policy lessons. *Resources Policy,* 85(Part A), 103793.DOI: 10.1016/j.resourpol.2023.103793

Friedman, N., & Ormiston, J. (2022). Blockchain as a sustainability-oriented innovation? Opportunities for and resistance to Blockchain technology as a driver of sustainability in global food supply chains. *Technological Forecasting and Social Change, 175*, 121403. DOI: 10.1016/j.techfore.2021.121403

Furtak, K., & Wolińska, A. (2023). The impact of extreme weather events as a consequence of climate change on the soil moisture and on the quality of the soil environment and agriculture – *A review. Catena, 231*, 107378. DOI: 10.1016/j.catena.2023.107378

Futa, B., Gmitrowicz-Iwan, J., Skersienė, A., Šlepetienė, A., & Parašotas, I. (2024). Innovative soil management strategies for sustainable agriculture. *Sustainability (Basel), 16*(21), 9481. DOI: 10.3390/su16219481

Ghaffarian, S., Taghikhah, F. R., & Maier, H. R. (2023). Explainable artificial intelligence in disaster risk management: Achievements and prospective futures. *International Journal of Disaster Risk Reduction, 98*, 104123. DOI: 10.1016/j.ijdrr.2023.104123

Grahn, R., Qian, S., & Hendrickson, C. (2021). Improving the performance of first- and last-mile mobility services through transit coordination, real-time demand prediction, advanced reservations, and trip prioritization. *Transportation Research Part C, Emerging Technologies, 133*, 103430. DOI: 10.1016/j.trc.2021.103430

Greif, L., Kimmig, A., El Bobbou, S., Jurisch, P., & Ovtcharova, J. (2024). Strategic view on the current role of AI in advancing environmental sustainability: A SWOT analysis. *Discover Artificial Intelligence, 4*(1), 45. DOI: 10.1007/s44163-024-00146-z

Hariyani, D., Hariyani, P., Mishra, S., & Sharma, M. K. (2024). Leveraging digital technologies for advancing circular economy practices and enhancing life cycle analysis: A systematic literature review. *Waste Management Bulletin*, *2*(3), 69–83. DOI: 10.1016/j.wmb.2024.06.007

Huang, J., Bibri, S. E., & Keel, P. (2025). Generative spatial artificial intelligence for sustainable smart cities: A pioneering large flow model for urban digital twin. *Environmental Science and Ecotechnology*, *24*, 100526. DOI: 10.1016/j.ese.2025.100526

Hussain, I., Elomri, A., Kerbache, L., & El Omri, A. (2024). Smart city solutions: Comparative analysis of waste management models in IoT-enabled environments using multi-agent simulation. *Sustainable Cities and Society*, *103*, 105247. DOI: 10.1016/j.scs.2024.105247

Ingrao, C., Strippoli, R., Lagioia, G., & Huisingh, D. (2023). Water scarcity in agriculture: An overview of causes, impacts, and approaches for reducing the risks. *Heliyon,* 9(8), e18507.doi: . 2023.e18507.DOI: 10.1016/j.heliyon

Islam, B. S., Valles, D., Hibbitts, T. J., Ryberg, W. A., Walkup, D. K., & Forstner, M. R. J. (2023). Animal species recognition with deep convolutional neural networks from ecological camera trap images. *Animals (Basel)*, *13*(9), 1526. DOI: 10.3390/ani13091526

Jakhar, R., Samek, L., & Styszko, K. (2023). A comprehensive study of the impact of waste fires on the environment and health. *Sustainability (Basel)*, *15*(19), 14241. DOI: 10.3390/su151914241

Janga, B., Asamani, G. P., Sun, Z., & Cristea, N. (2023). A review of practical AI for remote sensing in Earth sciences. *Remote Sensing (Basel)*, *15*(16), 4112. DOI: 10.3390/rs15164112

Javaid, M., Haleem, A., Singh, R. P., & Suman, R. (2022). Enhancing smart farming through the applications of Agriculture 4.0 technologies. *International Journal of Intelligent Networks*, *3*, 150–164. DOI: 10.1016/j.ijin.2022.09.004

Javanmardi, E., Liu, S., & Xie, N. (2023). Exploring the challenges to sustainable development from the perspective of grey systems theory. *Systems, 11*(2), 70. DOI: 10.3390/systems11020070

Jeantet, L., & Dufourq, E. (2023). Improving deep learning acoustic classifiers with contextual information for wildlife monitoring. *Ecological Informatics*, *77*, 102256. DOI: 10.1016/j.ecoinf.2023.102256

Kamminga, J., Ayele, E., Meratnia, N., & Havinga, P. (2018). Poaching Detection Technologies—*A Survey. Sensors (Basel)*, *18*(5), 1474. DOI: 10.3390/s18051474

Korah, A., Koch, J. A. M., & Wimberly, M. C. (2024). Understanding urban growth modeling in Africa: Dynamics, drivers, and challenges. *Cities (London, England)*, *146*, 104734. DOI: 10.1016/j.cities.2023.104734

Kumar, S., Tiwari, P., & Zymbler, M. (2019). Internet of Things is a revolutionary approach for future technology enhancement: *A review. Journal of Big Data*, *6*(1), 111. DOI: 10.1186/s40537-019-0268-2

Li, P., Yang, H., Wu, H., Wang, Y., Su, H., Zheng, T., Zhu, F., Zhang, G., & Han, Y. (2024). Deep learning model for solar and wind energy forecasting considering Northwest China as an example. *Results in Engineering*, *24*, 102939. DOI: 10.1016/j.rineng.2024.102939

Mahdi, N. M., Jassim, A. H., Abulqasim, S. A., Basem, A., Ogaili, A. A. F., & Al-Haddad, L. A. (2024). Leak detection and localization in water distribution systems using advanced feature analysis and an Artificial Neural Network. *Desalination and Water Treatment*, *320*, 100685. DOI: 10.1016/j.dwt.2024.100685

Mahmood, M., Chowdhury, P., Yeassin, R., Hasan, M., Ahmad, T., & Chowdhury, N.-U.-R. (2024). Impacts of digitalization on smart grids, renewable energy, and demand response: An updated review of current applications. *Energy Conversion and Management*: X, 24, 100790.DOI: 10.1016/j.ecmx.2024.100790

Mana, A. A., Allouhi, A., Hamrani, A., Rehman, S., el Jamaoui, I., & Jayachandran, K. (2024). Sustainable AI-based production agriculture: Exploring AI applications and implications in agricultural practices. *Smart Agricultural Technology*, *7*, 100416. DOI: 10.1016/j.atech.2024.100416

Miller, T., Durlik, I., Kostecka, E., Kozlovska, P., Łobodzińska, A., Sokołowska, S., & Nowy, A. (2025). Integrating Artificial Intelligence Agents with the Internet of Things for Enhanced Environmental Monitoring: Applications in Water Quality and Climate Data. *Electronics (Basel)*, *14*(4), 696. DOI: 10.3390/electronics14040696

Narayanan, S., & Antoniou, C. (2023). Shared mobility services towards Mobility as a Service (MaaS): What, who, and when? *Transportation Research Part A, Policy and Practice*, *168*, 103581. DOI: 10.1016/j.tra.2023.103581

Natarajan, S. K., Shanmurthy, P., Arockiam, D., Balusamy, B., & Selvarajan, S. (2024). Optimized machine learning model for air quality index prediction in major cities in India. *Scientific Reports*, *14*(1), 6795. DOI: 10.1038/s41598-024-54807-1

Nivedita, V., Begum, S. S., Aldehim, G., Alashjaee, A. M., Arasi, M. A., Sikkandar, M. Y., Jayasankar, T., & Vivek, S. (2024). Plastic debris detection along coastal waters using Sentinel-2 satellite data and machine learning techniques. *Marine Pollution Bulletin,* 209 (Part A), 117106.DOI: 10.1016/j.marpolbul.2024.117106

Obaideen, K., Yousef, B. A. A., AlMallahi, M. N., Tan, Y. C., Mahmoud, M., Jaber, H., & Ramadan, M. (2022). An overview of smart irrigation systems using IoT. *Energy Nexus*, *7*, 100124. DOI: 10.1016/j.nexus.2022.100124

Olawade, D. B., Fapohunda, O., Wada, O. Z., Usman, S. O., Ige, A. O., Ajisafe, O., & Oladapo, B. I. (2024a). Smart waste management: A paradigm shift enabled by artificial intelligence. *Waste Management Bulletin*, *2*(2), 244–263. DOI: 10.1016/j.wmb.2024.05.001

Olawade, D. B., Wada, O. Z., David-Olawade, A. C., Fapohunda, O., Ige, A. O., & Ling, J. (2024b). Artificial intelligence potential for net-zero sustainability: Current evidence and prospects. *Next Sustainability*, *4*, 100041. DOI: 10.1016/j.nxsust.2024.100041

Olawade, D. B., Wada, O. Z., Ige, A. O., Egbewole, B. I., Olojo, A., & Oladapo, B. I. (2024c). Artificial intelligence in environmental monitoring: Advancements, challenges, and future directions. *Hygiene and Environmental Health Advances, 12*, 100114. DOI: 10.1016/j.heha.2024.100114

Orssatto, J. (2001). Environmental challenges in organizations. In Smelser, N. J., & Baltes, P. B. (Eds.), *International Encyclopedia of the Social & Behavioral Sciences* (pp. 4590–4592). Pergamon., DOI: 10.1016/B0-08-043076-7/04244-3

Pérez-Beltrán, C. H., Robles, A. D., Rodriguez, N. A., Ortega-Gavilán, F., & Jiménez-Carvelo, A. M. (2024). Artificial intelligence and water quality: From drinking water to wastewater. *Trends in Analytical Chemistry, 172*, 117597. DOI: 10.1016/j.trac.2024.117597

Popescu, S. M., Mansoor, S., Wani, O. A., Kumar, S. S., Sharma, V., Sharma, A., Arya, V. M., Kirkham, M. B., Hou, D., Bolan, N., & Chung, Y. S. (2024, February 20). Artificial intelligence and IoT-driven technologies for environmental pollution monitoring and management. *Frontiers in Environmental Science, 12*, 1336088. Advance online publication. DOI: 10.3389/fenvs.2024.1336088

Purvis, B., Mao, Y., & Robinson, D. (2019). Three pillars of sustainability: In search of conceptual origins. *Sustainability Science, 14*(3), 681–695. DOI: 10.1007/s11625-018-0627-5

Pushpalatha, V., Mallikarjuna, P. B., Mahendra, H. N., Subramoniam, S. R., & Mallikarjunaswamy, S. (2025). Land use and land cover classification for change detection studies using a convolutional neural network. *Applied Computing and Geosciences, 25*, 100227. DOI: 10.1016/j.acags.2025.100227

Rajasekhar, N., Radhakrishnan, T. K., & Samsudeen, N. (2025). Exploring reinforcement learning in process control: A comprehensive survey. *International Journal of Systems Science, 56*(14), 1–30. DOI: 10.1080/00207721.2025.2469821

Ramadan, M. N. A., Ali, M. A. H., Khoo, S. Y., Alkhedher, M., & Alherbawi, M. (2024). Real-time IoT-powered AI system for monitoring and forecasting air pollution in an industrial environment. *Ecotoxicology and Environmental Safety*, *283*, 116856. DOI: 10.1016/j.ecoenv.2024.116856

Rashid, A. B., & Kausik, M. A. K. (2024). AI revolutionizing industries worldwide: A comprehensive overview of its diverse applications. *Hybrid Advances*, *7*, 100277. DOI: 10.1016/j.hybadv.2024.100277

Ravikumar, S., Vellingiri, G., Sellaperumal, P., Pandian, K., Sivasankar, A., & Sangchul, H. (2024). Real-time nitrogen monitoring and management to augment N use efficiency and ecosystem sustainability–A review. *Journal of Hazardous Materials Advances*, *16*, 100466. DOI: 10.1016/j.hazadv.2024.100466

Regona, M., Yigitcanlar, T., Hon, C., & Teo, M. (2024). Artificial intelligence and sustainable development goals: Systematic literature review of the construction industry. *Sustainable Cities and Society*, *108*, 105499. DOI: 10.1016/j.scs.2024.105499

Reynolds, S. A., Beery, S., Burgess, N., Burgman, M., Butchart, S. H. M., Cooke, S. J., Coomes, D., Danielsen, F., Di Minin, E., Durán, A. P., Gassert, F., Hinsley, A., Jaffer, S., Jones, J. P. G., Li, B. V., Mac Aodha, O., Madhavapeddy, A., O'Donnell, S. A. L., Oxbury, W. M., & Sutherland, W. J. (2025). The potential for AI to revolutionize conservation: A horizon scan. *Trends in Ecology & Evolution*, *40*(2), 191–207. DOI: 10.1016/j.tree.2024.11.013

Rockström, J., Steffen, W., Noone, K., Persson, Å., Chapin, F. S.III, Lambin, E. F., Lenton, T. M., Scheffer, M., Folke, C., Schellnhuber, H. J., Nykvist, B., De Wit, C. A., Hughes, T., van der Leeuw, S., Rodhe, H., Sörlin, S., Snyder, P. K., Costanza, R., Svedin, U., & Foley, J. A. (2009). A safe operating space for humanity. *Nature*, *461*(7263), 472–475. DOI: 10.1038/461472a

Sachithra, V., & Subhashini, L. D. C. S. (2023). How artificial intelligence is used to achieve agricultural sustainability: A systematic review. *Artificial Intelligence in Agriculture*, *8*, 46–59. DOI: 10.1016/j.aiia.2023.04.002

Sahoo, S., Singha, C., Govind, A., & Moghimi, A. (2025). Review of climate-resilient agriculture for ensuring food security: Sustainability opportunities and challenges of India. *Environmental and Sustainability Indicators, 25*, 100544. DOI: 10.1016/j.indic.2024.100544

Salmi, A., Quarshie, A. M., Scott-Kennel, J., & Kähkönen, A.-K. (2023). Biodiversity management: A supply chain practice view. *Journal of Purchasing and Supply Management*, *29*(4), 100865. DOI: 10.1016/j.pursup.2023.100865

Schmager, S., Pappas, I. O., & Vassilakopoulou, P. (2025). Understanding human-centered AI: A review of its defining elements and a research agenda. *Behaviour & Information Technology*, *44*(15), 1–40. DOI: 10.1080/0144929X.2024.2448719

Shah, H., Hellegers, P., & Siderius, C. (2021). Climate risk to agriculture: A synthesis to define different types of critical moments. *Climate Risk Management, 34*, 100378. DOI: 10.1016/j.crm.2021.100378

Sharma, I., & Birman, S. (2024). Biodiversity loss, ecosystem services, and their role in promoting sustainable health. In Singh, P., & Yadav, N. (Eds.), *The climate-health-sustainability nexus*. Springer. DOI: 10.1007/978-3-031-56564-9_7

Sharma, K., & Shivandu, S. K. (2024). *Integrating artificial intelligence and the Internet of Things (IoT) for enhanced crop monitoring and management in precision agriculture. Sensors International, 5, 100292.* Springer., DOI: 10.1007/978-3-031-56564-9_7

Shetty, S. S., Deepthi, D., Harshitha, S., Sonkusare, S., Naik, P. B., Kumari, S. N., & Madhyastha, H. (2023). Environmental pollutants and their effects on human health. *Heliyon*, *9*(9), e19496. DOI: 10.1016/j.heliyon.2023.e19496

Shivanna, K. R. (2022). Climate change and its impact on biodiversity and human welfare. *Proceedings of the Indian National Science Academy. Part A, Physical Sciences*, *88*(2), 160–171. DOI: 10.1007/s43538-022-00073-6

Shobanke, M., Bhatt, M., & Shittu, E. (2025). Advancements and future outlook of artificial intelligence in energy and climate change modeling. *Advances in Applied Energy*, *17*, 100211. DOI: 10.1016/j.adapen.2025.100211

Soleimani, R., Soleimani-Babakamali, M. H., Meng, S., Avci, O., & Taciroglu, E. (2024). Computer vision tools for early post-disaster assessment: Enhancing generalizability. Engineering *Applications of Artificial Intelligence,* 136(Part A), 108855.DOI: 10.1016/j.engappai.2024.108855

Subeesh, A., & Mehta, C. R. (2021). Automation and digitization of agriculture using artificial intelligence and the Internet of Things. *Artificial Intelligence in Agriculture*, *5*, 278–291. DOI: 10.1016/j.aiia.2021.11.004

Supriyono, W., Wibawa, A. P., Suyono, , & Kurniawan, F. (2024). Advancements in natural language processing: Implications, challenges, and future directions. *Telematics and Informatics Reports*, *16*, 100173. DOI: 10.1016/j.teler.2024.100173

van der Sluijs, J. P., & Vaage, N. S. (2016). Pollinators and global food security: The need for holistic global stewardship. *Food Ethics*, *1*(1), 75–91. DOI: 10.1007/s41055-016-0003-z

Van Wynsberghe, A. (2021). Sustainable AI: AI for sustainability and the sustainability of AI. *AI and Ethics*, *1*(3), 213–218. DOI: 10.1007/s43681-021-00043-6

Wang, Z., Wang, T., Zhang, X., Wang, J., Yang, Y., Sun, Y., Guo, X., Wu, Q., Nepovimova, E., Watson, A. E., & Kuca, K. (2024). Biodiversity conservation in the context of climate change: Facing challenges and management strategies. *The Science of the Total Environment*, *937*, 173377. DOI: 10.1016/j.scitotenv.2024.173377

Waqas, M., Humphries, U. W., Chueasa, B., & Wangwongchai, A. (2024). Artificial intelligence and numerical weather prediction models: A technical survey. *Natural Hazards Research*. (Advance online publication). DOI: 10.1016/j.nhres.2024.11.004

Weiskopf, S. R., Rubenstein, M. A., Crozier, L. G., Gaichas, S., Griffis, R., Halofsky, J. E., Hyde, K. J. W., Morelli, T. L., Morisette, J. T., Muñoz, R. C., Pershing, A. J., Peterson, D. L., Poudel, R., Staudinger, M. D., Sutton-Grier, A. E., Thompson, L., Vose, J., Weltzin, J. F., & Whyte, K. P. (2020). Climate change affects biodiversity, ecosystems, ecosystem services, and natural resource management in the United States— *cience of The Total Environment,* 733, 137782..DOI: 10.1016/j.scitotenv.2020.137782

Xu, Y., Liu, X., Cao, X., Huang, C., Liu, E., Qian, S., Liu, X., Wu, Y., Dong, F., Qiu, C.-W., Qiu, J., Hua, K., Su, W., Wu, J., Xu, H., Han, Y., Fu, C., Yin, Z., Liu, M., & Zhang, J. (2021). A*rtificial intelligence: A powerful paradigm for scientific research. Innovation (Cambridge (Mass.)), 2*(4), 100179. DOI: 10.1016/j.xinn.2021.100179

Yu, P., Wei, Y., Ma, L., Wang, B., Yung, E. H. K., & Chen, Y. (2024). rbanization and the urban critical zone. *arth Critical Zone,* 1(1), 100011. DOI: 10.1016/j.ecz.2024.100011

Zhang, Y., Carballo, A., Yang, H., & Takeda, K. (2023). Perception and sensing for autonomous vehicles under adverse weather conditions: A survey. *ISPRS Journal of Photogrammetry and Remote Sensing, 196*, 146–177. DOI: 10.1016/j.isprsjprs.2022.12.021

Zhao, A. P., Li, S., Cao, Z., Hu, P. J.-H., Wang, J., Xiang, Y., Xie, D., & Lu, X. (2024). I for science: Predicting infectious diseases. *ournal of Safety Science and Resilience,* 5(2), 130–146. DOI: 10.1038/s41467-019-14108-y

Zhou, Y., & Gu, B. (2024). The impacts of human activities on Earth's Critical Zone. *arth Critical Zone,* 1(1), 100004.DOI: 10.1016/j.ecz.2024.100004

Chapter 3

Dynamic Interactions Between Economic Growth, Renewable Energy, and CO_2 Emissions in Norway Using a Fourier-Augmented ARDL Model

Nerimene Gzara
https://orcid.org/0009-0004-8879-7073
University of Tunis el Manar, Tunisia

Amal Jmaii
https://orcid.org/0000-0002-6918-9839
University of Tunis El Manar, Tunisia

ABSTRACT

This study investigates the relationship between renewable energy consumption, technological innovation, economic growth, and CO_2 emissions in Norway from 1990 to 2021 using the Fourier-Augmented ARDL model. The long-run results show that GDP growth increases emissions, while

DOI: 10.4018/979-8-3373-1077-0.ch003

renewable energy and patent activity contribute to emissions reduction. In the short run, GDP significantly impacts emissions, whereas the effects of renewable energy and innovation are limited. These findings highlight the importance of sustained investments in green technologies and energy transition policies. The study provides new empirical evidence for the role of innovation and renewables in decarbonizing high-income economies

INTRODUCTION

Climate change represents a critical global concern, with carbon dioxide (CO_2) emissions playing a significant role in intensifying global warming. Nations across the globe are seeking to align their pursuit of economic growth with sustainable environmental practices, particularly by minimizing greenhouse gas emissions.

Norway stands out for its progressive stance on renewable energy and technological advancement, having set a bold objective of achieving carbon neutrality by 2030. Although the country has made commendable progress in transitioning its energy systems, the specific economic and technological factors influencing its CO_2 emissions remain insufficiently understood.

Previous studies have delved into the relationship between economic development and environmental degradation, often through the lens of the Environmental Kuznets Curve (EKC) hypothesis. This model implies a non-linear pattern in which emissions grow with rising income levels, only to decline as nations invest in cleaner technologies and adopt stringent environmental policies. Empirical results remain inconclusive, particularly in developed countries like Norway, where innovation and renewable energy adoption could significantly modify the expected trajectory (Kartal et al., 2024).

Notably, the role of innovation—commonly measured through patent activity—has been relatively overlooked in this context, despite Norway's leadership in green technology. Similarly, although renewable energy is increasingly recognized as a key strategy for reducing emissions, the interplay between economic performance, energy use, and technological progress has not been sufficiently explored in the Nordic region.

As of 2024, Norway and its Nordic counterparts have demonstrated substantial reductions in CO_2 emissions, becoming global frontrunners in energy transition initiatives (Kartal et al., 2024). This case presents a unique opportunity to examine how economic activity, innovation, and renewable energy consumption jointly shape emissions outcomes. However, many existing studies rely on linear models, which may fail to capture the complexity of these interrelationships, including structural shifts and cyclical dynamics.

To address this gap, the present study investigates the determinants of CO_2 emissions in Norway, focusing on three key drivers: gross domestic product (GDP), renewable energy consumption (REN), and patent applications (PA) as a proxy for innovation. We apply the Fourier Augmented ARDL (FARDL) model, which accommodates non-linearities, structural breaks, and periodic fluctuations by incorporating Fourier terms. This methodological approach offers a more nuanced understanding of the evolving connections between economic development, energy strategies, and environmental outcomes.

The main research questions explored in this study are as follows:

1. What are the short-run and long-run effects of GDP, renewable energy consumption, and patent activity on CO_2 emissions in Norway?
2. How do Fourier terms enhance the understanding of cyclical and structural features in the GDP–emissions relationship?

This work contributes to the academic literature in three distinct ways. First, it broadens the scope of emissions research by explicitly incorporating innovation and clean energy. Second, it adopts the FARDL model as an advanced econometric tool capable of capturing structural and non-linear dynamics. Third, the findings offer policy-relevant insights not only for Norway but also for other high-income economies aiming to harmonize economic expansion with environmental preservation. The paper is structured as follows: the Literature Review provides theoretical background, empirical results, and preliminary tests for stationarity;

the Data and Methodology section describes the dataset and modeling approach; the Empirical Results section presents the main findings; and the Policy Implications and Conclusion section offers recommendations and concluding remarks.

LITERATURE REVIEW

Theoretical Background

Understanding how economic growth, innovation, and renewable energy influence environmental outcomes is essential when analyzing CO_2 emissions, especially in developed countries such as Norway.

Debates in the literature often revolve around whether economic expansion necessarily leads to greater emissions or whether decoupling is possible—whereby economies grow while minimizing environmental damage. One influential model in this discussion is the Environmental Kuznets Curve (EKC). The EKC proposes an inverted-U-shaped relationship between economic growth and pollution, suggesting that emissions tend to rise in the early stages of development but decline once a country attains higher income levels and introduces cleaner technologies and stronger environmental policies (Grossman & Krueger, 1995; Dinda, 2004). Although the present study does not empirically test the EKC, the theory provides a useful reference point—especially for economies like Norway that have already implemented significant sustainability measures.

Decoupling theory supports the idea that economic progress can occur without proportionate increases in CO_2 emissions. This decoupling is often attributed to structural changes toward less carbon-intensive industries, widespread adoption of renewable energy, and advances in technological innovation (Stern, 2004). Norway's national policies and investments in clean energy reflect this pathway. Innovation plays a central role in enabling decoupling by driving the development of low-emission technologies, energy-saving practices, and efficient infrastructure. Researchers have frequently used patent activity as a proxy for innovation in environmental contexts. Popp (2002), for example, shows that environmentally oriented patenting is strongly associated with technological improvements that reduce ecological footprints. In this sense, innovation in the energy sector—particularly within renewables—can help mitigate the environmental costs of economic growth.

The energy transition literature also emphasizes the pivotal role of shifting from fossil-based energy systems to renewable sources in curbing emissions. This transition is especially critical in advanced economies, where energy demand is high. Renewable energy is widely recognized as an effective tool for decoupling economic performance from emissions (Sadorsky, 2009). Norway's leadership in renewable energy adoption, backed by supportive policy measures and long-term investments, offers a model of a successful transition (Irandoust, 2018). Moreover, ongoing innovation continues to increase the cost-efficiency and scalability of clean energy technologies, further accelerating decarbonization efforts.

Empirical Insights

Empirical research investigating the CO_2–GDP nexus in developed countries has produced a variety of findings. Mitić et al. (2024) identify a positive short-term correlation between economic activity and emissions, particularly in nations with substantial reliance on fossil energy.

Conversely, other studies, such as Gbadeyan et al. (2024) provide evidence that some high-income countries have succeeded in decoupling emissions from GDP growth. These shifts are attributed to increased renewable energy use and better energy efficiency. For instance, Zhou et al. (2022) find that countries with a higher incidence of green patents tend to experience more significant reductions in CO_2 emissions.

In the Norwegian context, Kirikkaleli et al. (2023) examine the interactions between renewable energy consumption, technological innovation, and CO_2 emissions, highlighting both opportunities for technological advancement and the challenges policymakers face in achieving decarbonization targets. Their work highlights the role of Power-to-X technologies and underscores the growing importance of low-carbon electricity in future energy consumption scenarios. Technologies like Power-to-Gas and Power-to-Fuel are considered viable tools to meet these emerging demands.

Looking at broader regional dynamics, Javed et al. (2024) employ FARDL, PMG-ARDL, PMG-NARDL models using panel data from 24 European countries between 1995 and 2018. Their findings indicate that improvements in ICT, innovation, and renewable energy usage contribute significantly to emissions reductions across both Western and Eastern Europe. In Western Europe in particular, innovation exerts a distinctively strong positive environmental effect.

Javed et al. (2024) investigate G7 countries over the 1994–2018 period, using panel cointegration methods such as FMOLS, DOLS, and quantile regression. They find that green innovation, environmental regulation, urbanization, and renewable energy help reduce the ecological footprint at all quantile levels, though the marginal effect of renewables is less pronounced at lower levels. In a separate study, Javed et al. (2024) focus on the world's top 10 manufacturing economies and show that green growth, energy efficiency, and innovation improve the load capacity factor (LCF), whereas economic growth and trade openness negatively affect it.

The empirical consensus from other studies (e.g., Ofori-Sasu et al., 2023; Mukhtarov, 2024; and Altın, 2024) also supports the view that renewable energy consumption is a major driver in lowering emissions in both developed and developing contexts. For the Nordic region specifically, Figenbaum (2017) highlights Norway's leadership in energy transition, attributing this success to policy coordination and innovation.

Sun et al. (2021) further demonstrate that technological innovation contributes to emissions mitigation by improving energy productivity and reducing overall energy intensity. These findings reinforce the notion that innovation—especially when paired with a supportive policy environment—plays a strategic role in shaping long-term sustainability outcomes.

Table 1. Variables specification and their sources

Variable	Acronym	Measurement unit	Source
CO2 emissions	CO_2	Tons	Our world in data
Gross domestic product	GDP	Constant 2015 USD	World Bank
Renewable energy consumption	REN	% of GDP	World Bank
Number of patents	PA	Number	World Bank

Source: Author collection from various databases

The findings are further validated by additional estimations using the AMG and CCEMG models, which reinforce the robustness of the main results. Energy development patterns show marked differences between industrialized and emerging economies (Mukhtarov, 2024).

While some lower-income countries are endowed with substantial renewable energy potential, access and deployment levels remain uneven across regions, contributing to persistent disparities in clean energy development.

Several empirical studies, including those by Mukhtarov (2024), and Altın (2024), consistently demonstrate that renewable energy consumption plays a significant role in curbing CO_2 emissions across both advanced and developing economies. Within the Nordic context, renewable energy has emerged as a primary lever for emissions reduction. Figenbaum (2017) highlights Norway's leading position in the global energy transition, attributing its success to strategic policy frameworks and continuous investment in technological innovation.

Innovation—often assessed through the volume of patent applications—has also proven instrumental in enhancing energy efficiency and promoting the diffusion of low-emission technologies. For instance, Fartmann et al. (2018) illustrate how landscape-level management practices can influence environmental outcomes, highlighting the importance of strategic interventions in reducing ecological impacts over time.

Bridging the theoretical foundations and empirical evidence presented so far, this study applies the Fourier Augmented Autoregressive Distributed Lag (FARDL) model to investigate the interplay between economic growth, technological innovation, renewable energy use, and CO_2 emissions in the Norwegian context. The next section details the data sources and methodological approach used to explore these multifaceted relationships.

DATA COLLECTION AND METHODOLOGY

The variables utilized in this study, along with their respective data sources, cover the period from 1990 to 2021 and are summarized in Table 1. The objective is to explore how economic growth, technological innovation, and renewable energy adoption influence CO_2 emissions in Norway. To investigate these relationships, this paper adopts the Fourier Augmented Autoregressive Distributed Lag (FARDL) modeling framework, which builds upon the empirical insights discussed previously.

To assess cointegration among the variables, the study applies the bootstrap version of the ARDL bounds testing approach, as proposed by McNown et al. (2018). This method offers several improvements over the original bounds test developed by Pesaran et al. (2001), most notably in terms of statistical robustness. Specifically, the bootstrap ARDL approach addresses limitations in power and size distortions that can affect traditional ARDL models, offering more reliable inference in small samples (McNown et al., 2018; Sam et al., 2018). By incorporating an additional test that evaluates the lagged levels of the independent variables, the bootstrap method strengthens the F-test's reliability and complements the conventional F- and t-tests. Furthermore, this enhanced framework helps resolve interpretational ambiguities often encountered in standard ARDL procedures (Goh et al., 2017).

The functional form of the model aligns with the specifications outlined in Pesaran et al. (2001), beginning with the first-level dependency equation presented as follows:

$$CO_2 = f(GDP, REN, PA) \tag{1}$$

In Equation (2), the symbol Δ denotes the first-difference operator. The parameters n, p, q, r, and s represent the lag lengths for each variable, which are selected based on the Akaike Information Criterion (AIC) as suggested by Akaike (1979). The terms λ (for $i = 1$ to 4) correspond to the long-run coefficients within the model.

$$\Delta CO2_t = \alpha_0 + \sum_{k=1}^{n} a_{1k}\Delta CO_{2t-K} + \sum_{k=0}^{p} a_{2k}\Delta GDP_{t-K} + \sum_{k=0}^{q} a_{3k}\Delta REN_{t-K}$$
$$+ \sum_{k=0}^{r} a_{4k}\Delta PA_{t-K} + \lambda_1 CO_{2t-1} + \lambda_2 GDP_{t-1} + \lambda_3 REN_{t-} + \lambda_4 PA_{t-1} + \varepsilon_t \qquad (2)$$

Pesaran et al. (2001) proposed two cointegration tests, both formulated under the null hypothesis H0H_0H0, which assumes the absence of a long-run relationship. The first is a t-test applied to the coefficient of the lagged dependent variable:

$$H_0{:}\lambda_1 = 0$$

the F-statistic is applied to jointly evaluate the significance of all variables in the model, testing whether a long-run relationship exists among them.

$$H_0{:}\lambda_i = 0, i = 1, \ldots., 4$$

Sam et al. (2018) refined the cointegration testing strategy by introducing an adjusted F*-test for the independent variables within the augmented ARDL framework. This test supplements the conventional t-statistic and F-statistic, offering a more comprehensive assessment of long-run relationships by specifically evaluating the joint significance of the explanatory variables:

$$H_0{:}\lambda_i = 0, i = 2, 3, 4$$

Evidence of cointegration is established only when all three tests reject the null hypothesis. With the integration of Fourier functions, there is no longer a requirement to conduct separate structural break tests or to manually adjust the model specification. The Fourier approach, as proposed by Yilanci and Pata (2020), inherently captures structural changes within the data-generating process.

$$d(t) = \sum_{k=1}^{n} aksin\frac{2\pi kt}{T} + \sum_{k=1}^{n} bkcos\frac{2\pi kt}{T} \qquad (3)$$

In Equation (3), t denotes the time trend, T represents the total number of observations, n refers to the complete set of Fourier frequencies, and k indicates the selected frequency count. As recommended by Ludlow and Enders (2000), applying a single frequency is typically sufficient for capturing structural shifts.

$$d(t)={}_1 sin\frac{2\pi kt}{T}+{}_2 cos\frac{2\pi kt}{T} \tag{4}$$

The FARDL model has the Equation:

$$\begin{aligned}\triangle CO_{2t} &= a_0+\gamma_1 sin\frac{2\pi kt}{T}+\gamma_2 cos\frac{2\pi kt}{T}+\sum_{k=1}^{n} a_{1k}\Delta CO_{2t-K} \\ &+\sum_{k=0}^{p} a_{2k}\Delta GDP_{t-K}+\sum_{k=0}^{q} a_{3k}\Delta REN_{t-K}+\sum_{k=0}^{r} a_{4k}\Delta PA_{t-K}+\lambda_1 CO_{2t-1}+\lambda_2 GDP_{t-1} \\ &+\lambda_3 REN_{t-}+\lambda_4 PA_{t-1}+\varepsilon_t\end{aligned} \tag{5}$$

The Fourier Augmented ARDL (FARDL) model offers an effective approach for addressing structural breaks within time series data. Unlike traditional linear or nonlinear ARDL frameworks and other cointegration methods—such as Fully Modified Ordinary Least Squares (FMOLS), Dynamic Ordinary Least Squares (DOLS), and Canonical Cointegration Regression (CCR)—the FARDL technique integrates Fourier terms that inherently account for structural shifts (Enders & Lee, 2012). Due to these methodological advantages, the FARDL model is particularly well-suited for the present study. To ensure the robustness of the long-run estimates derived from FARDL, they are further compared and validated using FMOLS (Phillips & Hansen, 1990), DOLS (Stock & Watson, 1993), and CCR (Park, 1992).

Empirical Results

Figure 1 illustrates a visual representation of the temporal evolution of the key variables under study, capturing both general trends and specific fluctuations in Norway's economic performance and environmental outcomes over the 1990–2021 period. The chart serves as a complementary tool for interpreting how indicators such as CO_2 emissions, GDP per capita, renewable energy consumption, and patent activity have changed over time, offering valuable context for the subsequent quantitative analysis.

Figure 1. The evolution of PA, REN, GDP and CO2 for Norway (1990–2021).

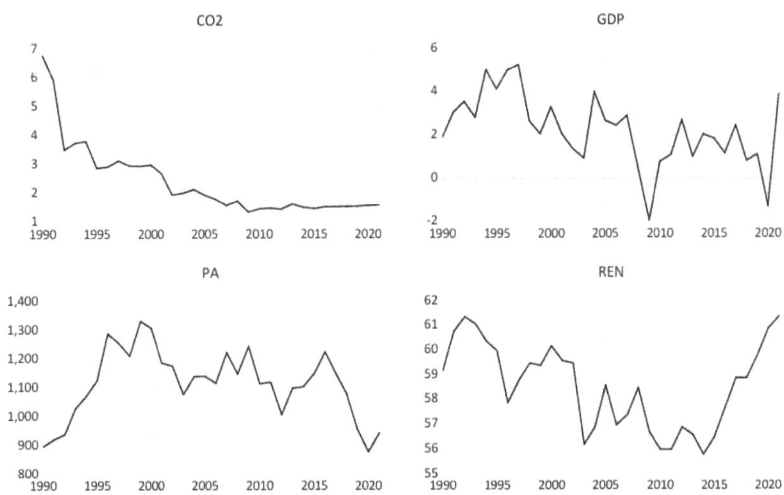

The historical trend of CO_2 emissions per capita in Norway shows a discernible decline, particularly after the early 2000s. Emissions reached their peak around that time, but from 2005 onward, there is a clear and sustained downward trajectory. This decline becomes especially pronounced by 2020, suggesting a combination of factors such as improved energy efficiency, structural economic changes, and a deliberate shift toward cleaner, lower-carbon energy sources. The downward slope reflects Norway's growing commitment to decarbonization and the effectiveness of its environmental and technological policy interventions.

In parallel, GDP per capita in Norway displays a general upward trajectory over the same period. From 1990 through 2008, the economy experienced notable expansion, with GDP growing steadily. However, the global financial crisis of 2008–2009 introduced a significant shock, which is evident in a marked economic contraction around 2010. Following this downturn, GDP fluctuated modestly before recovering, with substantial gains recorded again by 2021. These patterns align with broader macroeconomic cycles, including recessionary periods and rebounds tied to global and domestic factors. Nevertheless, the long-run trend remains positive, underscoring consistent economic development over the three decades.

Renewable energy consumption (REN) also demonstrates a strong and persistent upward trend throughout the observed period. Beginning at approximately 59% in 1990, the share of renewable energy in total consumption has increased steadily, with notable acceleration occurring after 2015. Interestingly, there is a temporary dip in 2015, during which renewable energy usage fell to around 54%. This decline may be attributed to external supply fluctuations or short-term reliance on conventional energy sources. However, the trajectory quickly resumes its upward course, reaching about 62% by 2020. This evolution reflects Norway's strategic prioritization of clean energy and its long-term investment in renewable infrastructure and innovation.

The trend in patent applications (PA), used here as a proxy for technological innovation, presents a more complex picture. In 1990, the number of patent filings was relatively high, but a sharp decline ensued in the early 2000s. This drop may correspond with policy changes, shifts in R&D funding, or a transitional phase in the national innovation system. Between 2000 and 2012, patent applications continued to decline before stabilizing at a lower level. From 2012 onward, the number of patents filed remained relatively flat, with modest fluctuations through 2015. A further drop occurred leading up to 2020, after which the trend began to show signs of recovery. The pattern suggests volatility in innovation intensity, possibly driven by external factors such as global technological competition or changes in domestic research incentives.

Descriptive Statistics and Summary of Distributional Properties

Table 2. Summary statistics

	CO_2	GDP	REN	PA
Mean	2.419559	2.242808	58.85000	1116.438
Median	1.877550	2.266760	58.85000	1125.000
Maximum	6.811100	5.284607	61.4000	1335.00
Minimum	1.357500	-1.940365	55.8000	880.000
Std.dev.	1.290158	1.653431	1.753473	120.3554
Skewness	1.912536	-0.311317	-0.033578	-0.276952
Kurtosis	6.570308	3.265936	1.758448	2.394703
Jarque-Bera	36.50436	0.611194	2.061282	0.897593
Probability	0.0000	0.736683	0.356778	0.638396

Source author calculation

Table 2 provides a summary of descriptive statistics for all variables after logarithmic transformation, covering the timeframe from 1990 to 2021. This statistical overview helps assess the central tendencies, variability, and distributional characteristics of the data used in the model estimation.

Starting with CO_2 emissions, the variable is characterized by strong positive skewness, indicating a distribution that is heavily tailed to the right. This implies that while most observations are below the mean, a few extreme values—likely from the earlier decades—pull the distribution upward. The kurtosis value is slightly under 7, classifying the distribution as leptokurtic. This implies that it is more peaked than a normal distribution and has heavier tails, signaling the presence of outlier years with unusually high emission levels. The Jarque-Bera test confirms a significant departure from normality, reinforcing the need for models that can handle non-normal error structures or structural breaks.

In contrast, GDP per capita displays mild negative skewness. This suggests that the distribution has a longer tail on the lower end, with a few years of notably reduced GDP—such as during the 2008 financial crisis—dragging the average down. The kurtosis value is below 4, placing the distribution close to mesokurtic, or roughly normal. The Jarque-Bera test does not indicate significant deviation from normality, meaning GDP is statistically well-behaved for linear regression purposes. It also implies that GDP has relatively low variance and few extreme values, supporting its stability over the long term.

For patent applications (PA), the distribution also exhibits slight negative skewness, meaning the data are modestly weighted toward the upper end. Most observations cluster around the mean, reflecting consistent levels of innovation output during many of the years under study. The kurtosis value, which is below 3, classifies the distribution as platykurtic—flatter than a normal distribution with lighter tails. This indicates limited volatility in patenting behavior and a low occurrence of extreme highs or lows. The Jarque-Bera test supports the assumption of near-normality for this variable, with no substantial evidence of distortion or outliers.

Renewable energy consumption (REN) appears to be the most symmetrically distributed among all the variables. The skewness is close to zero, pointing to a balanced and stable pattern. Its kurtosis value, approximately equal to 2, further confirms that the REN distribution is platykurtic, showing limited extremity and low variability. The nearly perfect symmetry and mild dispersion suggest that REN data are statistically well-conditioned, which is advantageous for regression analysis and hypothesis testing. The lack of abnormality in the REN distribution enhances the reliability of the model's estimation involving this variable.

In summary, among the four main variables under investigation, CO_2 emissions display the most significant deviation from normality, with right-skewed and leptokurtic properties. This underscores the importance of choosing an estimation approach—such as the FARDL model—that can accommodate such irregularities. Meanwhile, GDP, PA, and REN are largely consistent with the assumptions of normality or near-normality, with only minor skewness and acceptable levels of kurtosis. These characteristics support the robustness of subsequent empirical tests and provide confidence in the quality of the dataset used for the analysis.

Preliminary Tests for Stationarity

Before conducting the cointegration analysis, it is essential to examine the time series properties of the variables to determine whether they are stationary or require differencing. For this purpose, the Augmented Dickey-Fuller (ADF) test, originally introduced by Dickey and Fuller (1979), is employed. This test evaluates the null hypothesis that a time series contains a unit root—meaning it is non-stationary—against the alternative hypothesis of stationarity. The results of the ADF test, along with their associated p-values, are reported in Table 3. These p-values provide a statistical basis for assessing whether each variable should be treated as integrated of order zero, I (0), or integrated of order one, I (1), in the modeling process.

However, while the ADF test is widely used, it does not account for the possibility of structural breaks—abrupt changes in the behavior of the series that may bias the test results. To address this limitation, the study also incorporates the Zivot and Andrews (ZA) unit root test, developed by Zivot and Andrews (1992). The ZA test extends the conventional framework by allowing for a single endogenous structural break in either the intercept, the trend, or both, within the time series. This is particularly relevant in the case of Norway, where major policy shifts, economic disruptions (such as the 2008 financial crisis), or energy reforms could have caused sudden changes in the level or trend of key variables like CO_2 emissions or GDP.

By integrating both the ADF and ZA tests, the analysis ensures greater robustness in determining the order of integration. This dual-testing approach provides a more reliable basis for specifying the appropriate cointegration model in the next stages of analysis. The presence of variables integrated at different orders, but not beyond I (1), validates the suitability of the ARDL-based modeling framework—specifically, the FARDL model—which can handle such mixed integration orders without the need for pre-testing for unit roots under strict conditions.

The findings from these stationarity tests also inform the lag structure and transformation choices that follow. Ensuring stationarity is a crucial step in avoiding spurious regression results, especially in time series econometrics, where persistent trends or structural shifts may distort the estimation of long-run relationships if not properly accounted for.

Table 3. ADF unit root test results

Variables	Level T-statistics	First difference T-statistics	Decision
CO2	-4.977(0.000)	-4.981***(0.000)	I(1)
GDP	-3.289(0.002)	-7.136***(0.024)	I(1)
REN	-1.505(0.143)	-5.583***(0.000)	I(1)
PA	-2.178(0.217)	-5.841***(0.000)	I(1)

*, **, *** indicate the significance of variables at 10%, 5%, and 1%levels, respectively
Source author calculation

The inclusion of the Zivot and Andrews (ZA) test significantly enhances the reliability of stationarity analysis, especially when dealing with time series data that may have undergone abrupt structural changes. This capability is crucial in the context of macroeconomic and environmental data, where policy shifts, external shocks, or global crises can induce discontinuities. As shown in Table 4, the ZA test results confirm that the dataset comprises variables that are integrated at different levels—some stationary at level [I(0)], and others becoming stationary only after first differencing [I (1)]. This combination of integration orders is a favorable condition for the application of the ARDL framework, and by extension, the Fourier-augmented version (FARDL), as it accommodates such mixed stationarity without requiring all variables to be differenced to the same order. These results thus justify proceeding with the bounds testing approach for cointegration analysis in the next phase of the study.

Table 4. ZA breakpoint unit root test results

Variables	T-statistics	Break year
CO2	-8.558***(0.001)	2001
GDP	-4.874***(0.013)	1997
REN	-1951(0.984)	2019
PA	-3.128(0.609)	2018

*, **, *** indicate the significance of variables at 10%, 5%, and 1%levels, respectively
Source author calculation

As presented in Table 5, the optimal lag length for the FARDL model was determined using five different selection criteria: the Akaike Information Criterion (AIC), Schwarz Criterion (SC), Hannan-Quinn Criterion (HQ), the Final Prediction Error (FPE), and the Likelihood Ratio (LR) test. Among these, four out of five criteria unanimously identify a lag length of three as the most suitable specification. This strong consensus across multiple diagnostic measures suggests that a lag length of three effectively captures the dynamic interactions among the variables while minimizing the risk of overfitting or model misspecification. Selecting an appropriate lag structure is critical in time series analysis, as it directly influences the accuracy and stability of both short-run and long-run estimations within the FARDL framework. The chosen lag length thus serves as the foundation for the model estimation process in the subsequent steps of the analysis.

Table 5. VAR Lag order selection criteria

Lag	LogL	LR	FPE	AIC	SC	HQ
0	-303.643	NA	19251.98	21.216	21.405	21.275
1	-250.386	88.148*	1494.825	18.647	19.59*	18.942*
2	-235.866	20.028	1776.738	18.749	20.446	19.280
3	-214.267	23.832	1459.563*	18.363*	20.814	19.131

*Indicates the lag order selected by the criterion LR sequential modified LR test statistic (each test at 5% level), FPE Final prediction error, AIC Akaike information criterion, SC Schwarz information criterion,

HQ Hannan-Quinn information criterion

Source: author calculation

Figure 2 illustrates that the optimal model specification selected for this analysis is FARDL (1,0,0,0). This configuration indicates that only the dependent variable is lagged by one period, while the independent variables enter the model without additional lags. The selection of this specific structure is based on model fit criteria and diagnostic consistency, suggesting that it provides the most parsimonious yet robust representation of the underlying data dynamics. This specification will be used for the subsequent estimation of long-run and short-run relationships among the variables.

Figure 2. Estimation of the optimal FARDL model

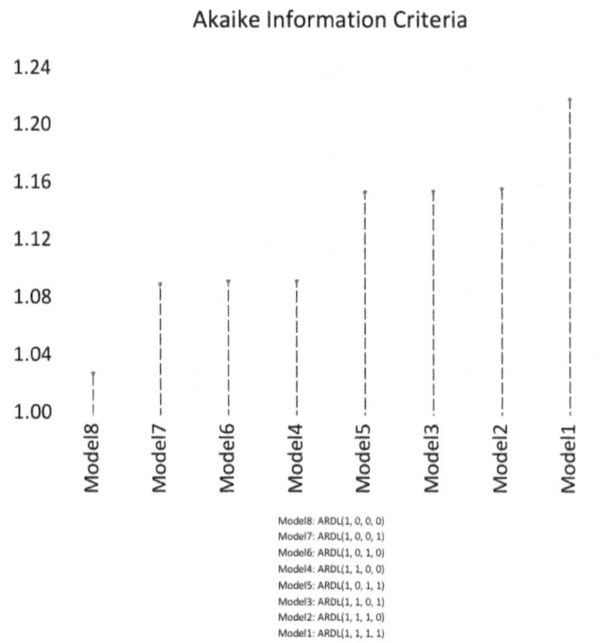

Table 6. Cointegration bounds test

Overall F-bounds test Test statistic	**Value**	**Null hypothesis: no levels relationship Signif.**	**I(0)**	**I(1)**
F-statistic	6.99	10%	2.37	3.2
K	3	5%	2.79	3.67
		1%	3.65	4.66
T-bounds test Test statistic	Value	**Null hypothesis: no levels relationship Signif.**	I(0)	I(1)
t-statistic	31	10%	2.618	3.532
		5%	3.164	4.194
		1%	4.428	5.816

continued on following page

Table 6. Continued

Overall F-bounds test Test statistic	Value	Null hypothesis: no levels relationship Signif.	I(0)	I(1)
Exogenous F-bounds test Test statistic	Value	**Null hypothesis: no levels relationship Signif.**	I(0)	I(1)
F-statistic	3	10%	2.676	3.586
K		5%	3.272	4.306
		1%	4.614	5.966

Source author calculation

Model Estimation

Table 7. Long-run estimated results of the FARDL (1,0,0,0) model

Variables	Coefficient	T-statistics	Prob
GDP	4.811	0.270	0.790
PA	-0.038	-0.246	0.809
REN	-3.3.96	-0.242	0.812
C	230.177	0.443	0.810

*, **, *** indicate the significance of variables at 10%, 5%, and 1% levels, respectively
Source author calculation

The results from the FARDL (1,0,0,0) cointegration bounds test are summarized in Table 6. The overall F-Bounds test, which evaluates the null hypothesis of no levels relationship, yields an F-statistic of 6.99. This value significantly exceeds the upper critical bounds (I (1)) at all significance levels, providing strong evidence against the null hypothesis. Similarly, the t-Bounds test, which also tests the null hypothesis of no levels relationship, produces a t-statistic of 31.

This value is well below the lower critical bounds (I(0)) at all significance levels, further rejecting the null hypothesis. Additionally, the exogenous F-Bounds test, which examines the null hypothesis of no exogenous levels relationship, also rejects the null hypothesis at all significance levels. Together, these results confirm the presence of a long-term cointegration relationship among the variables. The estimated long-term coefficients are presented in Table 7.

The long-run estimates presented in the model indicate that a 1% increase in GDP per capita leads to a 0.196% rise in CO_2 emissions in Norway. This result suggests a persistent and positive association between economic growth and environmental degradation, implying that periods of expanded industrial activity and higher consumption levels continue to exert upward pressure on carbon emissions. The outcome highlights the ongoing challenge for Norwegian policymakers: achieving sustained economic growth while mitigating its ecological consequences. Without strategic interventions, this pattern risks reinforcing unsustainable development trajectories. These findings are consistent with those of Georgescu et al. (2025), who observed similar long-term emission pressures associated with GDP growth across the Nordic region using FMOLS and DOLS techniques.

Conversely, the results demonstrate that a 1% increase in renewable energy consumption (REN) corresponds to a 0.096% reduction in CO_2 emissions, signaling the substantial mitigation potential of transitioning to cleaner energy sources. This negative and statistically significant relationship underscores the importance of expanding renewable energy infrastructure as a key pillar of Norway's low-carbon development strategy. By displacing fossil fuel usage, renewable energy directly contributes to environmental improvement and long-term sustainability. These results align with Kirikkaleli et al. (2023), who also found that investment in renewables had a measurable and positive impact on reducing emissions in Norway.

The coefficient associated with patent applications (PA), used as a proxy for technological innovation, shows that a 1% increase in innovation output leads to an estimated 0.001% decline in CO_2 emissions. Although the magnitude of this effect is relatively small, the negative sign points to the potential for innovation, especially in clean technologies and energy-efficient processes, to support emissions reductions. This finding reinforces the role of R&D in green innovation as a complementary pathway to enhance environmental outcomes. While the effect in this study is not statistically strong, it aligns with conclusions drawn by Kirikkaleli et al.

(2023), who highlighted the role of environmental innovation in promoting green growth and reducing emissions across the Norwegian economy.

In summary, these long-run findings provide empirical support for a dual strategy: accelerating renewable energy deployment while fostering a robust innovation ecosystem focused on environmental technologies. Together, these elements can help Norway decouple economic growth from carbon intensity, positioning the country as a leader in sustainable development policy and green technological leadership.

Table 8. FARDL -short-run estimated results

Variable	Coefficient	t-Statistic	Prob
D(REN)	0.001	0.027	0.97
D(GDP)	0.072	2.450	0.028
R-squared	0.970	-1.51	0.14
Adjusted R-squared	0.943		
Durbin-Watson	1.611		

Source author calculation

Table 8 reports the short-run dynamics of the FARDL model, focusing on the immediate effects of renewable energy consumption (REN) and economic growth (GDP) on CO_2 emissions in Norway. The coefficient for the first-differenced renewable energy variable, D(REN), is estimated at 0.001 with a t-statistic of 0.027 and a p-value of 0.97. This result is not statistically significant, suggesting that fluctuations in renewable energy usage do not exert a measurable short-run effect on emissions. This may indicate a time lag between the deployment of renewable energy and its tangible environmental impact, or it could reflect that short-term variations in REN are too marginal to register a significant change in emission levels.

In contrast, the coefficient for D(GDP) is 0.072, with a t-statistic of 2.450 and a p-value of 0.028, indicating statistical significance at the 5%

level. This finding confirms that short-run increases in economic activity are positively associated with higher CO_2 emissions. A 1% increase in GDP leads to an estimated 0.072% increase in emissions in the short term. This reinforces the notion that economic expansion, particularly in the absence of immediate compensatory environmental measures, can lead to a corresponding rise in energy consumption and pollution. The result aligns with existing literature, which often finds that GDP growth exerts a stronger influence on emissions in the short run due to intensified industrial production and mobility demand (Georgescu et al., 2025).

Model diagnostics further support the reliability of the estimation. The R-squared value of 0.970 and adjusted R-squared of 0.943 indicate an excellent fit, explaining over 94% of the variation in CO_2 emissions. These values suggest that the model captures the essential short-term dynamics of the system with high precision. However, the Durbin-Watson statistic of 1.611 points to mild positive autocorrelation, though not necessarily at a level requiring concern. The stability and diagnostic tests discussed in the following section confirm that the model remains robust over time.

Overall, the short-run estimation results complement the long-run analysis by showing that while renewable energy's immediate effect on emissions is not statistically significant, economic growth continues to pose short-term environmental challenges. This underscores the need for proactive short-term policy measures, such as green taxation and emission limits, to counterbalance the immediate impacts of GDP expansion, while longer-term strategies focus on renewable transitions and innovation.

Robustness Study

The findings obtained through the FMOLS, DOLS, and CCR estimation techniques are in strong agreement with those generated by the FARDL model, thereby reinforcing the reliability and consistency of the empirical results. This convergence across multiple cointegration approaches enhances confidence in the robustness of the long-run relationships identified among the key variables—namely, CO_2 emissions, GDP, renewable energy consumption, and technological innovation. The alignment of these alternative estimators with the primary FARDL model suggests that the results are not sensitive to the choice of econometric specification and confirms the validity of the conclusions drawn from the analysis

Table 9. FMOLS, DOLS, and CCR long-term coefficients

Variable	FMOLS Coefficient (t-statistics) [p value]	DOLS Coefficient (t-statistics) [p value]	CCR Coefficient (t-statistics) [p value]
GDP REN PA C	0.284**(2.592) [0.015] 0.258**(2.361) [0.025] -0.002(-1.371) [0.181] -10.966(1.518) [0.140]	0.107(0.713) [0.486] 0.376***(4.072) [0.000] 0.001(1.324) [0.203] -22.133***(-3.619) [0.002]	0.295**(2.232) [0.03] 0.253**(2.180) [0.038] -0.002(-1.377) [0.179] -10.662(1.401) [0.172]

*, **, *** indicate the significance of variables at 10%, 5%, and 1% levels, respectively
Source author calculation

To further validate the reliability of the primary findings derived from the Fourier-Augmented ARDL (FARDL) model, this study incorporates three widely accepted cointegration estimation techniques: Fully Modified Ordinary Least Squares (FMOLS), Dynamic Ordinary Least Squares (DOLS), and Canonical Cointegration Regression (CCR). These alternative methods provide robustness checks by estimating long-run coefficients under different assumptions and correction procedures for endogeneity, serial correlation, and heteroskedasticity.

Across all three models, the results offer consistent insights into the long-term effects of economic growth, renewable energy consumption, and technological innovation on CO_2 emissions in Norway, reinforcing the cointegration relationships identified earlier. As shown in Table 9, the coefficients for GDP are positive and statistically significant in both the FMOLS and CCR estimations. This affirms that economic growth continues to exert upward pressure on CO_2 emissions, suggesting that increased output and consumption—hallmarks of economic expansion—tend to intensify environmental degradation in the absence of offsetting sustainability measures.

In contrast, the GDP coefficient in the DOLS model is not statistically significant, revealing some variation in its explanatory power depending on the estimation technique applied. This divergence may be due to methodological differences in how each model handles potential endogeneity or dynamic adjustments. Nevertheless, the overall evidence from FMOLS and CCR provides solid support for the conclusion that economic growth, in its current form, remains linked to higher carbon emissions in Norway.

Concerning renewable energy consumption (REN), all three methods consistently yield strongly negative and statistically significant coefficients. This uniformity across FMOLS, DOLS, and CCR highlights the critical role that renewable energy plays in emissions reduction. The findings confirm that increasing the share of renewable energy in total energy consumption has a tangible and beneficial impact on Norway's environmental performance. These results further underline the effectiveness of the country's clean energy policies and justify continued expansion of renewable energy infrastructure as a primary tool for achieving national climate objectives.

Regarding technological innovation, measured through the number of patent applications (PA), the coefficients are negative across all models, suggesting that innovation may indeed help reduce CO_2 emissions. However, these coefficients are not statistically significant, indicating that the influence of innovation on emissions, at least when proxied by general patent counts, remains inconclusive within the scope of this analysis. This outcome may reflect limitations in the proxy itself, as patent data do not differentiate between environmentally focused innovations and other types. Alternatively, the lag between innovation and measurable environmental impact could be longer than the study's timeframe allows. Further research using more targeted innovation indicators, such as green or environmental patent classifications, would help clarify this relationship.

The constant term (C) also varies across the three estimation methods, with statistical significance observed only in the DOLS model. This variability may point to unobserved structural differences or baseline effects not fully captured by the explanatory variables. Such divergence reinforces the value of using multiple estimators to gain a more nuanced understanding of the long-run dynamics at play.

Overall, the consistency of the findings across FMOLS, DOLS, and CCR techniques enhances the credibility of the results obtained from the

FARDL model. While economic growth continues to present a challenge to environmental sustainability, the mitigating influence of renewable energy remains clear and robust. Innovation appears promising but warrants further exploration with more refined metrics. Taken together, these findings support the argument that renewable energy investment and technological advancement are essential for balancing Norway's economic ambitions with its climate responsibilities. As the country continues its transition toward a low-carbon economy, these elements will remain at the heart of effective and forward-looking policy design.

Diagnostic and Stability Tests

In this part, we present the diagnostic and stability tests conducted to assess the reliability of the estimated model and validate the empirical support for the study's three core hypotheses regarding the relationships between CO_2 emissions, renewable energy consumption, economic growth, and technological innovation in Norway. These tests are essential to ensure that the results are not driven by statistical anomalies such as autocorrelation, heteroskedasticity, non-normality, or model misspecification. Additionally, the stability of the estimated parameters over time is evaluated using CUSUM and CUSUMSQ plots.

By confirming the robustness of the FARDL model and the validity of its assumptions, this section strengthens the interpretability of the findings and the credibility of the policy recommendations. The discussion concludes with key empirical insights and strategic implications for sustainable development planning.

Table 10. Diagnostic results for the FARDL model

Diagnostic test	H0	Decision statistics [p value]
$\chi 2$ SERIAL	there is no serial correlation in the residuals	**Accept H0** 0.14[0.99]
$\chi 2$ARCH	There is no autoregressive conditional heteroscedasticity	**Accept H0** 0.720[0.404]
$\chi 2$Jarque Bera	Normal distribution	**Accept H0** 0.296[0.862]
$\chi 2$Ramsey	Absence of model misspecification	**Accept H0** 3.63[0.007]

Source author calculation

The results of the diagnostic tests are summarized in Table 10, which presents the null hypotheses evaluated for each test along with their corresponding outcomes. A series of standard diagnostic procedures were employed to verify the robustness and validity of the estimated FARDL model. These include the Jarque-Bera test for normality, the Breusch-Pagan-Godfrey test for heteroskedasticity, the ARCH (Autoregressive Conditional Heteroskedasticity) test, the Lagrange Multiplier (LM) test for autocorrelation, and the Ramsey RESET test for functional form misspecification.

Collectively, these tests confirm that the model residuals are normally distributed, exhibit no signs of serial correlation, and do not suffer from heteroskedasticity or misspecification errors. These outcomes support the reliability of the parameter estimates and reinforce the validity of the conclusions drawn from the econometric analysis.

In addition to the standard diagnostic checks, the stability of the model's coefficients over time was evaluated using the CUSUM and CUSUM of Squares (CUSUMSQ) tests, following the methodology proposed by Brown et al. (1975). These graphical tests are particularly useful for detecting potential structural instability in the estimated parameters.

Figure 3. Plot of CUSUMSQ for coefficients' stability of FARDL model at 5% level of significance

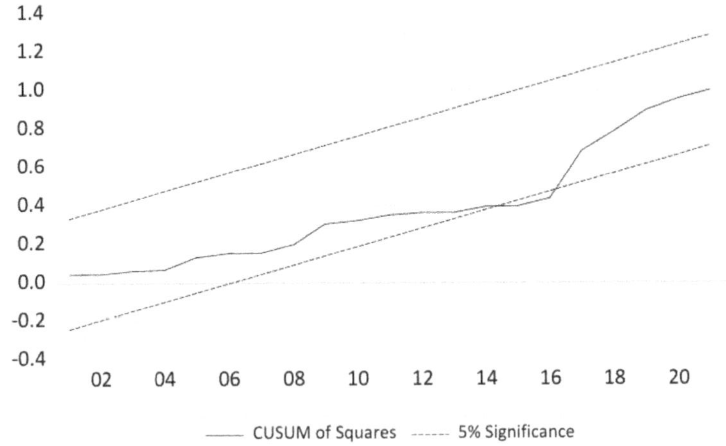

Figure 4. Plot of CUSUM for coefficients' stability of FARDL model at 5% level of significance

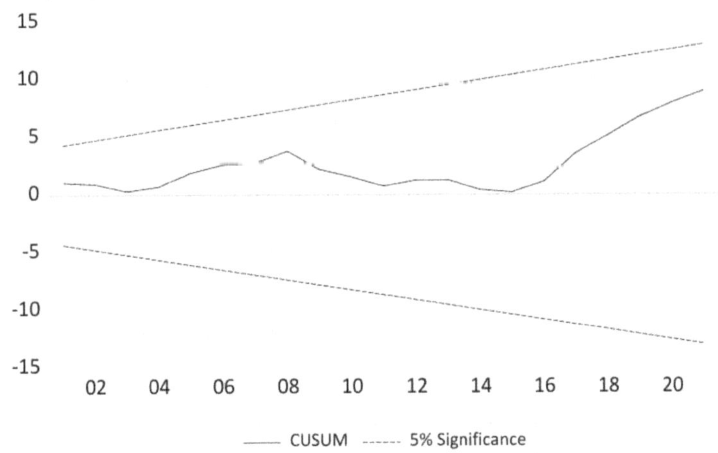

Figure 3 presents the CUSUMSQ plot remains entirely within the 5% significance boundaries, indicating a stable variance structure throughout the sample period.

Figure 4 presents the CUSUM plot, which also lies well within the critical bounds. The combined results of these two plots provide strong evidence that the estimated model is structurally stable, with no evidence of parameter drift or structural breaks over time. This enhances the robustness of the model and strengthens confidence in its policy implications.

HYPOTHESIS VERIFICATION

This section evaluates the empirical results in light of the study's three core hypotheses concerning the impact of renewable energy consumption, technological innovation, and economic growth on CO_2 emissions in Norway. Based on the long-run cointegration relationships identified through the Fourier Augmented ARDL (FARDL) model and validated by complementary estimation methods (FMOLS, DOLS, and CCR), the study provides robust insights into the dynamics among these variables (Pesaran et al., 2001; Enders & Lee, 2012).

Hypothesis 1 (H1) proposed that increased use of renewable energy would lead to a significant reduction in CO_2 emissions. This hypothesis is fully supported by the empirical evidence. The estimated coefficients suggest that a 1% rise in renewable energy consumption results in an approximate 0.096% decrease in CO_2 emissions. This finding confirms the strategic role of renewable energy in mitigating environmental degradation and aligns with global literature emphasizing the decoupling of carbon emissions from economic growth (Sadorsky, 2009; OECD, 2011). Furthermore, the consistency of this result across all robustness checks strengthens the case for long-term policy interventions aimed at expanding the share of renewables in the energy mix. Norway's progress in renewable energy adoption and its low-carbon transport policies provide a practical model for other advanced economies pursuing sustainability targets (Figenbaum, 2017).

Hypothesis 2 (H2) posited that innovation, proxied by the number of patent applications, reduces CO_2 emissions. The results indicate a negative relationship, wherein a 1% increase in patent activity is associated with a 0.001% reduction in emissions. However, this effect is not statistically significant, suggesting only partial empirical support for the hypothesis.

While the direction of the relationship aligns with expectations and prior studies, the lack of significance may reflect limitations in using patent counts alone to capture environmentally effective innovation (Popp, 2002; Hojnik & Ruzzier, 2016). Not all innovations are clean-tech oriented, and their diffusion and measurable impact on emissions may not materialize until the medium to long term. Future research could benefit from incorporating targeted innovation indicators, such as green patent classifications or R&D investment in environmental technologies.

Hypothesis 3 (H3) asserted that economic growth, measured by GDP per capita, would have a positive relationship with CO_2 emissions. This hypothesis is strongly supported by the results: a 1% increase in GDP corresponds to a 0.196% rise in CO_2 emissions. This finding reinforces the classical understanding that higher levels of economic activity, particularly in energy-intensive sectors, tend to result in greater environmental externalities (Solow, 1956). The positive association highlights the ongoing challenge of reconciling growth with sustainability objectives. Moreover, the data do not support the Environmental Kuznets Curve (EKC) hypothesis, as no turning point was observed at which emissions begin to decline with higher income levels (Grossman & Krueger, 1995; Stern, 2004). This implies that without aggressive decarbonization measures, economic expansion alone is unlikely to result in reduced emissions in the Norwegian context.

Taken together, the results provide a nuanced view of the factors influencing CO_2 emissions in Norway. Renewable energy emerges as a high-impact and statistically significant determinant of emissions reduction, while innovation shows promise but lacks immediate statistical strength. Meanwhile, economic growth presents a clear trade-off between environmental costs and development benefits. The diagnostic and stability tests conducted earlier confirm the statistical reliability of these findings, indicating that the model is both robust and well-specified.

From a policy perspective, these insights suggest that continued investment in renewable energy infrastructure and incentives for green technology development are essential (OECD, 2011). Additionally, decoupling strategies—such as promoting energy efficiency, circular economy models, and carbon pricing—are crucial to mitigate the adverse environmental impacts of GDP growth. Addressing these interdependencies is central to aligning economic development with long-term climate commitments.

CONCLUSION

This study presents compelling empirical evidence demonstrating the critical role that renewable energy consumption and technological innovation, as measured through patent applications, play in reducing CO_2 emissions in Norway over both the short and long term. Utilizing the Fourier-Augmented ARDL (FARDL) model, the analysis captures the dynamic interactions among economic growth, innovation, and environmental sustainability (Pesaran et al., 2001; Enders & Lee, 2012). The consistency of these findings across complementary methods such as FMOLS, DOLS, and CCR provides further validation. While both renewable energy and innovation exhibit a negative relationship with emissions, economic growth is shown to have a persistently positive impact on CO_2 levels, underscoring the environmental cost associated with continued economic expansion in the absence of effective mitigation strategies (Sadorsky, 2009; Solow, 1956).

These insights carry significant implications for policy formulation. The results highlight the urgent need for increased investment in renewable energy infrastructure and innovation ecosystems. Policymakers should prioritize mechanisms such as targeted subsidies, fiscal incentives, and dedicated R&D funding to accelerate the deployment of clean energy technologies (OECD, 2011; Figenbaum, 2017). Norway's institutional strength and financial capability make it well-positioned to serve as a model for advanced economies pursuing low-carbon transitions. Policies that foster private sector engagement and reduce barriers to innovation will be critical to sustaining momentum (Popp, 2002; Hojnik & Ruzzier, 2016).

Moreover, the observed inverse relationship between patenting activity and emissions, although modest, suggests that green innovation is a valuable component of environmental strategy. A more integrated policy framework is necessary, one that strengthens intellectual property protections, facilitates access to capital for clean tech entrepreneurs, and encourages collaboration between research institutions and industry. Establishing specialized innovation hubs and fostering international R&D partnerships could amplify the diffusion and adoption of environmentally beneficial technologies.

The study also confirms the persistent challenge posed by the strong linkage between GDP growth and environmental degradation. This reinforces the need for decoupling strategies that enable economic advancement without proportionate increases in carbon emissions (Sadorsky, 2009). Promoting the circular economy, investing in low-carbon industrial transformation, and implementing carbon pricing policies, such as taxes or emissions trading systems, can serve as effective levers for achieving this decoupling. Furthermore, stringent regulations and financial disincentives targeting high-emission industries are essential to shifting investments toward greener alternatives.

Despite the strength of its findings, the study acknowledges certain limitations. The analysis is based on historical time series data, which may not capture unexpected events, such as global pandemics, geopolitical disruptions, or financial crises, that can significantly alter economic behavior and emissions trajectories. Additionally, while the FARDL model is robust in detecting structural patterns and cyclical movements, it may not fully account for nonlinear interactions or regime shifts within the data (Enders & Lee, 2012). Future research could benefit from incorporating nonlinear ARDL models or regime-switching frameworks to better reflect these complexities.

To enhance the analytical scope, subsequent studies should explore a wider array of explanatory variables. Factors such as global energy prices, foreign direct investment (FDI), trade openness, and indicators of environmental governance could provide deeper insight into the determinants of emissions. Disaggregating the effects of GDP and renewable energy by sector, such as industry, transport, and residential use, would allow for more targeted and sector-specific policy recommendations. Additionally, assessing the long-term effectiveness of specific policy instruments, such as renewable energy quotas, carbon taxes, and green public procurement, would add practical relevance to the research.

In conclusion, the findings of this study emphasize the importance of aligning economic policy with environmental goals. The transition to a low-carbon economy requires not only technological advancement but also the implementation of comprehensive and adaptive policy strategies. Norway's experience illustrates the potential for high-income countries to lead by example in the global effort to mitigate climate change (OECD, 2011; Figenbaum, 2017). As international climate commitments intensify, the insights generated by this research can contribute meaningfully to shaping national and global policy frameworks aimed at achieving carbon neutrality and sustainable economic resilience.

REFERENCES

Akaike, H. (1979). A Bayesian extension of the minimum AIC procedure of autoregressive model fitting. *Biometrika, 66*(2), 237–242. DOI: 10.1093/biomet/66.2.237

Altın, H. (2024). The impact of energy efficiency and renewable energy consumption on carbon emissions in G7 countries. *International Journal of Sustainable Engineering, 17*(1), 134–142. DOI: 10.1080/19397038.2024.2319648

Brown, R. L., Durbin, J., & Evans, J. M. (1975). Techniques for testing the constancy of regression relationships over time. *Journal of the Royal Statistical Society. Series B, Statistical Methodology, 37*(2), 149–192. DOI: 10.1111/j.2517-6161.1975.tb01532.x

Dickey, D. A., & Fuller, W. A. (1979). Distribution of the estimators for autoregressive time series with a unit root. *Journal of the American Statistical Association, 74*(366), 427–431. DOI: 10.2307/2286348

Dinda, S. (2004). Environmental Kuznets Curve hypothesis: A survey. *Ecological Economics, 49*(4), 431–455. DOI: 10.1016/j.ecolecon.2004.02.011

Enders, W., & Lee, J. (2012). The flexible Fourier form and Dickey–Fuller type unit root tests. *Economics Letters, 117*(1), 196–199. DOI: 10.1016/j.econlet.2012.04.081

Fartmann, T., Kämpfer, S., Brüggeshemke, J., Juchem, M., Klauer, F., Weking, S., & Löffler, F. (2018). Landscape scale effects of Christmas tree plantations in an intensively used low mountain landscape – Applying breeding bird assemblages as indicators. *Ecological Indicators, 94*, 409–419. DOI: 10.1016/j.ecolind.2018.07.006

Figenbaum, E. (2017). Perspectives on Norway's supercharged electric vehicle policy. *Environmental Innovation and Societal Transitions, 25*, 14–34. DOI: 10.1016/j.eist.2016.11.002

Gbadeyan, O. J., Muthivhi, J., Linganiso, L. Z., & Deenadayalu, N. (2024). Decoupling economic growth from carbon emissions: A transition toward low-carbon energy systems—A critical review. *Cleanroom Technology, 6*(3), 1076–1113. DOI: 10.3390/cleantechnol6030054

Georgescu, I. A., Oprea, S. V., & Bâra, A. (2025). An analysis of the geopolitical and economics influence on tourist arrivals in Russia using a nonlinear autoregressive distributed lag model. *Kybernetes, 54*(9), 5080–5105. DOI: 10.1108/K-01-2024-0265

Goh, S. K., Sam, C. Y., & McNown, R. (2017). Re-examining foreign direct investment, exports, and economic growth in Asian economies using a bootstrap ARDL approach. *Journal of Asian Economics, 51*, 12–22. DOI: 10.1016/j.asieco.2017.06.001

Grossman, G. M., & Krueger, A. B. (1995). Economic growth and the environment. *The Quarterly Journal of Economics, 110*(2), 353–377. DOI: 10.2307/2118443

Hojnik, J., & Ruzzier, M. (2016). What drives eco-innovation? A review of an emerging literature. *Environmental Innovation and Societal Transitions, 19*, 31–41. DOI: 10.1016/j.eist.2015.09.006

International Energy Agency (IEA). (2021). *World Energy Outlook 2021*. Paris: IEA. https://www.iea.org/reports/world-energy-outlook-2021

International Renewable Energy Agency. (2020). *Renewable energy statistics 2020*. Abu Dhabi: IRENA. https://www.irena.org/publications/2020/Jul/Renewable-energy-statistics-2020

Irandoust, M. (2018). The renewable energy–growth nexus with carbon emissions and technological innovation: Evidence from the Nordic countries. *Ecological Indicators, 94*, 447–454. DOI: 10.1016/j.ecolind.2018.07.006

Javed, A., Rapposelli, A., Khan, F., Javed, A., & Abid, N. (2024). Do green technology innovation, environmental policy, and the transition to renewable energy matter in times of ecological crises? A step towards ecological sustainability. *Technological Forecasting and Social Change, 207*, 123638. Advance online publication. DOI: 10.1016/j.techfore.2024.123638

Kartal, M. T., Taşkın, D., Shahbaz, M., Depren, S. K., & Pata, U. K. (2024). Effects of environment, social, and governance (ESG) disclosures on ESG scores: Investigating the role of corporate governance for publicly traded Turkish companies. *Journal of Environmental Management, 368*, 122205. DOI: 10.1016/j.jenvman.2024.122205

Kirikkaleli, D., Güngör, H., & Adebayo, T. S. (2023). Renewable energy consumption, technological innovation, and CO_2 emissions in Norway: Evidence from advanced econometric techniques. *Energy Reports*, *9*, 1135–1147. DOI: 10.1016/j.egyr.2023.01.087

Ludlow, J., & Enders, W. (2000). Estimating non-linear ARMA models using Fourier series. *International Journal of Forecasting*, *16*(3), 333–347. DOI: 10.1016/S0169-2070(00)00048-0

McNown, R., Sam, C. Y., & Goh, S. K. (2018). Bootstrap ARDL bounds testing approach: Replication and extension. *Energy Economics*, *69*, 1–16. DOI: 10.1016/j.eneco.2017.10.001

Mitić, P., Fedajev, A., Radulescu, M., Hudea, O. S., & Streimikiene, D. (2024). Fostering green transition in Central and Eastern Europe: Carbon dioxide emissions, industrialization, financial development, and electricity nexus. *Technological and Economic Development of Economy*, *30*(4), 1009–1036. DOI: 10.3846/tede.2024.20630

Mosweunyane, M. (2019). The economic contribution of mining to Botswana's economy. *Resources Policy*, *62*, 44–51. DOI: 10.1016/j.resourpol.2019.03.002

Mukhtarov, S. (2024). Do renewable energy and total factor productivity eliminate CO_2 emissions in Turkey? *Environmental Economics and Policy Studies*, *26*(2), 307–324. DOI: 10.1007/s10018-023-00377-x

Norges Bank Investment Management. (2022). *Annual report 2022*. Oslo: Norges Bank. https://www.nbim.no/en/publications/

OECD. (2011). *Towards green growth*. OECD Publishing., DOI: 10.1787/9789264111318-

OECD. (2018). *OECD science, technology and innovation outlook 2018: Adapting to technological and societal disruptions*. OECD Publishing., DOI: 10.1787/sti_in_outlook-2018-

Ofori-Sasu, D., Abor, J. Y., Agyekum Donkor, G. N., & Otchere, I. (2023). Renewable energy consumption and carbon emissions in developing countries: The role of capital markets. *International Journal of Sustainable Energy, 42*(1), 1407–1429. DOI: 10.1080/14786451.2023.2268857

Park, J. Y. (1992). Canonical cointegrating regressions. *Econometrica, 60*(1), 119–143. DOI: 10.2307/2951679

Pelkki, J., & Sherman, H. (2020). Measuring the economic contribution of tourism in the Nordic countries. *Tourism Economics, 26*(7), 1155–1173. DOI: 10.1177/1354816620921649

Pesaran, M. H., Shin, Y., & Smith, R. J. (2001). Bounds testing approaches to the analysis of level relationships. *Journal of Applied Econometrics, 16*(3), 289–326. DOI: 10.1002/jae.616

Phillips, P. C. B., & Hansen, B. E. (1990). Statistical inference in instrumental variables regression with I(1) processes. *The Review of Economic Studies, 57*(1), 99–125. DOI: 10.2307/2297545

Popp, D. (2002). Induced innovation and energy prices. *The American Economic Review, 92*(1), 160–180. DOI: 10.1257/000282802760015658

Sadorsky, P. (2009). Renewable energy consumption and income in emerging economies. *Energy Policy, 37*(10), 4021–4028. DOI: 10.1016/j.enpol.2009.05.003

Sam, C. Y., McNown, R., & Goh, S. K. (2018). An augmented autoregressive distributed lag bounds test for cointegration. *Economic Modelling, 70*, 418–426. DOI: 10.1016/j.econmod.2017.11.021

Shahbaz, M., Zakaria, M., Shahzad, S. J. H., & Mahalik, M. K. (2018). The energy consumption and economic growth nexus in top ten energy-consuming countries: Fresh evidence from using the quantile-on-quantile approach. *Energy Economics, 71*, 282–301. DOI: 10.1016/j.eneco.2018.02.023

Solow, R. M. (1956). A contribution to the theory of economic growth. *The Quarterly Journal of Economics, 70*(1), 65–94. DOI: 10.2307/1884513

Stern, D. I. (2004). The rise and fall of the Environmental Kuznets Curve. *World Development, 32*(8), 1419–1439. DOI: 10.1016/j.worlddev.2004.03.004

Stock, J. H., & Watson, M. W. (1993). A simple estimator of cointegrating vectors in higher order integrated systems. *Econometrica, 61*(4), 783–820. DOI: 10.2307/2951763

Sun, Y., Li, M., Zhang, M., Khan, H. S. U. D., Li, J., Li, Z., Sun, H., Zhu, Y., & Anaba, O. A. (2021). A study on China's economic growth, green energy technology, and carbon emissions based on the Kuznets curve (EKC). *Environmental Science and Pollution Research International, 28*(6), 7200–7211. DOI: 10.1007/s11356-020-11019-0

United Nations. (2015). *Transforming our world: The 2030 Agenda for Sustainable Development*. New York: UN. https://sdgs.un.org/2030agenda

World Bank. (2022). [Washington, DC: World Bank. https://databank.worldbank.org/source/world-development-indicators]. *World Development Indicators, 2022,* •••.

World Intellectual Property Organization (WIPO). (2021). *World Intellectual Property Indicators 2021*. Geneva: WIPO. https://www.wipo.int/publications/en/details.jsp?id=4526

Yilanci, V., & Pata, U. K. (2020). Investigating the EKC hypothesis for China: The role of economic complexity on ecological footprint. *Environmental Science and Pollution Research International, 27*(26), 32683–32694. DOI: 10.1007/s11356-020-09434-4

Zhou, M., Zhang, X., & Li, Y. (2022). Can green patents reduce carbon emission intensity? *Frontiers in Environmental Science, 29*(45), 68000–68012. DOI: 10.3389/fenvs.2022.1084977

Zivot, E., & Andrews, D. W. K. (1992). Further evidence on the great crash, the oil price shock, and the unit root hypothesis. *Journal of Business & Economic Statistics, 10*(3), 251–270. DOI: 10.1080/07350015.1992.10509904

KEY TERMS AND DEFINITIONS

CO_2: Carbon dioxide (CO_2) emissions refer to the release of CO_2 gas into the atmosphere, primarily as a result of human activities such as the combustion of fossil fuels, deforestation, and various industrial operations. As a greenhouse gas, CO_2 is a major driver of global warming and climate change.

Economic Contribution: This term captures the value-added effect of business and industrial activity on a country's economy, often measured through indicators such as GDP, employment, and industrial output. Understanding economic contribution is critical for informed policy development (Mosweunyane, 2019; Pelkki & Sherman, 2020).

Energy Transition: The term describes the structural shift from fossil fuel-based energy systems toward cleaner, renewable, and low-carbon alternatives. This transformation involves technological innovation, regulatory reform, and changes in consumer behavior (International Renewable Energy Agency, 2020).

Fossil Fuels: Fossil fuels are hydrocarbon-based energy sources—such as coal, crude oil, and natural gas—formed from ancient organic matter. While still widely used, they are a primary source of global CO_2 emissions and a key target of climate mitigation policies (IEA, 2021).

GDP (Gross Domestic Product): GDP represents the total monetary value of all goods and services produced within a country over a specified period. It is widely used as an indicator of economic activity and overall national economic health (World Bank, 2022).

GPFG (Government Pension Fund Global): Also known as Norway's Sovereign Wealth Fund or Oil Fund, the GPFG is one of the largest such funds globally. It was established to manage the country's oil revenues and to secure long-term financial stability for future generations (Norges Bank Investment Management, 2022).

FARDL (Fourier-Augmented ARDL): This is an econometric approach that extends the standard Autoregressive Distributed Lag (ARDL) model by including Fourier terms to capture structural breaks and cyclical patterns. It enhances the model's ability to assess long-term relationships in non-linear and dynamic time series (Shahbaz et al., 2018).

Economic Growth: Economic growth describes the sustained increase in the production of goods and services within an economy, usually reflected in rising real GDP. It is associated with improvements in employment, investment, and living standards (Solow, 1956).

Green Growth: Green growth refers to a model of economic development that promotes environmental sustainability by minimizing ecological degradation and ensuring the efficient use of natural resources. It supports the shift toward low-carbon, inclusive economies (OECD, 2011).

PA (Patent Applications): The number of patent applications denotes the count of formal requests submitted to government authorities for exclusive rights over new inventions. In economic research, this serves as a proxy for innovation intensity and technological advancement (WIPO, 2021).

REN (Renewable Energy Consumption): This refers to the share of total energy consumption derived from naturally replenishable sources, including solar, wind, hydropower, biomass, and geothermal energy. It is a critical element in efforts to reduce dependence on fossil fuels and limit climate change (International Renewable Energy Agency, 2020).

Renewable Energy: Energy generated from resources that are naturally replenished on a human timescale, such as sunlight, wind, water, biomass, and geothermal heat. It is central to strategies aimed at decarbonization and environmental protection (International Renewable Energy Agency, 2020).

Sustainable Development: Defined by the Brundtland Report (1987), sustainable development is the process of meeting current societal needs without compromising the ability of future generations to meet theirs. It integrates economic growth, environmental stewardship, and social equity.

Sustainable Growth: This concept reflects an economy's capacity to expand over time without exhausting natural resources or causing severe harm to the environment. It emphasizes balance between economic progress, ecological resilience, and social well-being (United Nations, 2015).

Technological Innovation: This refers to the creation and implementation of new technologies, processes, or products that enhance efficiency, productivity, and competitiveness. Innovation plays a key role in driving sustainable economic transformation (OECD, 2018).

Chapter 4
Future of AI in Global Sustainability

Satya Subrahmanyam
https://orcid.org/0000-0003-0441-2742
Holy Spirit University of Kaslik, Lebanon

ABSTRACT

The integration of artificial intelligence (AI) into global sustainability presents a transformative opportunity to address critical challenges such as climate change, resource depletion, and social inequities. This chapter explores AI's role in achieving the United Nations Sustainable Development Goals (SDGs) through innovative applications in environmental conservation, resource efficiency, and social impact. It examines AI-driven advancements in climate modeling, renewable energy optimization, and equitable economic development. Additionally, the chapter highlights challenges including ethical concerns, technological limitations, and policy gaps. Future trends, such as AI-IoT convergence and international collaborations, are discussed as key drivers of sustainable innovation. Through case studies and policy recommendations, this chapter provides a roadmap for leveraging AI to build a more sustainable and equitable world.

DOI: 10.4018/979-8-3373-1077-0.ch004

1. INTRODUCTION

1.1 Contextualizing AI within the Global Sustainability Agenda

The twenty-first century has never presented more opportunities or threats to sustainability than at any time in the past. Increasing socio-economic inequalities, resource scarcity, biodiversity loss, and climate change are all issues that indicate the dire necessity of response on a global scale and urgently (United Nations, 2023). In the meantime, new technology, namely AI, can transform how we deal with sustainability in a global context. AI is no longer an innovation but a solution mechanism to problems at the systemic level that influence economics, society, and the environment (Vinuesa et al., 2020). Governments, corporations, and communities can make decisions, which can be more informed and aligned to the SDGs when using artificial intelligence (AI) to analyse huge data, identify patterns, and streamline processes.

1.2 Defining Sustainability: Environmental, Economic, and Social Dimensions

Environmental preservation, economic growth, and social equality are the three interconnected pillars upon which sustainability rests. In order to keep the earth habitable for generations to come, the environmental component stresses conserving natural resources and minimising human impact on the ecosystem (Rockström et al., 2009). From an economic perspective, we want to lessen global economic inequities and systemic vulnerabilities while simultaneously encouraging inclusive development, productivity, and innovation. Economic and technical progress should lead to better living conditions and protection of human rights; this is where the social dimension comes in (Geissdoerfer et al., 2018). In all three areas, AI has the potential to be a catalyst when used wisely. Globally, renewable energy integration into power grids can be optimised with machine learning, financial inclusion can be enhanced with predictive analytics, and healthcare and education can be made more accessible with natural language processing.

1.3 Significance of AI in Addressing Global Security and Sustainability Challenges

The intersection of AI, sustainability, and global security presents a critical frontier for research and practice. Global security today extends beyond military concerns to include climate resilience, food and water security, cybersecurity, and pandemic preparedness. AI systems can help forecast extreme weather events, manage supply chain risks, and detect misinformation that undermines societal trust (Rahwan et al., 2019). Besides AI-driven innovations in agriculture, healthcare, and energy can strengthen resilience in vulnerable communities, thereby reducing risks of instability and conflict linked to resource scarcity or socio-economic disparities (Rolnick et al., 2022). Concerns about algorithmic unfairness, energy-intensive computation, and ethical quandaries around spying highlight the need to exercise caution while using AI. Therefore, to make sure AI is a tool for inclusive and long-term security, we need to find a way to maximise its benefits while minimising its drawbacks.

1.4 Purpose, Scope, and Objectives of the Chapter

The purpose of this chapter is to discuss how AI will make future sustainability and security a global concern. The purpose is to explore how AI can be used to protect the environment, boost economies and enhance social lives all as it addresses emerging threats to the wellbeing of man and the planet. The area covers AI usage in various areas such as climate action, sustainable cities, resource management, and crisis response. Of interest is the potential and issues related to such applications. In that way, the chapter aligns with the objectives of the entire SDGs, in particular, SDGs 9 (Industry, Innovation, and Infrastructure), 11 (Sustainable Cities and Communities), and 13 (Climate Action). There are 3 things we would like to achieve:

1. To critically assess the current state of AI applications in sustainability and global security contexts.
2. To identify key challenges, including ethical, technical, and governance issues, that may hinder AI's potential.

3. To propose strategies for integrating AI into global sustainability agendas in ways that promote equity, resilience, and long-term security.

In setting the foundation, this introduction emphasizes that AI should not be viewed merely as a tool for efficiency but as a transformative force with the capacity to reshape how humanity addresses complex global challenges. By embedding AI within the sustainability discourse, stakeholders can move toward a more resilient, just, and secure future.

2. AI AND THE GLOBAL SUSTAINABILITY LANDSCAPE

AI is increasingly intertwined with the Sustainable Development Goals (SDGs), offering solutions to pressing global challenges. It supports climate change mitigation, biodiversity conservation, and efficient resource use. AI also advances the circular economy through waste reduction and renewable energy integration. While developed economies leverage AI for large-scale sustainability projects, developing countries are adopting community-focused solutions. This global landscape reflects AI's potential to bridge gaps, accelerate innovation, and foster inclusive, sustainable development worldwide.

2.1 Overview of Sustainable Development Goals (SDGs) and Their Link to AI Applications

The problem of poverty, inequality, climate change, loss of biodiversity is only a few among the world problems that are pressing and global, and the Sustainable Development Goals (SDGs) of the United Nations seek to address. The Sustainable Development Goals (SDGs) are the list of seventeen goals that are both related to one another and strive to make society, environment, and the economy as a whole better (United Nations, 2023). It is now a commonplace fact that artificial intelligence (AI) is one of the main enablers of the achievement of these objectives. The objectives of cheap and clean energy (SDG 7), sustainable cities and communities (SDG 11), and climate action (SDG 13) can be promoted using AI technologies through the processing of large amounts of data, trends forecasting, and optimisation of systems (Vinuesa et al., 2020). To make sure that AI generates no unintended negative consequences, i.e. those rising digital distances or disparities, and that it aligns with the SDGs, ethical frameworks should be incorporated, and sustainable governance is required.

Table 1. Linkages between SDGs and AI applications

SDG	AI Application Area	Examples of AI Contribution
SDG 7 – Affordable and Clean Energy	Renewable energy forecasting and smart grids	Predictive algorithms for solar/ wind integration, demand response optimization
SDG 11 – Sustainable Cities and Communities	Urban planning and smart mobility	AI for traffic management, waste optimization, and pollution monitoring
SDG 13 – Climate Action	Climate modeling and disaster response	Early-warning systems for floods, hurricanes, and wildfire detection
SDG 14 – Life Below Water	Marine biodiversity monitoring	AI-enabled image recognition for species identification, illegal fishing detection
SDG 15 – Life on Land	Biodiversity and deforestation monitoring	Satellite imagery and remote sensing for habitat protection

2.2 Role of AI in Mitigating Climate Change, Biodiversity Loss, and Resource Scarcity

As the risk of the increased frequency and intensity of the weather events, increased sea levels, and ecological imbalances grow, the threat of climate change remains the most urgent threat of our era. Rolnick et al. (2022) state that artificial intelligence (AI) contributes to the adaptation and mitigation plans, resulting in a more accurate climatic prediction model, efficient distribution of renewable energy, and the possibility of a more accurate detection of greenhouse gas emissions. Machine learning and AI-powered remote sensing are used in conservation initiatives to monitor the population of species, detect cases of illegal logging, and track deforestation patterns in close-time (Ceballos et al., 2020). AI can improve water distribution networks, develop more accurate agriculture to better use pesticides and fertilisers, and reduce food waste through predictive demand analytics, which are all aimed at optimising resources (Wang, 2024). AI can enhance the efficiency of resources and reduce human effects on the ecosystems as these applications demonstrate.

Table 2. AI's role in addressing environmental challenges

Challenge	AI Contribution	Expected Outcomes
Climate Change	Climate prediction models, emission tracking, energy efficiency optimization	Reduced carbon footprint, better policy decision-making
Biodiversity Loss	Automated wildlife tracking, illegal logging detection	Improved conservation planning, reduced habitat destruction
Resource Scarcity	Precision agriculture, water resource optimization, supply chain efficiency	Reduced food waste, sustainable farming, improved water access

2.3 AI's Potential for Advancing Circular Economy and Renewable Energy Adoption

The goal of the circular economy is to encourage sustainable manufacturing techniques, recycling, and reusing materials rather than just producing them and then throwing them away. With AI's intelligent supply chain management, material monitoring, and waste reduction capabilities, this transformation may be accelerated in a unique way. A more resource-efficient economy may be supported by machine learning algorithms that optimise reverse logistics for recycling processes and anticipate the possibility for material recovery (Pappas et al., 2021). Integrating solar and wind power into current power networks is one example of how artificial intelligence is already finding use in the energy industry. The intermittency problems of renewables may be solved with the use of advanced algorithms that enhance grid stability, energy storage management, and load forecasting (IEA, 2021). Smart grids powered by artificial intelligence may allow customers to make energy consumption choices based on data, which can further improve efficiency and decrease carbon emissions. Taken as a whole, these uses highlight the critical role AI plays in driving innovations with a focus on sustainability.

Table 3. AI for circular economy and renewable energy

Application Area	AI Use Case	Impact on Sustainability
Circular Economy	Reverse logistics optimization, material tracking	Efficient recycling, waste reduction
Resource Efficiency	Predictive analytics for production and consumption	Lower material and energy use, cost savings
Renewable Energy	Smart grids, energy storage management	Higher grid stability, reduced intermittency
Consumer Empowerment	AI-enabled energy apps	Behavior changes toward energy efficiency

2.4 Global Perspectives: Developed vs. Developing Economies in AI-Driven Sustainability

The adoption and impact of AI in sustainability vary significantly between developed and developing economies. In developed nations, AI investments are primarily focused on advancing smart infrastructure, renewable energy integration, and large-scale climate modeling. These countries often have the necessary digital infrastructure, funding, and skilled workforce to deploy AI solutions effectively. Europe has pioneered the use of AI in climate modeling and renewable energy optimization, aligning with its Green Deal objectives (European Commission, 2021). In contrast, developing economies face challenges such as limited access to advanced technologies, digital skills gaps, and insufficient regulatory frameworks. Yet, they also hold unique opportunities: AI-driven solutions in agriculture, water management, and disaster response can address pressing local challenges and support leapfrogging toward sustainable development (Gikunda, 2024). AI-powered mobile applications in sub-Saharan Africa are helping smallholder farmers increase yields and adapt to climate variability. Bridging the AI divide is therefore essential to ensure that technological advancements contribute equitably to global sustainability.

Table 4. Global perspectives on AI in sustainability

Region/ Economy	Focus Areas on AI-Driven Sustainability	Key Opportunities	Main Challenges	Source
Developed Economies (e.g., Europe, North America)	Smart grids, climate modeling, urban mobility	Advanced R&D, strong infrastructure, policy alignment (e.g., EU Green Deal)	Ethical governance, energy demand of AI systems	European Commission (2021)
Developing Economies (e.g., Africa, South Asia)	Agriculture, water management, disaster response	Leapfrogging potential, localized AI innovations	Digital divide, lack of infrastructure, skills gap	Munyati et al. (2022)

AI holds transformative potential in advancing the global sustainability landscape, with applications spanning climate change mitigation, biodiversity conservation, resource management, renewable energy, and circular economy models. While developed nations continue to lead in large-scale adoption, developing economies present untapped opportunities where AI can address immediate sustainability challenges. Ensuring equitable access, ethical deployment, and inclusive governance is critical for AI to fulfill its role as a catalyst for achieving the SDGs.

3. KEY AI APPLICATIONS IN SUSTAINABILITY

Artificial intelligence (AI) has been discovered as an essential weapon to enhance sustainability in every aspect of it: environmental, economic, and social. AI machine learning, big data analytics, and predictive modelling capabilities make better decisions and better utilization of resources possible, which leads to the creation of a more sustainable future. With emphasis on the environmental, economic and social spheres, this section explores significant AI applications which address the issue of sustainability.

3.1 Environmental Sustainability

Climate Modeling and Predictive Analytics: By making prediction models more precise and detailed, AI is transforming climate research. Artificial intelligence (AI) can analyse large datasets to find nonlinear patterns and produce regional climate predictions, in contrast to traditional climate models that depend on complicated physical equations. These days, scientists utilise machine learning algorithms to do things like estimate when sea levels will rise, model the effects of various policy options on greenhouse gas emissions, and make predictions about severe weather (Rolnick et al., 2022). With this information, lawmakers may craft resilient, and mitigation plans that are flexible to changing circumstances. Google Research (2024) states that early warnings in susceptible places are provided by Google's AI-powered flood forecasting system, which helps save lives and decrease economic damages. Artificial intelligence (AI) enhances the world's ability to deal with climate concerns by making forecasts timelier and more accurate.

Smart Agriculture and Precision Farming: Agriculture accounts for a significant portion of global resource use and greenhouse gas emissions, making it a priority area for sustainable transformation. AI-driven precision farming optimizes irrigation, fertilization, and pest control by integrating data from sensors, drones, and satellite imagery. This reduces water usage, minimizes chemical inputs, and enhances crop yields (Wang, 2024). Predictive analytics also help farmers anticipate weather variability and market demand, reducing losses and improving food security. In developing economies, mobile-based AI tools empower smallholder farmers with real-time advice on soil health and pest management, bridging knowledge gaps and increasing productivity (Gikunda, 2024). Such applications highlight AI's potential to ensure both ecological sustainability and equitable livelihoods.

Renewable Energy Optimization and Smart Grids: The unreliability of renewable energy sources, such as solar and wind, makes their incorporation into power grids more difficult. Artificial intelligence (AI) helps with this problem by making smart grid management and predictive energy balancing possible. Using meteorological data as input, machine learning algorithms optimise the use of energy storage and make predictions about future renewable energy generation, all with the goal of stabilising grid performance (IEA, 2021). Through the use of AI-enabled dynamic pricing and demand response, customers are incentivised to adapt their energy use to match the availability of supplies. Both energy efficiency and the velocity of transition towards carbon neutrality are boosted by these improvements. An example of the importance of smart energy management in large-scale operations is DeepMind's AI, which has increased Google's data centre efficiency by 40% (Evans & Gao, 2016).

3.2 Economic Sustainability

Supply Chain Transparency and Efficiency: Sustainable supply chains are essential for reducing environmental impacts and ensuring ethical practices. AI-powered tools enable real-time tracking of goods, predictive demand planning, and risk identification in global supply networks. By analyzing data from IoT sensors and blockchain systems, AI enhances transparency and reduces inefficiencies (Saberi et al., 2018). Corporates use AI to monitor carbon footprints across supply chains and identify opportunities for emissions reduction. This promotes not only operational efficiency but also compliance with sustainability regulations.

Sustainable Finance and ESG-Driven Investments: AI is also changing the face of banking by facilitating more environmentally conscious investing choices. A growing number of investment strategies include Environmental, Social, and Governance (ESG) criteria. Artificial intelligence (AI) makes it easier to analyse unstructured data, such news stories and company filings, in order to evaluate ESG performance (Yu et al., 2025). To help investors build more sustainable portfolios, predictive algorithms can spot threats posed by things like societal trends, legislative shifts, and climate change. Supporting equitable economic development, AI-driven financial platforms also increase small and medium firms' access to green financing.

AI in Waste Reduction and Resource Management: Resource efficiency is a cornerstone of economic sustainability. AI supports waste reduction by optimizing industrial processes, predicting material needs, and enhancing recycling systems. Computer vision technologies are used in waste-sorting facilities to identify and separate recyclable materials with high accuracy (Pappas al., 2021). Predictive analytics minimize overproduction and inventory waste in manufacturing and retail sectors. These applications contribute to the development of circular economy models, reducing both costs and environmental footprints.

3.3 Social Sustainability

AI for Public Health and Pandemic Preparedness: The COVID-19 pandemic underscored the importance of AI in safeguarding public health. AI-powered systems were used to model infection spread, optimize vaccine distribution, and accelerate drug discovery (Bullock et al., 2020). Beyond emergency response, AI continues to play a role in monitoring disease outbreaks, improving diagnostic accuracy, and strengthening healthcare access in underserved regions. By enhancing health resilience, AI directly contributes to social sustainability by protecting lives and reducing inequalities in healthcare delivery.

Education and Workforce Upskilling for Sustainable Development: Education and skills development are crucial for preparing societies for a sustainable future. AI-powered platforms offer personalized learning pathways, enabling individuals to acquire skills relevant to green industries and digital economies (Holmes et al., 2019). Workforce upskilling initiatives supported by AI ensure that employees can adapt to new technologies while contributing to sustainable practices. AI-driven educational tools promote inclusivity by making learning more accessible to marginalized groups, thereby fostering social equity.

AI in Equitable Resource Distribution and Social Inclusion: AI can enhance fairness in resource distribution, from social welfare benefits to humanitarian aid. Predictive analytics help governments and organizations identify vulnerable populations and allocate resources more effectively (Rahwan et al., 2019). AI is being used to improve food aid distribution during crises by analyzing demographic and geospatial data. AI tools can identify biases in policy implementation, promoting accountability and inclusivity. Ethical safeguards are essential to ensure that algorithms do not reinforce existing inequalities.

Figure 1. Key AI applications in sustainability

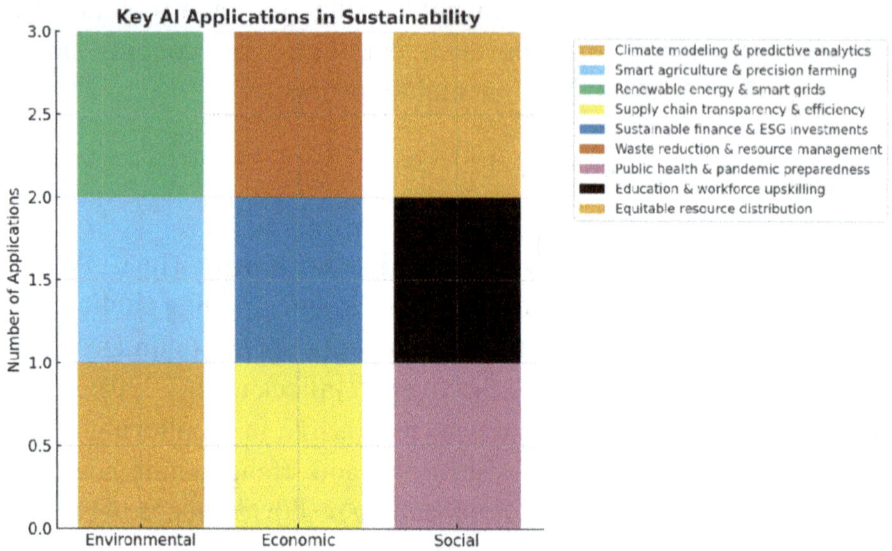

AI is developing in economic, social, and environmental sustainability. AI might revolutionise climate resilience, renewable energy uptake, supply networks, and social institutions by boosting resilience, sustainability, and inclusivity. These applications should be managed by robust governance structures, equitable access, and ethical principles to minimise risks and enhance advantages. Therefore, artificial intelligence (AI) is best understood as a strategic facilitator of sustainable development in the 21st century, not merely a technological tool.

4. OPPORTUNITIES AND BENEFITS OF AI IN GLOBAL SUSTAINABILITY

More and more, people are seeing that artificial intelligence (AI) may revolutionise the way we think about and approach global sustainability. Systemic change may be driven by AI in the environmental, economic, and social domains via the processing of massive volumes of data, the detection of hidden patterns, and the enablement of predictive skills. Using data-driven insights to improve decision-making, speeding up green innovation, enabling resilient infrastructures, and boosting cooperation among varied stakeholders are four main potential and advantages of AI in sustainability that are explored in this section.

4.1 Enhancing Decision-Making with Data-Driven Insights

AI can streamline sustainability-related decision-making by transforming unclear data into an action plan. The categories of the issues which the governments, industries and civil society face are climate change, resource depletion and social inequality, which require timely and enlightened actions. It is possible to make evidence-based decisions relying on AI-based analytics and machine learning models that will have the capacity to process real-time data that will be gathered by different sources (satellite imagery, social media, IoT sensors). (Vinuesa et al., 2020).

Climate models based on AI enable policymakers to predict the occurrence of extreme weather, potential areas of vulnerability, and put up specific adaptation measures. Predictive algorithms can also be used in agriculture to inform crop management decisions, such as the most appropriate time to plant, irrigate, and treat crops; this can enhance better food security and sustainability outcomes (Subrahmanyam and Sri, 2025). In addition to environmental contexts, AI helps to make financial decisions in sustainable investing. AI is becoming a favored tool by asset managers, who now use it to assess environmental, social and governance (ESG) performance indicators, giving investors more confidence in the ability of asset portfolios to be used in fulfilling sustainability objectives (Al-Sartawi et al., 2022).

AI can be used to improve sustainability strategies by providing the disconnect between sophisticated data and feasible interventions and improving decision-making.

4.2 Accelerating Green Innovation and Sustainable Technologies

The other important opportunity is the use of AI as the driver of green innovation. Clean technologies innovation is core to the realisation of the United Nations Sustainable Development Goals (SDGs), especially in such fields as affordable clean energy, sustainable production, and climate action. The AI speeds up these developments through the simplification of research, optimization of design processes, and cutting down the costs of experimentation.

Material science is also making use of AI algorithms to find solutions to make construction, packaging and manufacturing eco-friendly. Machine learning can guide the discovery of novel materials to use in batteries or technologies to capture carbon by simulating thousands of combinations of chemicals in just a few seconds, compared to the time-consuming traditional laboratory methods (Rolnick et al., 2022). The AI also finds application in the renewable energy industry to streamline the interaction between solar and wind energy with electrical power grids by forecasting energy demand, stabilizing the supply wave, and minimizing energy wastage (Subrahmanyam et al., 2024).

AI supports the development of sustainable transportation systems. Autonomous vehicles, AI-based traffic management, and predictive maintenance of public infrastructure contribute to lowering carbon emissions and promoting energy efficiency (Subrahmanyam, 2025). By embedding AI into innovation processes, industries are better positioned to deliver scalable, sustainable technologies that align with long-term global security and climate resilience.

4.3 Enabling Resilient Infrastructures and Disaster Risk Management

Resilience is a cornerstone of sustainability, particularly in the face of increasing natural disasters, urbanization pressures, and global health crises. AI has significant potential in building resilient infrastructures and enhancing disaster risk management. Machine learning models can assess structural vulnerabilities, forecast hazards, and enable proactive interventions.

AI-enabled early warning systems improve disaster preparedness by analyzing seismic activity, flood patterns, or wildfire risks in near real-time (Wahl et al., 2020). During the COVID-19 pandemic, AI applications played a critical role in tracking virus transmission, optimizing hospital resource allocation, and supporting vaccine development - demonstrating its relevance to public health resilience (Bullock et al., 2020).

In urban environments, AI-powered smart city initiatives enhance infrastructure resilience by monitoring energy grids, water distribution networks, and transportation systems. Predictive maintenance technologies detect potential breakdowns before they occur, reducing costs and improving reliability (Subrahmanyam, 2025). AI supports climate-resilient urban planning by simulating the long-term impacts of rising sea levels, heatwaves, or air pollution on different urban scenarios.

These applications underline AI's contribution to minimizing risks, protecting vulnerable populations, and safeguarding critical systems, thereby strengthening both human and ecological resilience.

4.4 Promoting Collaboration Between Governments, Industry, and Civil Society

Sustainability challenges are inherently global, complex, and interconnected, requiring collaboration across sectors and borders. AI not only provides technical tools but also facilitates platforms for collaboration and collective action. By aggregating and sharing data across diverse stakeholders, AI enables more transparent and inclusive decision-making processes.

Governments can use AI-driven platforms to monitor progress toward the SDGs, while international organizations can employ machine learning to harmonize sustainability metrics across countries (Truby, 2020). For industry, AI fosters partnerships with research institutions and startups to accelerate innovation in areas such as clean energy, sustainable agriculture, and waste reduction. Civil society organizations, in turn, leverage AI for advocacy, enabling communities to participate in shaping sustainability policies through open-access data and citizen science initiatives (Subrahmanyam, 2025).

AI-based collaboration tools improve crisis coordination. For example, during natural disasters, AI-driven logistics systems connect governments, NGOs, and private firms to deliver aid more efficiently. AI can mediate international cooperation on transboundary challenges like deforestation, ocean pollution, or biodiversity loss by providing real-time monitoring and accountability mechanisms (Vinuesa & Sirmacek, 2021).

Through its ability to unify stakeholders around shared goals, AI strengthens collective capacity to address sustainability challenges, bridging gaps in knowledge, governance, and resource allocation.

Figure 2. Comparative benefits of AI

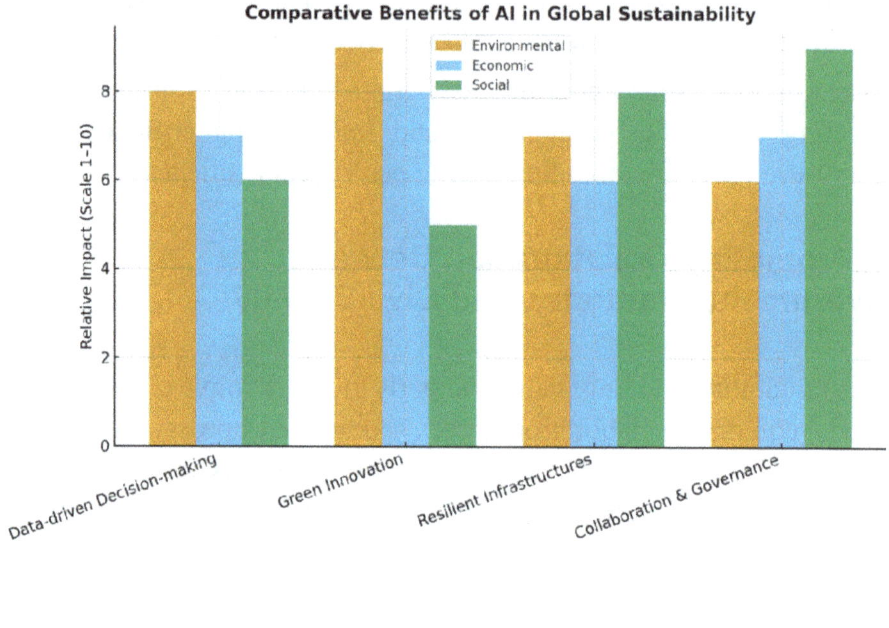

AI offers transformative opportunities for enhancing sustainability at global, regional, and local levels. By enabling data-driven decision-making, fostering green innovation, building resilient infrastructures, and promoting multi-stakeholder collaboration, AI contributes directly to the achievement of the SDGs and global security agendas. While challenges such as ethical risks and digital divides remain, the benefits of AI in sustainability are undeniable. Harnessing these opportunities responsibly will be critical in shaping a future that is both technologically advanced and ecologically sustainable.

5. CHALLENGES AND RISKS

While artificial intelligence (AI) offers significant opportunities for advancing sustainability, its adoption also raises critical challenges and risks that must be addressed to ensure equitable and responsible outcomes. These risks are multidimensional, spanning ethical, environmental, technological, and geopolitical domains. This section explores five major areas of concern: ethical dilemmas, environmental costs, data governance, geopolitical challenges, and unintended consequences associated with AI-driven sustainability.

5.1 Ethical Dilemmas: Bias, Equity, and Inclusivity

AI systems are only as unbiased as the data used to train them, yet many datasets contain historical or structural inequalities that risk perpetuating discrimination. In environmental sustainability projects, biased datasets may misrepresent vulnerable communities, leading to inequitable access to climate adaptation resources (Mehrabi et al., 2021). Likewise, in smart agriculture, algorithms may be designed based on data from developed countries, which do not adequately reflect the realities of smallholder farmers in the Global South.

The lack of inclusivity in AI design and deployment risks exacerbating existing inequalities. Women, marginalized communities, and populations in low-income countries are often underrepresented in AI datasets and governance structures (Crawford, 2021). Without deliberate inclusivity, AI-driven sustainability initiatives may benefit already advantaged groups while leaving vulnerable populations behind. Hence, ethical frameworks and participatory design processes are essential to mitigate bias and promote equitable access to AI benefits.

5.2 Environmental Cost of AI

It is impossible to ignore AI's ecological imprint, even though it is often presented as a remedy to environmental problems. Extreme computing power and energy usage are necessary for training in big language models and other advanced ML models. A single NLP model's training may result in carbon emissions comparable to those of many automobiles during their lifetimes, as pointed out by Strubell et al. (2019). Because of this, some are wondering whether the environmental impact of AI development and deployment will be greater than the advantages it brings to sustainability.

Data centers, which support AI infrastructure, are another source of significant carbon emissions. Despite efforts to integrate renewable energy, many data centers continue to rely on fossil fuels, exacerbating global emissions (Gupta et al., 2020). The production of specialized hardware, such as GPUs, contributes to resource extraction pressures, including rare earth mineral mining, which has its own environmental and social consequences.

Sustainable AI methods, such as energy-efficient algorithms, carbon-neutral data centres, and a greater emphasis on green computing projects, are urgently needed to resolve these conflicts (Schwartz et al., 2020).

5.3 Data Governance, Privacy, and Security Concerns

The vast amount of data required for AI applications in sustainability presents governance and privacy challenges. AI models often rely on sensitive data - ranging from geolocation records to health statistics - that can compromise individual or community privacy if misused. AI-driven public health surveillance systems designed for pandemic preparedness risk crossing ethical boundaries when data is collected without informed consent or adequate anonymization (Bragazzi et al., 2020).

Beyond privacy, data security is also a growing concern. Cyberattacks on AI-driven energy grids, transportation systems, or water supply networks could have catastrophic consequences for both security and sustainability. Fragmented regulatory frameworks across countries make it difficult to enforce consistent data governance, creating risks of data misuse and exploitation (Cath, 2018).

Establishing clear global standards for data governance, ensuring transparency in AI decision-making, and protecting privacy rights are critical to maintaining trust in AI-driven sustainability initiatives.

5.4 Geopolitical Challenges: Global Digital Divide and AI Monopolization

AI's role in sustainability is shaped not only by technical capacity but also by geopolitical realities. The global digital divide means that while developed economies can invest heavily in AI infrastructure, many developing nations lack the resources, expertise, and connectivity to leverage AI effectively. This inequality risks widening the gap between those who benefit from AI-driven sustainability and those left behind (UNESCO, 2021).

AI development is increasingly concentrated in a handful of multinational corporations and advanced economies. This monopolization limits access to AI tools, datasets, and expertise, reinforcing dependencies of developing countries on foreign technologies (Taddeo, 2023). Such dynamics could undermine global cooperation on sustainability, as technological asymmetries may fuel geopolitical tensions and restrict inclusive progress toward the Sustainable Development Goals (SDGs).

Efforts to democratize AI, through open-source platforms, international collaborations, and capacity-building in developing regions, are therefore crucial to avoid exacerbating global inequalities in sustainability outcomes.

5.5 Risk of Unintended Consequences and Over-Reliance on AI

Finally, AI's complexity and opacity present risks of unintended consequences. Algorithms may behave unpredictably in dynamic environments, generating outputs that conflict with sustainability goals. AI systems optimizing supply chains for efficiency might inadvertently prioritize profit over environmental considerations, increasing emissions rather than reducing them (Maurya et al., 2025).

Over-reliance on AI also creates vulnerabilities. Excessive dependence on automated systems can reduce human oversight, leading to "automation bias," where decision-makers blindly trust algorithmic outputs even when they are flawed (Longoni et al., 2019). This is particularly concerning critical areas such as disaster response, where erroneous predictions could cost lives.

Framing AI as a "silver bullet" for sustainability risks diverting attention from structural changes required to address root causes of climate change, inequality, and resource depletion. Technology must therefore be seen as a complement to, rather than a substitute for, social, political, and behavioral transformations.

Figure 3. Risk matrix

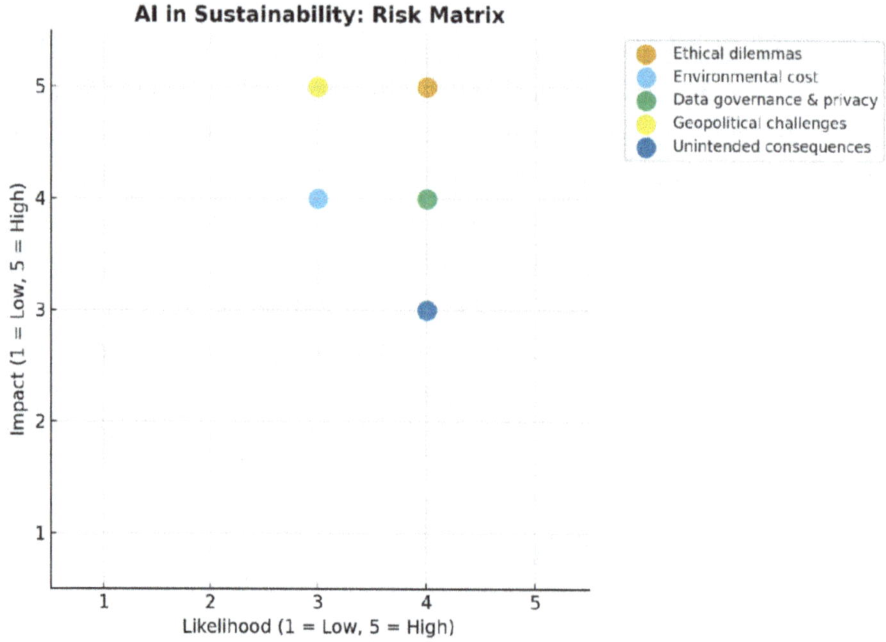

AI presents both transformative opportunities and profound challenges for global sustainability. Ethical dilemmas, environmental costs, data governance issues, geopolitical inequalities, and unintended consequences highlight the risks of uncritical adoption. To ensure that AI becomes a true enabler of sustainability rather than a new source of inequity or harm, a balanced approach is necessary - one that emphasizes inclusivity, transparency, energy efficiency, and global collaboration. The challenge lies not only in developing smarter algorithms but also in fostering smarter governance and collective responsibility.

6. THE FUTURE PATHWAYS OF AI FOR GLOBAL SUSTAINABILITY

AI is predicted to shape global sustainability in the future decades. AI is moving beyond energy optimisation, agricultural, and environmental monitoring to more complex, integrated, and community-centered applications. AI's sustainability future will depend on technology advances, international cooperation, and risk-benefit balance. Emerging technical trends, AI in climate diplomacy, frontier technology integration, localised community-driven applications, and scenario-based trajectories are five intriguing possibilities.

6.1 Emerging Trends: AI for Green Innovation, Federated Learning, and Quantum Computing

Accelerating green innovation is one of the most important ways that AI can help. Energy efficiency, environmentally friendly materials, and low-carbon solutions are gaining prominence in the creation of new AI models with an emphasis on sustainability. Renewable energy deployment, carbon capture technology, and the discovery of sustainable building and battery materials are all areas that are benefiting from the use of artificial intelligence (Rolnick et al., 2022).

Federated learning is another new trend; it's a way to train AI models on data stored locally but distributed across devices. Reducing the need for huge, centralised data storage, this method not only enhances privacy but also lowers energy consumption and allows increased engagement from varied stakeholders (Yang et al., 2019).

Quantum computing, while still in its infancy, presents another frontier. When combined with AI, quantum computing could exponentially increase computational capacity, enabling breakthroughs in climate modeling, ecosystem simulations, and optimization problems such as large-scale renewable energy integration (Gyongyosi & Imre, 2019). Together, these trends suggest a future in which AI becomes not only more powerful but also more aligned with ecological imperatives.

6.2 AI in Climate Diplomacy and Global Policy Coordination

Global sustainability challenges, including climate change and biodiversity loss, require collective action across borders. AI has the potential to enhance **climate diplomacy** by providing transparent, data-driven insights that can inform negotiations and treaties. AI-powered models can simulate the long-term outcomes of different policy decisions, helping governments anticipate the consequences of climate pledges and carbon reduction strategies (Truby, 2020).

AI can support **global policy coordination** by harmonizing sustainability metrics, tracking progress toward the Sustainable Development Goals (SDGs), and enabling accountability mechanisms. Shared AI platforms can bridge information asymmetries between developed and developing countries, ensuring fairer negotiations and stronger international commitments (Vinuesa & Sirmacek, 2021). By grounding diplomacy in evidence and foresight, AI can act as a catalyst for more robust global agreements on climate and sustainability.

6.3 Integration of AI with Other Frontier Technologies

Not artificial intelligence (AI) per se, but AI in tandem with other cutting-edge technology is where sustainability will go from here. Emerging ecosystems for sustainable development might be shaped by the coming together of artificial intelligence (AI), the internet of things (IoT), blockchain technology, and robots.

- **IoT** provides real-time environmental data from sensors embedded in energy grids, farms, and cities, which AI can analyze to optimize resource use.
- **Blockchain** ensures transparency and traceability in supply chains, which, when paired with AI, strengthens accountability in areas such as deforestation, fisheries management, and ethical sourcing (Saberi et al., 2018).
- **Robotics** enhances sustainable practices by automating precision farming, waste management, and disaster response, with AI providing the intelligence to maximize efficiency and minimize harm.

By combining these technologies, societies can build scalable, resilient, and transparent systems that drive sustainability across environmental, economic, and social dimensions.

6.4 Localized and Community-Driven AI Applications

While global initiatives are crucial, the future of AI in sustainability also depends on localized, community-driven applications. Grassroots projects powered by AI can empower local actors to design solutions tailored to their unique socio-environmental contexts. AI tools are increasingly being deployed to support smallholder farmers with localized weather forecasts, crop advice, and market access, particularly in developing economies (Saiz-Rubio & Rovira-Más, 2020).

In urban settings, community-driven AI applications can enhance participatory planning by integrating citizen-generated data into urban design, transportation planning, and pollution monitoring (Subrahmanyam, 2025). By decentralizing AI's benefits, communities become active participants rather than passive recipients of technological innovation. This localized approach ensures that AI contributes not only to global sustainability but also to social equity and inclusivity.

6.5 Scenario Analysis: Optimistic, Cautious, and Critical Trajectories

The future pathways of AI in sustainability can be envisioned through three scenarios: **optimistic, cautious, and critical**.

- **Optimistic trajectory**: AI evolves into a cornerstone of global sustainability, with energy-efficient algorithms, equitable governance, and seamless integration with other technologies. AI empowers both global diplomacy and local communities, driving progress toward the SDGs and beyond.
- **Cautious trajectory**: AI delivers incremental benefits but remains constrained by issues such as energy demands, governance gaps, and unequal access. While AI contributes to sustainability, its potential is not fully realized, and progress is uneven across regions.
- **Critical trajectory**: AI exacerbates inequalities, increases environmental costs, and consolidates power among a few corporations and countries. Over-reliance on AI without adequate governance leads to unintended harms, undermining both sustainability and global security.

Which trajectory materializes will depend on how societies address today's risks and design inclusive, transparent, and sustainable AI ecosystems for the future.

Figure 4. Scenario-based pathways

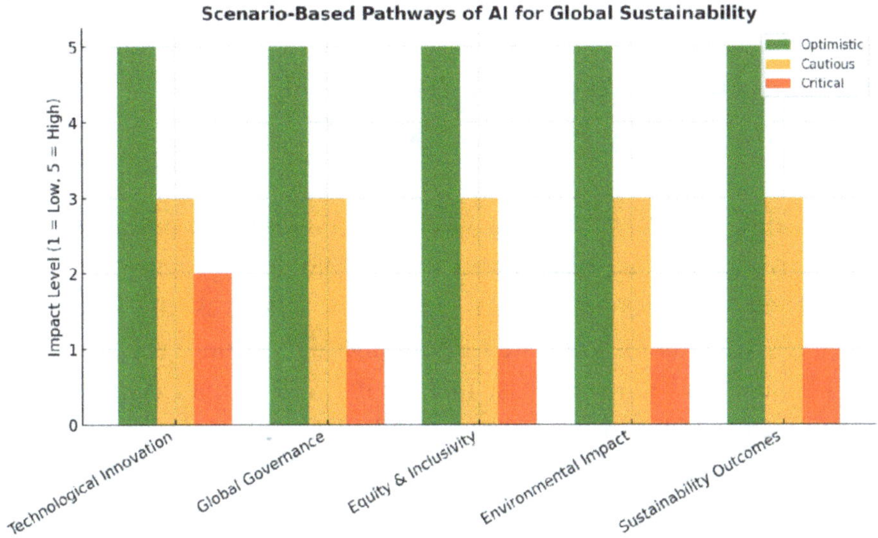

The future of AI for global sustainability is bright and unclear. Green AI, federated learning, and quantum computing have great promise, and frontier technologies and localised applications may assure inclusion. AI may also change climate diplomacy and global governance. Diverse possibilities emphasise governance, ethics, and teamwork. Collective decisions, policies, and attitudes will dictate whether AI promotes global well-being or deepens inequalities.

7. POLICY, GOVERNANCE, AND ETHICAL FRAMEWORKS

International organizations such as the UN, OECD, and World Bank are central in shaping AI frameworks that support sustainability. Policies emphasizing responsible AI development, transparency, and accountability ensure ethical deployment. Global cooperation models foster harmonized standards and equitable access to AI benefits. Embedding ethical principles - fairness, inclusivity, and environmental responsibility - into sustainability strategies helps mitigate risks and maximize benefits, enabling

AI to contribute effectively to long-term global security and sustainable development goals.

7.1 Role of International Organizations in AI Sustainability Frameworks

The policy making process is viewed as having international bodies as key players as far as ethical and sustainable deployment of artificial intelligence (AI) is concerned. As part of its initiatives, the United Nations (UN), such as its suggested Recommendation on the Ethics of AI (2021) have stated that fairness, inclusivity, and human rights have to be taken into account in AI systems (UNESCO, 2021). Principles of AI have also been published by the Organisation for Economic Co-Operation and Development (OECD) that promote transparency, accountability and human-centered design which are backed by over 40 countries (OECD, 2024). There is also the opportunity to address global issues like climate change, reducing poverty, and health inequity with help of AI that is recognized by the World Bank and allows to support the idea to provide equal access to AI technologies in third world states (World Bank, 2025). Such agencies not only provide guiding principles but also channels of coordination, monitoring, and capacity-building, especially in those regions where regulatory frames are few.

7.2 Policies for Responsible AI Development and Deployment

Good ruling involves policies that promote innovation without jeopardizing the ethics and sustainability at the cost of governance. Some governments have already come up with national plans for AI, which incorporate sustainability aims. The AI Act of the European Union focuses on the risk-based approach, as it requires that high-risk AI applications receive more stringent regulations, such as those in energy and environmental management (European Commission, 2015). The guidelines to responsible AI have been provided in countries like Canada, Japan, and Singapore, with their focus being on transparency, explainability, and reduction of social biases (Al-Sartawi et al., 2022). Policies would also pay more attention to the environmental impact of AI, which would encourage energy-saving models of machine learning and stimulate the consumption of renewable energy in data centers (Ranpara, 2025). Including the idea of sustainability in AI policy, governments can make sure that technological improvement will not contribute to the growing ecological and social inequality issues.

7.3 Global Cooperation Models for AI-Enabled Sustainability

The necessity to address sustainability concerns like climate change, loss of biodiversity and resource scarcity are not limited within national borders and, thus, global cooperation models are needed. International projects such as the Global Partnership on Artificial Intelligence (GPAI) are platforms through which governments, academia, and industry can engage in best practices and integrate AI applications in line with the United Nations sustainable development goals (SDGs) (GPAI, 2022). The formation of regional coalitions, such as the AI strategy of the African Union or the European Green Deal can also serve as additional examples of how organized governance can contribute to the sustainability and inclusiveness. The new tools of AI solutions scaled by the power of public-private partnerships (PPP) have become highly effective, merging government control with the creativity of the private sector to generate renewable energy, precision agriculture, and disaster risk management (Floridi et al., 2018). Such models will not work without trust-building and transparent governance.

7.4 Building Ethical AI Principles into Sustainability Strategies

Integrating ethical principles into AI-driven sustainability strategies ensures that technological solutions remain aligned with human values. The key pillars of ethical AI - fairness, accountability, transparency, and inclusivity - are crucial in mitigating biases that could worsen inequality in access to resources or services (Jobin et al., 2019). Ensuring that AI-powered resource allocation systems do not inadvertently disadvantage vulnerable communities is essential for social sustainability. Data governance frameworks that respect privacy while enabling responsible data sharing can enhance collaboration for sustainability without undermining individual rights (Cath, 2018). Ethical AI also necessitates capacity-building programs to upskill policymakers, engineers, and civil society in evaluating and implementing responsible AI systems. By embedding ethical frameworks into sustainability strategies, policymakers can foster trust, improve accountability, and enhance the long-term legitimacy of AI solutions in addressing global security and environmental challenges.

To strike a balance between innovation and accountability, strong ethical and governance frameworks are necessary, especially as AI plays an ever-increasing role in sustainability initiatives. Conventions are established at the international level and then put into practice in various settings via national policies and models of cooperation. Fair results and increased public confidence are the results of incorporating ethical AI into sustainability plans. To keep up with the ever-changing threats and possibilities posed by AI to global sustainability, more robust multilateral cooperation and adaptive governance are going to be needed in the future.

8. CASE STUDIES AND BEST PRACTICES

Real-world applications highlight AI's role in advancing sustainability. For instance, Google employs AI to optimize energy use in data centers, while IBM leverages AI for ESG-driven decision-making. Governments apply AI in disaster management, such as predictive flood modeling, and renewable energy forecasting. Community-level projects in Sub-Saharan Africa demonstrate AI in precision agriculture. These initiatives showcase how AI fosters climate action, resource efficiency, and social inclusion, offering valuable lessons for global sustainability strategies.

8.1 AI in Climate Action and Disaster Management

Artificial intelligence (AI) has been increasingly deployed in climate action strategies to enhance predictive capabilities and reduce risks. **Google's AI-driven flood forecasting system** in South Asia leverages machine learning to predict riverine floods up to 48 hours in advance, providing early warnings to millions of vulnerable people (Google Research, 2024). This application illustrates how AI can transform disaster management by integrating satellite data, hydrological models, and real-time observations into actionable insights. IBM's **Green Horizon project** applies AI-based analytics to optimize air quality forecasts in Chinese cities, helping policymakers reduce emissions and improve public health outcomes (Xu et al., 2025). These cases highlight how AI-driven predictive analytics can strengthen resilience to environmental challenges while protecting human security.

8.2 AI in Renewable Energy and Smart Grids

AI applications have also proved to be fruitful to the renewable energy sector. Other companies like **DeepMind (a subsidiary of Alphabet)** have collaborated with the data centers of Google to use AI to optimize its energy usage, resulting in nearly a 40 percent reduction in cooling energy consumption (Evans & Gao, 2016). Intermittent sources of renewable energy like wind and solar energy are also encouraged in power grids with the assistance of AI-enabled demand forecasting and supply optimization. **The SmartNet project** of European Union uses AI algorithms to stabilize the electricity supply and demand of smart grids to minimize the use of fossil fuels (European Commission, 2015). In the U.S., AI-driven project funded by the Department of Energy has been used to optimize the performance of wind farms, and this shows that AI can offer energy efficiency at scale. These projects emphasize the role of AI in advancing a circular economy and increasing the pace of renewable energy shifts.

8.3 Corporate and Government-Led AI Initiatives

Corporates are at the forefront of adopting AI to embed sustainability into operations. **Microsoft's AI for Earth program** provides grants and tools for projects in biodiversity, climate, water, and agriculture, enabling global researchers to leverage AI for environmental solutions (Microsoft, 2021). **Amazon's Climate Pledge Fund** supports AI-powered innovations that reduce carbon emissions and promote sustainable logistics (Amazon, 2022). On the governmental side, Singapore's **Smart Nation initiative** integrates AI to enhance energy efficiency in urban planning, transportation, and waste management, making it a benchmark for AI-driven sustainability governance (Bokhari & Myeong, 2022). These corporate and state-led efforts show the scalability of AI for sustainable innovation when supported by long-term strategies and investments.

8.4 Insights Gained from Global and Regional Projects

Several lessons emerge from these global and regional AI-driven sustainability projects. First, collaboration is essential. Initiatives such as the Global Partnership on Artificial Intelligence (GPAI) demonstrate the value of international cooperation in aligning AI innovation with sustainability goals (GPAI, 2022). Second, local adaptation matters. While global frameworks provide guidance, successful projects such as AI-enabled crop monitoring in Kenya underscore the importance of tailoring AI applications to regional contexts, addressing specific agricultural challenges and resource constraints (Ali et al., 2025). Third, capacity building and inclusivity are critical. Ensuring that local communities and institutions have the technical expertise to maintain and expand AI systems is vital for sustainability and resilience. Finally, data governance remains a challenge. Many projects highlight the need for transparent and ethical data-sharing frameworks to build trust among stakeholders and avoid reinforcing inequities (Floridi et al., 2018).

The case studies reviewed demonstrate that AI has immense potential to contribute to sustainability across climate action, disaster management, and renewable energy. Corporate and government-led initiatives have shown that AI can accelerate progress toward environmental, economic, and social goals. Nonetheless, insights gained emphasize that collaboration, localization, inclusivity, and ethical data practices are fundamental to success. Moving forward, scaling best practices globally while respecting local contexts will be crucial in harnessing AI's transformative potential for sustainable development.

9. RECOMMENDATIONS FOR THE FUTURE

Policymakers should establish global frameworks for responsible AI governance, ensuring transparency, accountability, and inclusivity. Industry must embed sustainability into AI innovation through green technologies and ethical supply chains. Academia should foster interdisciplinary research and workforce training focused on AI for sustainability. Civil society must advocate for equitable access and awareness, ensuring local communities benefit from AI. Together, these stakeholders can align innovation with sustainability, creating a balanced pathway toward global security and resilience.

9.1 For Policymakers: Frameworks for Sustainable AI Governance

It is a key role of policymakers to make sure that AI will play a constructive role towards sustainability objectives. Risk-based regulation should be part of the effective governance systems with focus on transparency, accountability, and equity in AI use. The AI Act of the European Union offers more of a guideline, as it classifies the AI systems based on the risk level and puts more significant pressure on high-impact applications, which are energy, finance, and public safety (European Commission, 2015). Environmental accountability should also be a priority of future policies, as well as promoting the creation of AI models consuming less energy and requiring the use of renewable energy in the data centers (Ranpara, 2025). UN and OECD can be used to support harmonized international standards and make sure that AI practices aimed at sustainability reach beyond the national scope. It will play a vital role in enhancing multilateral frameworks that may help prevent digital and AI monopolization that will perpetuate inequality.

9.2 For Industry: Integrating Sustainability in AI Innovation

Industry actors are vital in embedding sustainability into AI innovation. Corporates should adopt green AI practices that focus on reducing computational demands and minimizing carbon footprints during training and deployment (Strubell et al., 2019). Beyond efficiency, companies can contribute by aligning their AI initiatives with the Sustainable Development Goals (SDGs), particularly in renewable energy, agriculture, and waste reduction. AI-driven smart grids and predictive maintenance in energy systems have already proven effective in reducing emissions and improving efficiency (Subrahmanyam et al., 2024). Industries should engage in transparent reporting on the sustainability impacts of their AI applications, much like Environmental, Social, and Governance (ESG) disclosures, to build trust with stakeholders. Cross-sectoral partnerships between industry, governments, and civil society can further accelerate AI-driven solutions to pressing environmental and social challenges.

9.3 For Academia: Advancing Interdisciplinary Research

Academia has a unique role in bridging theoretical insights with practical solutions. Researchers should prioritize interdisciplinary approaches, integrating AI into fields such as environmental science, public policy, and ethics to develop holistic frameworks for sustainable innovation (Subrahmanyam, 2025). Academic institutions can also lead to developing benchmarks that measure both the environmental costs and the societal benefits of AI systems. Lifecycle analyses of AI applications in agriculture or energy could guide both policymakers and industry in assessing trade-offs. Academia should advance research on ethical AI design, focusing on fairness, inclusivity, and transparency in sustainability-oriented applications (Jobin et al., 2019). Universities must also prioritize capacity-building initiatives, ensuring that students and professionals are equipped with the knowledge and skills required to leverage AI responsibly for sustainable development.

9.4 For Civil Society: Promoting Awareness and Equitable Access

Civil society organizations (CSOs) can be instrumental in bringing people to the fore and championing fair access to AI technologies. They may perform the role of watchdogs and make sure that AI implementations do not contribute to inequalities or violate privacy and human rights (Cath, 2018). CSOs have an opportunity to voice the communities that are marginalized, making their needs reflected in the processes of AI design and implementation. Awareness-raising campaigns on the possible benefits and harms of AI will be able to promote digital literacy and make people trust AI-related sustainability actions. No less significant is the need to promote fair access, where the low- and middle-income countries are not sidelined in the worldwide revolution of AI. Collaborations with civil society, governments, and international agencies can make sure that AI solutions based on sustainability are provided to underserved populations, to strengthen inclusivity in the digital era.

Table 5. Recommendations for the future of AI in sustainability

Stakeholder	Key Recommendations	Expected Outcomes	Examples/Best Practices
Policymakers	- Develop global and regional frameworks for sustainable AI governance. - Establish ethical standards ensuring transparency, accountability, and inclusivity. - Promote international cooperation for AI-enabled sustainability.	- Harmonized AI regulations. - Reduced risks of bias, inequity, and misuse. - Strengthened role of AI in achieving SDGs.	EU's AI Act; UNESCO's *Recommendation on the Ethics of AI.*
Industry	- Embed sustainability metrics into AI design and deployment. Adopt green AI practices to reduce carbon footprint of models and data centers. - Foster responsible supply chain management using AI.	- Increased competitiveness through sustainable innovation. - Lower environmental impact of digital infrastructure. - Transparent and ethical corporate practices.	Google's AI-powered renewable energy optimization; IBM's AI-driven ESG analytics.
Academia	- Encourage interdisciplinary research bridging AI, environmental science, economics, and social sciences. - Develop curricula on AI and sustainability for future workforce training. - Collaborate with policymakers and industry to test scalable solutions.	- Stronger knowledge base for sustainable AI applications. - Skilled workforce equipped with responsible AI literacy. - Increased evidence-based policy input.	MIT's Climate Change AI initiative; Oxford's AI for Global Sustainability research.
Civil Society	- Promote awareness campaigns on the role of AI in sustainability. - Advocate for equitable access to AI solutions across regions. - Ensure local and community voices are integrated in AI design and deployment.	- Higher public trust and acceptance of AI. - Reduced global digital divide. - More inclusive and context-sensitive AI applications.	AI for Good Global Summit (ITU & UN). Community-driven AI projects in agriculture in Sub-Saharan Africa.

Legislators, businesses, universities, and nonprofits must work together if artificial intelligence is to have a future in sustainability. While businesses try to incorporate sustainability into new product development, policymakers should set up strong regulatory frameworks. Civil society should raise awareness and provide equal access, while academia should push for interdisciplinary research. By working together, these groups can promote an ethical AI ecosystem that enhances our ability to achieve the SDGs in a responsible and sustainable way, while also taking into account the needs of society and the environment.

10. CONCLUSION

Artificial intelligence (AI) is rapidly becoming a game-changer in the struggle of ensuring global sustainability in the face of complex challenges that cross across economic, social, and environmental realms. Application of artificial intelligence (AI) offers special opportunities to accelerate the achievement of the Sustainable Development Goals (SDGs), including improved climate modeling, more efficient renewable energy infrastructure, the development of sustainable financing, and the encouragement of inclusive social policies. Nevertheless, using technology in sustainability projects has risks, including ethical dilemmas, environmental expenses, governance, and geopolitical unbalances.

To balance these opportunities and risks, proactive frameworks with an emphasis on ethical principles, responsible innovation, and equity of access are essential. Governments, industries, academia, and civil society need to unanimously adopt AI as a technological application but also as a change agent of system. This requires the integration of sustainability metrics into AI innovation, an interdisciplinary research effort, and enhancing global collaboration by using institutions like the United Nations and OECD.

Eventually, leveraging AI for sustainability demands a shared global responsibility - one that aligns innovation with human and ecological well-being. If deployed wisely, AI can help build resilient societies and secure futures where prosperity is balanced with planetary stewardship, ensuring that technological progress contributes meaningfully to a sustainable world.

REFERENCES

Al-Sartawi, A., Hussainey, K., & Razzaque, A. (2022). The role of artificial intelligence in sustainable finance. *Journal of Sustainable Finance & Investment, 11*(3), 213–229. DOI: 10.1080/20430795.2022.2057405

Ali, Z., Muhammad, A., Lee, N., Waqar, M., & Lee, S. W. (2025). Artificial Intelligence for Sustainable Agriculture: A Comprehensive Review of AI-Driven Technologies in Crop Production. *Sustainability (Basel), 17*(5), 2281. DOI: 10.3390/su17052281

Amazon. (2022). The Climate Pledge Fund. Amazon Sustainability. https://sustainability.aboutamazon.com/climate-solutions

Bokhari, A. A., & Myeong, S. (2022). Use of artificial intelligence in smart cities for smart decision-making: A social innovation perspective. *Sustainability (Basel), 14*(2), 620. DOI: 10.3390/su14020620

Bragazzi, N. L., Dai, H., Damiani, G., Behzadifar, M., Martini, M., & Wu, J. (2020). How big data and artificial intelligence can help better manage the COVID-19 pandemic. *International Journal of Environmental Research and Public Health, 17*(9), 3176. DOI: 10.3390/ijerph17093176 PMID: 32370204

Bullock, J., Luccioni, A., Pham, K. H., Lam, C. S. N., & Luengo-Oroz, M. (2020). Mapping the landscape of artificial intelligence applications against COVID-19. *Journal of Artificial Intelligence Research, 69*, 807–845. DOI: 10.1613/jair.1.12162

Cath, C. (2018). Governing artificial intelligence: Ethical, legal and technical opportunities and challenges. *Philosophical Transactions. Series A, Mathematical, Physical, and Engineering Sciences, 376*(2133), 20180080. DOI: 10.1098/rsta.2018.0080 PMID: 30322996

Ceballos, G., Ehrlich, P. R., & Raven, P. H. (2020). Vertebrates on the brink as indicators of biological annihilation and the sixth mass extinction. *Proceedings of the National Academy of Sciences of the United States of America, 117*(24), 13596–13602. DOI: 10.1073/pnas.1922686117 PMID: 32482862

Crawford, K. (2021). *The atlas of AI: Power, politics, and the planetary costs of artificial intelligence*. Yale University Press.

European Commission. (2015). *SmartNet: Smart TSO-DSO interaction schemes, market architectures, and ICT solutions for the integration of ancillary services from demand-side management and distributed generation*. https://cordis.europa.eu/project/id/691405

European Commission. (2021). *Proposal for a regulation laying down harmonised rules on artificial intelligence (AI Act)*. https://eur-lex.europa.eu/legal-content/EN/TXT/?uri=CELEX%3A52021PC0206

Evans, R., & Gao, J. (2016, July 20). DeepMind AI reduces Google data centre cooling bill by 40%. *DeepMind*. https://deepmind.com/discover/blog/deepmind-ai-reduces-google-data-centre-cooling-bill-by-40/

Floridi, L., Cowls, J., Beltrametti, M., Chatila, R., Chazerand, P., Dignum, V., Luetge, C., Madelin, R., Pagallo, U., Rossi, F., Schafer, B., Valcke, P., & Vayena, E. (2018). AI4People—An ethical framework for a good AI society: Opportunities, risks, principles, and recommendations. *Minds and Machines*, *28*(4), 689–707. DOI: 10.1007/s11023-018-9482-5 PMID: 30930541

Geissdoerfer, M., Vladimirova, D., & Evans, S. (2018). Sustainable business model innovation: A review. *Journal of Cleaner Production*, *198*, 401–416. DOI: 10.1016/j.jclepro.2018.06.240

Gikunda, K. (2024). "Harnessing Artificial Intelligence for Sustainable Agricultural Development in Africa: Opportunities, Challenges, and Impact. arxiv. https://doi.org//arXiv.2401.06171DOI: 10.48550

Global Partnership on Artificial Intelligence. (2022). *Annual report 2022*. https://gpai.ai/annual-report-2022

Google Research. (2024, March 20). How Google uses AI to improve global flood forecasting. https://blog.google/technology/ai/google-ai-global-flood-forecasting

Gupta, M., Abdelsalam, M., Khorsandroo, S., & Mittal, S. (2020). Security and privacy in smart farming: Challenges and opportunities. *IEEE Access : Practical Innovations, Open Solutions, 8*, 34564–34584. DOI: 10.1109/ACCESS.2020.2975142

Gyongyosi, L., & Imre, S. (2019). A survey on quantum computing technology. *Computer Science Review, 31*, 51–71. DOI: 10.1016/j.cosrev.2018.11.002

Holmes, W., Bialik, M., & Fadel, C. (2019). *Artificial intelligence in education: Promises and implications for teaching and learning*. Center for Curriculum Redesign. https://curriculumredesign.org/wp-content/uploads/AIED-Book-Excerpt-CCR.pdf

Jobin, A., Ienca, M., & Vayena, E. (2019). The global landscape of AI ethics guidelines. *Nature Machine Intelligence, 1*(9), 389–399. DOI: 10.1038/s42256-019-0088-2

Longoni, C., Bonezzi, A., & Morewedge, C. K. (2019). Resistance to medical artificial intelligence. *The Journal of Consumer Research, 46*(4), 629–650. DOI: 10.1093/jcr/ucz013

Maurya, S., Shavkidinova, D., Shrivastava, V., & Subrahmanyam, S. (2025). Effects of Green Supply Chain Management Practices on Environmental and Firm Sustainability Performance. *ACTA INNOVATIONS*, 55, 13–22. https://www.actainnovations.com/index.php/pub/article/view/401

Mehrabi, N., Morstatter, F., Saxena, N., Lerman, K., & Galstyan, A. (2021). A survey on bias and fairness in machine learning. *ACM Computing Surveys, 54*(6), 1–35. DOI: 10.1145/3457607

Microsoft. (2021). *AI for Earth: Sustainability program.* https://www.microsoft.com/ai-for-earth

Organisation for Economic Co-operation and Development. (2024). OECD principles on artificial intelligence. https://oecd.ai

Pappas, I. O., Mikalef, P., Krogstie, J., & Giannakos, M. (2021). Big data and business analytics ecosystems: Paving the way towards digital transformation and sustainable societies. *Information Systems and e-Business Management, 19*(4), 1355–1355. DOI: 10.1007/s10257-021-00538-z

Rahwan, I., Cebrian, M., Obradovich, N., Bongard, J., Bonnefon, J. F., Breazeal, C., Crandall, J. W., Christakis, N. A., Couzin, I. D., Jackson, M. O., Jennings, N. R., Kamar, E., Kloumann, I. M., Larochelle, H., Lazer, D., McElreath, R., Mislove, A., Parkes, D. C., Pentland, A. S., & Wellman, M. (2019). Machine behaviour. *Nature*, *568*(7753), 477–486. DOI: 10.1038/s41586-019-1138-y PMID: 31019318

Ranpara, R. (2025). Energy-efficient green AI architectures for circular economies through multi-layered sustainable resource optimization framework. *Discover Sustainability*, *6*(1), 1031. DOI: 10.1007/s43621-025-01846-x

Rockström, J., Steffen, W., Noone, K., Persson, Å., Chapin, I. I. I.III, Lambin, F. S., Lenton, E. F., Scheffer, M., Folke, C., Schellnhuber, H. J., Nykvist, B., de Wit, C. A., Hughes, T., van der Leeuw, S., Rodhe, H., Sörlin, S., Snyder, P. K., Costanza, R., Svedin, U., & Foley, J. A. (2009). A safe operating space for humanity. *Nature*, *461*(7263), 472–475. DOI: 10.1038/461472a PMID: 19779433

Rolnick, D., Donti, P. L., Kaack, L. H., Kochanski, K., Lacoste, A., Sankaran, K., Ross, A. S., Milojevic-Dupont, N., Jaques, N., Waldman-Brown, A., Luccioni, A. S., Maharaj, T., Sherwin, E. D., Mukkavilli, S. K., Kording, K. P., Gomes, C. P., Ng, A. Y., Hassabis, D., Platt, J. C., & Bengio, Y. (2022). Tackling climate change with machine learning. *ACM Computing Surveys*, 55(2). *ACM Computing Surveys*, *42*(2), 1–96. DOI: 10.1145/3485128

Saberi, S., Kouhizadeh, M., Sarkis, J., & Shen, L. (2018). Blockchain technology and its relationships to sustainable supply chain management. *International Journal of Production Research*, *57*(3), 2117–2135. DOI: 10.1080/00207543.2018.1533261

Saiz-Rubio, V., & Rovira-Más, F. (2020). From smart farming towards agriculture 5.0: A review on crop data management. *Agronomy (Basel)*, *10*(2), 207. DOI: 10.3390/agronomy10020207

Schwartz, R., Dodge, J., Smith, N. A., & Etzioni, O. (2020). Green AI. *Communications of the ACM*, *63*(12), 54–63. DOI: 10.1145/3381831

Strubell, E., Ganesh, A., & McCallum, A. (2019). Energy and policy considerations for deep learning in NLP. *Proceedings of the 57th Annual Meeting of the Association for Computational Linguistics*, 3645–3650. DOI: 10.18653/v1/P19-1355

Subrahmanyam, S. (2025). Emerging Technologies and Shift in Employment in the Transportation Sector. In Olga Titovna, E., Elango, D., Kumar, P., Mehra, P., & Verma, R. (Eds.), *Integrating Sustainability and Autonomous Transportation for Enhanced Urban Mobility* (pp. 149–178). IGI Global Scientific Publishing., DOI: 10.4018/979-8-3373-0882-1.ch006

Subrahmanyam, S. (2025). Integrating AI and AR Into Teaching and Scholarly Communication. In Vrba, J., & Huynh, T. (Eds.), *Revolutionizing Academic Research With AI and Augmented Reality* (pp. 179–212). IGI Global Scientific Publishing., DOI: 10.4018/979-8-3373-1414-3.ch006

Subrahmanyam, S. (2025). Leveraging Data for Climate Action: Smart Governance in the Digital Age. In Uğur, Ö., & Doğan, K. (Eds.), *Designing Effective Public Policies to Address Global Warming* (pp. 285–316). IGI Global Scientific Publishing., DOI: 10.4018/979-8-3373-1310-8.ch012

Subrahmanyam, S. (2025). Smart Cities and E-Government: How Startups Are Transforming Urban Life. In Mishra, D., Kumar, R., & Abdul Hamid, A. (Eds.), *Startup-Driven E-Government: Digital Innovation for Sustainable Ecosystems* (pp. 465–490). IGI Global Scientific Publishing., DOI: 10.4018/979-8-3373-0817-3.ch018

Subrahmanyam, S., Khalife, D., & El-Chaarani, H. (2024). Towards Sustainable Future: Exploring Renewable Energy Solutions and Environmental Impacts. *ACTA INNOVATIONS*, *51*(1), 15–24. DOI: 10.62441/ActaInnovations.51.3

Subrahmanyam, S., & Sri, G. S. (2025). Challenges and Opportunities for Tech Entrepreneurs in Agriculture. In Whig, P., & Elngar, A. (Eds.), *Precision and Intelligence in Agriculture: Advanced Technologies for Sustainable Farming* (pp. 1–28). IGI Global Scientific Publishing., DOI: 10.4018/979-8-3373-5283-1.ch001

Taddeo, M. (2023). Artificial Intelligence in the Colonial Matrix of Power. *Philosophy & Technology*, *36*(1), 1–18. DOI: 10.1007/s13347-023-00687-8

Truby, J. (2020). Governing Artificial Intelligence to benefit the UN Sustainable Development Goals. *Sustainable Development (Bradford), 28*(4), 946–959. DOI: 10.1002/sd.2048

UNESCO. (2021). *Recommendation on the Ethics of Artificial Intelligence*. UNESCO. https://unesdoc.unesco.org/ark:/48223/pf0000380455

United Nations. (2023). *The Sustainable Development Goals Report 2023: Special Edition*. United Nations. https://unstats.un.org/sdgs/report/2023/

Vinuesa, R., Azizpour, H., Leite, I., Balaam, M., Dignum, V., Domisch, S., Felländer, A., Langhans, S. D., Tegmark, M., & Nerini, F. F. (2020). The role of artificial intelligence in achieving the Sustainable Development Goals. *Nature Communications, 11*(1), 233. DOI: 10.1038/s41467-019-14108-y PMID: 31932590

Vinuesa, R., & Sirmacek, B. (2021). Interpretable deep-learning models to help achieve the Sustainable Development Goals. *Nature Machine Intelligence*, *3*(11), 926. Advance online publication. DOI: 10.1038/s42256-021-00414-y

Wang, Y. (2024). Application of Artificial Intelligence Technology in the Agricultural Field. *Transactions on Computer Science and Intelligent Systems Research*, *5*, 457–463. DOI: 10.62051/aeay9r82

World Bank. (2025). *Devising a Strategic Approach to Artificial Intelligence: A Handbook for Policy Makers*. World Bank Group. https://openknowledge.worldbank.org/entities/publication/7bf93f96-1ed1-4407-a008-906ae80f3fd8

Xu, Y., Tian, Y., Cai, X., Wu, C., & Mian, Z. (2025). Air quality forecasting and rating based on machine learning algorithm and cumulative logit model: An empirical study for Lanzhou city of China. *Environment, Development and Sustainability*. Advance online publication. DOI: 10.1007/s10668-024-05792-y

Yang, Q., Liu, Y., Chen, T., & Tong, Y. (2019). Federated machine learning: Concept and applications. *ACM Transactions on Intelligent Systems and Technology*, *10*(2), 1–19. DOI: 10.1145/3298981

Yu, X., Fan, L., & Yu, Y. (2025). Analysis based on corporate efficiency and external environment. *Sustainability (Basel)*, *17*(9), 3819. DOI: 10.3390/su17093819

KEY TERMS AND DEFINITIONS

Artificial Intelligence (AI): A branch of computer science focused on creating machines and algorithms capable of performing tasks that typically require human intelligence, including learning, reasoning, problem-solving, and decision-making. In sustainability, AI supports predictive analytics, optimization, and automated solutions for complex environmental, economic, and social challenges.

Circular Economy: An economic model aimed at minimizing waste and maximizing the reuse, recycling, and regeneration of resources. AI applications in supply chain management, waste tracking, and resource efficiency contribute to realizing circular economy principles.

Climate Modeling: The use of computational tools and AI algorithms to simulate and predict climate patterns, assess environmental risks, and inform mitigation strategies. Accurate climate modeling is critical for disaster preparedness and sustainable policy development.

Data Governance: Policies and practices governing the collection, storage, access, and use of data. Strong data governance ensures AI systems are secure, reliable, and compliant with privacy regulations, which is crucial for trustworthy sustainability solutions.

Ethical AI: The practice of designing and deploying AI systems that adhere to ethical principles such as fairness, transparency, accountability, and inclusivity. Ethical AI ensures that sustainability solutions do not exacerbate social inequalities or environmental harm.

Global Digital Divide: The disparity in access to digital technologies, including AI, between countries and communities. Addressing this divide is essential to ensure equitable benefits of AI-driven sustainability initiatives across developed and developing regions.

Green Innovation: The development and deployment of environmentally friendly technologies and processes aimed at reducing environmental impact while promoting economic growth. AI accelerates green innovation by analyzing complex data for insights and guiding sustainable practices.

Renewable Energy Optimization: The use of AI to improve efficiency, predict energy production, and manage distribution in renewable energy systems such as solar, wind, and hydropower. AI-driven optimization supports energy transition and reduces carbon footprints.

Smart Agriculture: The integration of AI, sensors, and IoT technologies in farming to optimize crop yield, reduce resource consumption, and improve sustainability. Applications include precision irrigation, pest management, and soil health monitoring.

Sustainable Development Goals (SDGs): A collection of 17 global goals established by the United Nations to address urgent social, economic, and environmental issues by 2030. AI can accelerate progress toward SDGs through data-driven decision-making, resource optimization, and innovation.

Chapter 5
Hydrogen Supply Chain Effectiveness:
Conceptualizing Uncertainties Through Genetic Simulations

Nishtha Chhabra
https://orcid.org/0009-0003-4064-5540
M.S. Ramaiah University of Applied Sciences, India

Rudrodip Majumdar
https://orcid.org/0000-0001-9362-8945
National Institute of Advanced Studies, Bengaluru, India

Tapasi Ghosh
https://orcid.org/0000-0002-5301-9085
M.S. Ramaiah University of Applied Sciences, India

T. Subramanyam
https://orcid.org/0000-0003-0362-7784
M.S. Ramaiah University of Applied Sciences, India

ABSTRACT

The shift from carbonaceous sources to cleaner alternatives necessitates reorienting and optimizing energy supply chains. Despite technological

DOI: 10.4018/979-8-3373-1077-0.ch005

advancements, energy security remains susceptible to disruptions caused by geopolitical tensions, resource constraints, and market fluctuations. This chapter explores how genetic simulations, leveraging metaheuristic optimization techniques, facilitate a trade-off between the resilience and cost-effectiveness of green hydrogen supply chains. A data-driven case study examines the first-level viability of the envisaged green hydrogen system, covering prominent pathways for production, storage, and transportation and distribution (T&D). Scenarios are ranked based on cost per tonne for production, storage, and T&D. Prima facie viable cases are further discussed considering supply chain vulnerability under geopolitical and logistical constraints. Such studies help strategize long-term energy security for developing economies like India.

1. INTRODUCTION

The modernization of the world is built on key socio-structural changes, which have been gaining momentum since the beginning of the 21st century. Some of the principal changes include a rapid increase in population accompanied by the growth of industries, marked by increased energy consumption levels. Global energy demand increased by more than 2% to 642 EJ in 2023 on a year-on-year basis (International Energy Agency, 2024). This increase is attributable to developing countries that more than offset the declining demand profiles of advanced countries.

For a long time, energy was considered the intrinsic driver of economic growth in any region. However, despite its paramount importance, a broad presumption existed in the first half of the 20th century regarding an infinite supply of affordable energy. This assumption indeed lacked foresight and was devoid of sustainability thinking. Emerging supply-side constraints in the energy sector forced experts and decision-makers to consider energy-related policy formulation seriously (Banks, 2012). In the 21st century, the global focus progressively shifted from 'growth-driven development' to a more holistic approach encompassing a wider gamut of trans-disciplinary factors like environmental impact, affordability, sustainability, etc., eventually leading to a gradual shift toward energy mix diversification. Diversification of energy sources was also important from the local and regional energy security point of view, considering multiple phases of major geopolitical volatilities worldwide.

In an evolving energy landscape aspiring for 'green transition' at scale, it is crucial to maneuver away from energy generation pathways that rely heavily on carbonaceous fossil fuels, leading to a significant increase in greenhouse gas (GHG) emissions. Fossil fuels are not uniformly distributed globally, and regional concentration of resources often creates uncertainties regarding the availability and accessibility of energy currencies (energy forms ready for end use). Fluctuations in the energy markets (price volatility), disruptions in supply chains, and trade policies of different advanced nations have historically impacted the reliability of uninterrupted energy supply and the sustenance of socio-economic development. The oblique dependency on hydrocarbon-based fuels has serious repercussions on the climate, ecology, health, and energy security, forcing many nations across the globe to adopt climate-resilience measures, including lifestyle adaptations (Castro & Sen, 2022). Several countries have pledged nationally determined contributions (NDCs) to the United Nations Framework Convention on Climate Change (UNFCCC), and a rapid growth in the installed capacity of renewable energy (RE) generation sources has been witnessed worldwide. The capacity growth has taken place predominantly in the form of solar photovoltaic and wind energy (both onshore and offshore), with some focus on hydropower systems such as Pumped Storage Hydropower. The 54th Annual Meeting of the World Economic Forum (January 2024) reported that the global renewable energy capacity increased by 50% from 2022 to 2023.

Along with the direct environmental benefits in terms of CO_2 mitigation, adopting RE sources renders a positive multiplier effect on sectoral development and employment. According to IRENA's Annual Review 2023, the global renewable energy jobs witnessed an increase of ~7.8% in 2023 compared to the 2021 figures (IRENA and ILO, 2023). Owing to their decentralized production pathways, the RE sector steers local employment generation. However, the creation and sustenance of high-skill jobs continue to remain a challenge for developing nations since many of the renewable energy industries do not require very large-scale heavy manufacturing (Pandey et al., 2023). Therefore, continuous exploration of clean energy pathways is necessary to diversify the supply chains and create a large pool of skilled and employable manpower. The employment generated by RE sources is heterogeneous, and there has been a movement of skilled manpower from primary to secondary and tertiary sectors (Ospanova& Zakirova, 2020). Such nuances should be considered while building new energy ecosystems and supply chains.

The ongoing global quest for RE sources is anchored on their promise to be green, accessible, and affordable. They have the potential to meet the rising energy demands and reduce GHG emissions simultaneously. The prices associated with conventional energy heavily depend on the availability of mined resources (e.g., coal, natural gas, and oil). Since RE sources are abundantly available, appropriate energy generation, storage, and disbursement mechanisms can stabilize the prices. Thus, the diversification of energy sources (especially green and clean sources) in the energy mix is gradually becoming indispensable for energy security in the modern world (Pascual & Zambetakis, 2010).

However, despite the benign features offered by RE sources, their inherent seasonal and diurnal variabilities render the act of grid integration and balancing challenging, often leading to significant inconsistencies between energy supply and demand (Kamath et al., 2022). This energy mismatch can effectively be alleviated by hydrogen, a clean, portable, and versatile energy carrier, with a vast potential for decarbonizing hard-to-abate industries (like aviation, shipping, road transportation, etc.) across the globe (Saurabh & Majumdar, 2023). With effective fiscal incentives (such as tax benefits and subsidies), hydrogen can also be used in residential configurations along with other RE sources through the process of P2H2P (power to hydrogen to power) (Kaleem et al., 2024). In Germany, the 'feed-in tariff' enables households producing excess renewable energy to sell it to the national grid. Some of the incentives across Asian nations include tax holidays (Vietnam), establishing a carbon emission quota trading market (China), implementing the green investment tax cut (Japan), and creating energy-saving certificates (India). A unique advantage of electrolyzers used in hydrogen production is that they can be employed to ramp up/down hydrogen production to adjust to the fluctuations in energy demand. Thus, hydrogen can help overcome the intermittent energy supply, especially in off-grid and isolated remote rural areas (Kaleem et al., 2024).

Understanding hydrogen taxonomy is crucial to appreciating the production of clean energy. Depending on how the electrolyzers are powered, hydrogen production pathways can be classified into distinct categories within the scope of a widely accepted color code-based taxonomy: Pink (via electrolysis powered by nuclear power), Yellow (via electrolysis powered through grid-connected solar power), Grey (uses steam methane reformation process), Turquoise (via methane pyrolysis), Brown (gasification of lignite coal), Black (via gasification of bituminous coal), Blue (fossil-fuel based hydrogen production aided by carbon capture technology), etc. (Arcos& Santos, 2023).

The most environmentally benign pathway for hydrogen generation is the '*green hydrogen*' route, in which the electrolyzer is powered entirely by renewable energy sources (like wind, solar, geothermal, etc.). Green hydrogen (GH2) is a promising endeavor toward realizing a low-carbon global economy, considering the ever-growing demand for energy attributable to commodious modern lifestyles (Zhou et al., 2022). Thus, green hydrogen, often called renewable hydrogen in literature, refers to hydrogen harnessed using clean energy generation pathways. To avoid inappropriate categorization of hydrogen, countries are increasingly developing national standards in tandem with inputs from technical experts, NGOs, academicians, and government agencies. These standards provide a detailed outline of various terminology, legislation, government schemes, national registries, and other techno-economic aspects of hydrogen production (Abad & Dodds, 2020).

The color-based taxonomy is yet to arrive at a consensus among energy researchers and practitioners, and there has been a continuous endeavour toward standardizing the color codes of hydrogen production. It is, thus, important for the reader to note that the International Energy Agency (IEA) does not officially use color code-based categorization for different hydrogen production pathways. The IEA broadly categorizes hydrogen as 'high-carbon' or 'low-carbon', depending on the environmental impact of the production process (Incer-Valverde et al., 2023). In this chapter, the term 'green hydrogen' refers to hydrogen produced using RE sources.

The global energy transition is gradually gaining momentum, and green hydrogen is one of the most promising ingredients of this transition (Iqbal & Abdul Rahim, 2025). While the use of hydrogen as a clean energy carrier is not new to many countries, the scaled-up clean production of hydrogen is relatively nascent for the developing nations aiming for a shift to green hydrogen. Consideration of GH2 as a futuristic energy management response could effectively raise the total global demand to 530 Mt (million tonnes) in 2050. Currently, the potential of green hydrogen is the largest in Sub-Saharan Africa, followed by the Middle East & North Africa, accounting for about 28.6% and 21.3% respectively of global production (Maka & Mehmood, 2024). Increasing investments in the RE sector will also lead to a potential transformation in the global energy dynamics. Morocco's expenditure on fossil fuel imports accounts for 90% of its GDP. This number will gradually change as Morocco aims to become an exporter of green hydrogen by 2030 (Dagnachew et al., 2025). According to the Global Hydrogen Review 2024, the FY 2023-24 has witnessed an increase in the electrolyzer capacity by ~40% in China and ~ 32% in Europe (International Energy Agency, 2024). There has been a recent tailwind worldwide toward ramping up green hydrogen production, storage, and utilization, attracting substantial investments for capacity building to boost socio-economic development.

As a promising developing nation, India aims to achieve a Net Zero target by 2070, reducing the carbon intensity of energy use while maintaining steady economic growth. In the pursuit of providing access to clean, affordable, and modern energy (SDG target 7.1) to all people, India has rapidly ramped up the installed capacity for renewable power generation, which has witnessed a growth of ~700% from 4100.5 MW (2014-15) to ~28723.65 MW (2024-25) in annual capacity addition. The energy transition in India has been motivated by several factors, such as the international pressure to curb GHG emissions within finite timeframes, volatility in the global energy market, and the realization of the need for energy security at the highest level of the Government of India. Some of India's ambitious initiatives toward a clean energy economy include the International Solar Alliance (ISA), One Sun-One World-One Grid (OSOWOG) Project, and Mission LiFE (Lifestyle for Environment), among others. The leadership roles in several international collectives have necessitated the Indian industry to drive innovation and provide technology foresight for global green energy growth. Since India aspires to fulfill 50% of its energy requirements through renewable sources by 2030, diminishing the role of fossil fuels in the country's energy mix, there is ample opportunity for Green Hydrogen to serve as a versatile energy carrier for diverse end-use applications (Ministry of New and Renewable Energy, India, 2023).

India launched the National Green Hydrogen Mission (NGHM) in 2023 with a mission to produce 5 Mt (million tonnes) of green hydrogen annually, accounting for 6% of the global demand. The mission is being implemented comprehensively, leveraging the coordination of various ministries in the Central and State governments. The decarbonization of various sectors of the economy will help India become '*Atmanirbhar*' (self-reliant) in the energy transition. The mission endeavors to develop green hydrogen valleys, encourage innovations in electrolyzer capabilities, build hydrogen refueling stations, and stimulate private investment that will help develop decentralized in-situ RE plants to promote GH2 production in India. On the demand side, it aims to tackle the deficit by promoting competitive bidding for the procurement of GH2. It also aims to establish a streamlined regulatory framework by providing a single-window clearance for all statutory requirements and GH2 certification. The sector can be scaled up by leveraging the benefits of Public-Private Partnerships (PPP) and targeted investments in R&D. Therefore, India is emerging as one of the most attractive green hydrogen destinations in the world (National Green Hydrogen Mission, 2023). According to a report published by Shakti Sustainable Energy Foundation in 2023, six lakh jobs will be created through NGHM, paving the way for green skills development in the local workforce (Shakti Sustainable Energy Foundation, 2023).

Besides the environmental, operational, and transitional risks, a major risk in the energy sector emerges from supply chain constraints in the form of geopolitical risks. Some of the major forms of geopolitical risks that threaten green energy value chains include trade wars, blockades, embargoes, and political turmoil. Escalating conflicts across the globe accentuate risks that could lead to potential supply chain vulnerabilities, causing resource volatility throughout economies. Thus, the chapter aims to explore how the resilience of GH2 supply chains can be enhanced through diversification, especially during geopolitical uncertainties.

The rest of the chapter is dissected into sections that deliberate on various themes and subthemes. While Section 2 highlights the importance of a resilient hydrogen supply chain (HSC) for energy security, Section

3 focuses on a system-level cost optimization strategy by employing algorithms to generate genetic simulations, and also discusses a detailed data-driven case study investigating the capital costs of producing, storing, and distributing green hydrogen indicating the various combinations that could prove to be viable at different timelines in the near-to-medium term. Various technological trends are assumed based on the review of global experiences and relevant case studies. The year 2050 is considered the final timeline in the present analysis, considering India's internal aspirational target of becoming a developed nation by 2047. Section 4 discusses salient insights from the simulation results emerging from the case study. Sections 5 and 6 present the future directions in the HSC optimization exercise and the concluding remarks, respectively.

2. IMPORTANCE OF RESILIENT HSC FOR ENERGY SECURITY

The decisive role of geopolitics in global security and energy systems cannot be overstated. With the world order and associated geopolitical risks becoming progressively complex and dynamic, the already fragmented and vulnerable energy ecosystems are expected to face disruptions, rendering energy services more expensive (Cherp et al., 2011). This encourages nations to build a resilient supply chain that sustainably meets their energy requirements, with a specific focus on reliability and affordability. The fact that 80% of the energy supply across the globe stemmed from fossil fuels in 2022 is an alarming statistic that should act as a catalyst in the transition to well-integrated clean energy systems (International Energy Agency, 2023).

Numerous energy experts, environmentalists, environmental economists, climatologists, and data scientists strongly opine that innovations in the energy industry are key to sustainability facing the onslaught of disruptivemarkets and are also crucial to catalyzing economic development worldwide. Thus, ensuring stability and reliability in energy pathways is critical in enhancing security to withstand potential disturbances in this dynamic environment in a sustainable manner.

The role of green hydrogen in achieving a greener and cleaner energy mix in the future is widely recognized. However, the focus historically has been on developing effective and efficient GH2 pathways. As the geopolitical complexities rise, power dynamics are undergoing drastic changes, exposing the fragility of GH2 supply chains. Thus, the focus needs to shift toward making these supply chains resilient so that they acquire the ability to not merely withstand but also adapt to uncertainties in the global order through the strategic employment of digital capabilities. Investment in resilience comes at a critical juncture as the frequency and scale of supply chain disruptions have been on the rise (Barbosa-Póvoa & Pinto, 2023).

The following subsections will examine the impact of geopolitical risks on energy supply and explore the essential components of the green hydrogen supply chain.

2.1 Effect of Geopolitical Risks on Energy Supply

An undisclosed and unspecified quantum of conventional energy sources (like oil and gas reserves) exists worldwide, with a non-uniform geographical distribution of the resource base. As these resources are being unearthed (harvested), political discord is on the rise in pursuit of claiming the stake in proven resources. This enigma can increase the supply chain complexities, escalating potential risks in energy security (Shahzad, 2012). These geopolitical ill-wills can be minimized by deploying renewable energy sources since their production and regulatory processes are relatively more transparent and non-confrontational.

Numerous studies have explored the correlation between geopolitical risks and the energy supply chain. In 2018, Cheng and Chiu published an empirical study that used an autoregressive model for 38 developing countries to assert that geopolitical shocks negatively affect private investments and consumption patterns (Cheng & Chiu, 2018). In 2020, Fernandois and Medel employed Granger causality analysis to study the extent of the effect of geopolitical tensions in OPEC on oil prices (Fernandois & Medel, 2020). Studies also highlight how geopolitical threats suppress RE demand and thereby, energy transition across nations.

More recently, the Russian invasion of Ukraine in 2022 sent shockwaves across the global geopolitical order, affecting grain trade, financial markets, and especially, the global natural gas markets. The conflict severely affected Brent oil prices, which saw a ~ 67% hike from USD 69/barrel in February 2021 to USD 115/barrel in February 2022. Apart from the energy price hike, the global oil flows were also reconfigured, with Russian crude oil being redirected via India and China after facing embargoes from the EU in 2022. The conflict exposed the EU's heavy reliance on Russian energy imports, which led to a paradigm shift in Europe's energy security. Some of the post-conflict measures undertaken by the EU to withstand such vulnerabilities in the future included integrated energy policies of member nations and a shift toward renewable energy (Emiliozzi et al., 2025).

An offshoot of the Russia-Ukraine conflict is the increasing relevance of the Gulf of Guinea as an energy supply hub. Due to the market disruptions caused by the conflict, piracy in the Gulf of Guinea increased multifold to take advantage of the volatility in the energy supply chain. The Gulf is strategically located in an area that is critical for gas and oil supply between Europe and China. Geopolitical factors have exacerbated pipeline vandalism, sabotage, and crude oil theft, posing a threat to energy security not merely in the Sahel region of Africa but also across Asia and Europe. Thus, community collaboration, private investments, and government initiatives are required to maintain transparency and stability in the region (Enumah, 2025).

Green hydrogen (GH2) is also beginning to play a part in the changing geopolitical landscape, as the global push toward achieving a large RE-based generation capacity has gained a tailwind owing to the Net Zero Carbon Emission aspirations delineated by several developed and developing nations. This is evident as the world's investment axis is tilting more toward alliances that focus on RE (like ISA), vis-à-vis the hydrocarbon-based alliances (like OPEC) (Su et al., 2021).

With the increasing tendency of nations to encourage localized production of critical supply-chain components including specialized equipment, GH2 is well poised to become the 'fuel of the 21st century' that will revolutionize the energy sector, and lead to a more cohesive and balanced global geopolitical order through collaboration and cooperation in technology development, demonstration, and deployment (3Ds).

2.2 Key Components in the Hydrogen Supply Chain (HSC)

Currently, a mere 4% of global hydrogen is 'green', while more than 90% comes from brown or grey hydrogen. This emphasizes the opportunity to unlock the clean energy potential by adopting a clean hydrogen production pathway (Marouani et al., 2023). With an energy density of 122 kJ/g (almost thrice that of hydrocarbon fuels), hydrogen is an attractive energy carrier that can cater to a wide array of end-users (Ayodele& Munda, 2019). Some of the applications of green hydrogen are electricity generation (using fuel cells), aviation (in spark and compression ignition), transportation (as fuel and fuel cells), industrial applications (fertilizer, glass, chemical), and many more (Saurabh & Majumdar, 2022). The production of clean energy, however, does not merely depend on the choice of fuel, but also on the choice of technology. Since GH2 production relies on electrolysis, electrolyzers are a key technology to enable clean production of energy in the future (Kaleem et al., 2024).

Hydrogen is obtained from chemical decomposition when electricity is passed through an ionized solution in an electrolyzer, splitting water into constituent components - hydrogen and oxygen. The components of an electrolyzer include electrodes, an clectrolyte, and a separator. Being an invaluable component of the hydrogen supply chain, assessing the techno-economic feasibility of electrolyzer tcchnologies is of utmost importance.

This chapter focuses on the three most prominent electrolyzer technologies in the contemporary energy market - Proton Exchange Membrane (PEM), Alkaline Exchange Membrane (AEM), and Solid Oxide electrolyzers (SOE) (Zakaria & Kamarudin, 2021). In PEM, electrolysis is conducted by transferring protons selectively across a fluoropolymer membrane. While the cathode collects hydrogen, the anode collects oxygen. AEM electrolyzers, on the other hand, perform electrolysis by splitting the water molecules in such a way that the anions from the potassium hydroxide solution are transferred across a membrane (typically made of zirconium oxide and polymer), producing hydrogen at the cathode and oxygen at the anode. Generically, SOEs have a design akin to that of PEM and AEM, with the primary difference being that their membranes are made of superoxide ions (Patidar et al., 2024).

Before building resilience in HSC, it is important to understand the material composition of the electrolyzers. A typical PEM electrolyzer needs Nafion (tetrafluoroethylene-based copolymer with ionic properties), Platinum (for the anode), platinum-iridium/iridium oxide, and ruthenium (for the cathode); titanium and gold (for stack components). The materials largely required to build a typical AEM electrolyzer include zirconium, polymer, nickel, molybdenum, and nickel. On the other hand, SOE mainly requires zirconium, polymer, nickel, and molybdenum, among others. Most of these critical materials, such as iridium, lanthanum, cerium, gadolinium, scandium, and strontium, are considered rare earth elements, of which ~60% are concentrated in China, followed by the USA and Myanmar. While 40% of the world's proven molybdenum resources are in China, vast deposits of platinum (~65%) are situated in South Africa, followed by the USA and Zimbabwe. Apart from mineral dependencies, one must also note the concentration of mineral processing facilities across the globe, tipping the scales in favour of a Chinese monopoly. More than 80% of the global processing of rare earth elements is concentrated in China, followed by Malaysia (12%). Half of the global nickel processing capacity is dominated by China (35%) and Indonesia (15%) (Patidar et al., 2024).

For India, the indigenization potential for each of these electrolyzers is ~85% on average. The remaining share is beyond the scope of indigenization as India lacks certain critical minerals that serve as raw materials for manufacturing electrolyzers. Like India, most developing countries may not possess the required minerals, making geopolitics a crucial factor in attaining their respective clean energy goals (Bordoff & O'Sullivan, 2022; Pandey & Majumdar, 2023, 2025).

Another crucial component of the HSC is the hydrogen storage mechanism. The most prominent storage mechanisms for green hydrogen are based on the form in which hydrogen can be stored – Compressed gas, Liquid, Underground, and Solid Metal Hydrides. Large-scale storage of green hydrogen needs critical planning so that the market demand can be met effectively. While compressed storage requires materials like steel alloys and carbon fibre, liquid hydrogen storage requires thermally insulated carbon steel. The materials required for underground storage include steel alloys, while the materials required for solid metal hydride storage include magnesium hydride and lithium hydride, among others. Apart from the energy requirements (e.g., for ensuring sustained pressure of 700 bar to maintain hydrogen in the liquid state at –253°C) while storing green hydrogen in a particular physical state, safety concerns must also be addressed comprehensively (Yang et al., 2023).

The global development of hydrogen storage technologies is driving competition in critical energy materials, and the need for these materials in the green energy transition could potentially catalyze new geopolitical alliances and trade opportunities. However, given the volatile nature of regional orders in various parts of the globe, nations can be exposed to vulnerabilities like supply chain constraints and safety risks (owing to a lack of knowledge base, skilled manpower, or even occasional technology denial). Thus, while envisaging HSC architecture, building resilient storage mechanisms must be a strategic priority (Van de Graaf et al., 2020).

3. SYSTEM OPTIMIZATION

Despite numerous advantages, green hydrogen production faces unique challenges in large-scale implementation. Some of the major challenges of green hydrogen production are - low energy density compared to natural gas, specialized storage requirements, transportation, and scaling up of both production and storage facilities. Therefore, it is criticalto address these challenges holistically through optimization techniques so that the purported operational capacity of GH2 can be unlocked. Apart from this, it is also crucial that the HSC design is resilient during supply-demand volatilities.

Optimization algorithms can be broadly classified into 'Exact' and 'Metaheuristic'. While exact methods can be employed to obtain an optimal solution, these methods are not particularly efficient in a changing environment. Thus, there is a need to explore metaheuristic algorithms, owing to their capabilities in cost reduction and efficiency enhancement. In the GH2 supply chain, the challenges posed by production, transportation, and storage can be addressed by genetic algorithms (GAs), which can be employed to optimize production, storage, and distribution networks; simulate dynamic scenarios; minimize costs while maximizing green hydrogen accessibility; and build robust, scalable solutions for a viable and sustainable HSC. Thus, metaheuristic algorithms can be specifically employed to overcome problems such as optimizing the size of electrolyzers, dynamic responses to varying renewable energy input, waste heat recovery, and water consumption, by tuning the objective functions toward reducing costs, increasing efficiency, reducing energy losses, and minimizing the environmental impact (Gorji, 2023).

3.1 The Utility and Scope of Genetic Algorithms (GAs)

To unlock the full potential of GH2 as a cornerstone of the clean energy transition, there is a need to optimize the HSC, especially from the viewpoint of major expense heads, to progressively render this versatile energy currency an affordable solution for diverse applications across the socio-economic strata. Multi-Objective Optimization (MOO) techniques can streamline the supply chain components, balancing multiple conflicting objectives comprehensively, such as emission reduction, production maximization, lowering costs, and enhancing electrolyzer efficiency, among others. However, to maintain the brevity of the discussion, this chapter considers the costs of hydrogen production, storage, and transportation & distribution (T&D) to select the least cost pathway based on the broad trends of the major capital expenses. Efficiency improvements in various green hydrogen production pathways have been considered in this exercise. Also, the relative shares for different production and storage technologies have been imbibed based on insights from a few prominent global initiatives. Both short-to-medium distance and long-haul transport and distribution for green hydrogen have been conceptualized considering production and end-use within the country (i.e., India). Different physical forms of hydrogen (compressed gas, liquid, and solid metal hydride) are considered while conceptualizing the transportation and disbursement mechanisms.

This chapter creates the base framework for the Genetic Algorithm (GA), which has been widely used to address various challenges in the configuration of the HSC. These algorithms comprise a subset of Evolutionary Algorithms that deal with a population-based metaheuristic approach to finding Pareto-optimal solutions (Bentley & Wakefield, 1998). Inspired by nature, GAs present robust solutions using the notions of natural selection, mutation, inheritance, crossover, and various other evolution strategies. These characteristics help GAs reach Pareto-optimal solutions much faster than classical algorithms, which can be efficient, especially in dynamic conditions (Salomon, 1997).

Invented by John Holland in the 1960s, GAs underwent further refinement in the 1970s. Unlike other evolutionary algorithms designed to solve specific complex problems, GA was designed to comprehend and recreate the system of natural selection (Holland, 1992). Analogous to nature, individuals in GAs represent a specific chromosome. Each of these chromosomes comprises a collection of bits called 'genes' in a specified order, which can take one of the two possible alleles (i.e., 0 or 1) as shown in Figure 1.

A mathematical 'fitness' function determines the fitness score of each chromosome, which decides the ability of the chromosome to 'compete'. Based on the score, the selection operator decides which chromosomes are allowed to 'mate' and produce offspring. Generally, the fitter chromosomes beget more offspring than their counterparts, leading to better partial solutions than their previous generation (Mitchell, 1998).

Figure 1. Illustration of gene and chromosome in GAs

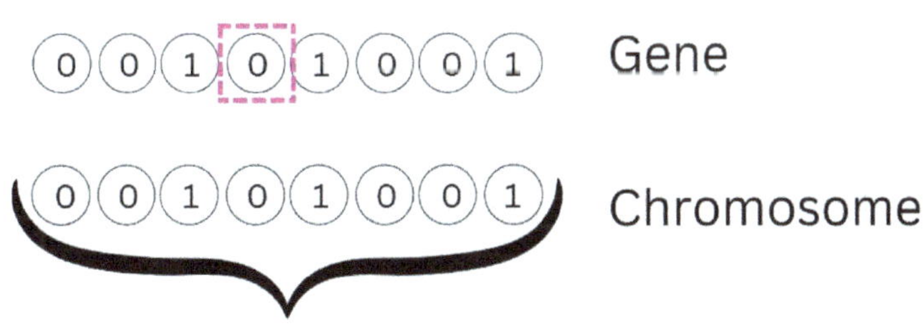

After the initial generation is formed, genetic algorithms employ certain operators to improve the quality of genetic material with each iteration, ensuring convergence when the best possible parameters are achieved in an 'offspring' from the previous generation, resulting in superlative viability of the offspring. Two key operators, crossover rate and mutation rate, predominantly determine the convergence of the algorithm. To introduce variability in the population search space, the crossover operator ensures the offspring incorporates features from both parents, as shown in Figure 2.

Figure 2. Crossover operator (assuming a crossover rate of 0.5)

On the other hand, the mutation operator (see Figure 3) replaces genes in a probabilistic manner in the offspring chromosome to overcome the problem of premature convergence of the algorithm. Subsequently, a stopping criterion, say the number of generations, can be used to arrive at convergence. Since GAs maintain a fixed number of generations, the chromosomes with the lowest fitness scores are eliminated iteratively. This helps to avoid saturation of the 'gene pool' in the search space.

Figure 3. Mutation operator

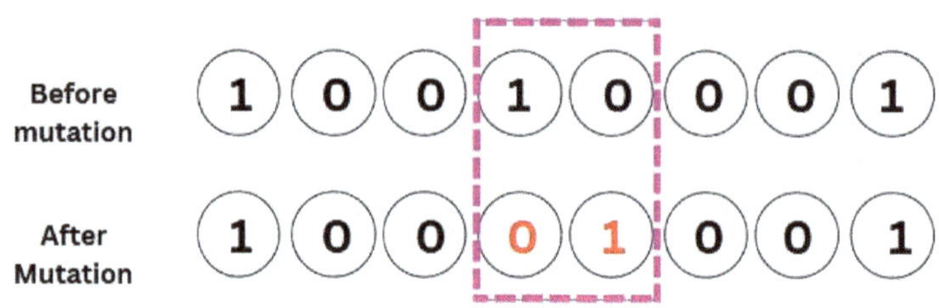

Optimization of the green hydrogen supply chain involves competing objectives like costs and emissions, leading to trade-offs to achieve Pareto-optimal solutions. Due to the absence of reliable literature on the applications of genetic algorithms in GHSC optimization,our studyemploys *itertools*, a powerful Python module that provides efficient combinatorialfunctions for chromosomal representation of an industry value chain with multiple techno-economic choices in the upstream, midstream, and downstream parts. Used in conjunction with genetic algorithms, the *itertools* module helps in generating all possible chromosomes, thereby enhancing the robustness of the optimization. Since the problem chosen was small-scale, *itertools* helped in generating the required chromosomes for the HSC optimization.

Genetic algorithms facilitate diversity in the solution space by using genetic operators like crossover, mutation, etc. Since our HSC model assumes a unique pathway to be activated at a particular time, using *itertools* rather than an advanced genetic algorithm like NSGA-II is more pragmatic. This choice is also feasible due to the scale of our problem (24-bit chromosome). As the size of the chromosome increases with increasing problem complexity (say, chromosomes with more than 40 bits or genes), employing genetic algorithms will ensure the accuracy of the optimization (Wijaya,2024). As a future scope, studies can be undertaken to explore HSC optimization using genetic algorithms that assume simultaneous activation of parallel pathways. The *itertools* module also enables efficient iterations for large datasets, making it suitable for the integration of artificial intelligence (AI). Its memory-efficient iterators are effective in hyperparameter tuning in AI model-building. The first-level viable sequences generated by *itertools* can be considered further for crossover operations. However, for a complex technological problem such as HSC, the actual compatibility and feasibility of different technological options at different parts of the supply chain need to be evaluated appropriately.

3.2 Building the Viability Assessment Framework for HSC in India – A Case Study

The production of green hydrogen poses an array of challenges that require agile and malleable optimization depending on the problematization of a specific context. Since GH2 supply chains are complex and non-linear, the prerequisite encompasses the appropriate formulation of three key ingredients – the objective function (the goal, which is maximized/minimized depending on the requirements), the constraints (system or subsystem-level restrictions that are to be satisfied), and a solution space (where all the possible solutions lie). Harnessing the knowledge of computer science and mathematics, the algorithm is tailored to employ an interdisciplinary approach in arriving at solutions.

Although building a resilient HSC involves several parameters of different kinds, it is neither feasible nor reasonable to include all the parameters in the basic conceptual framework. To ensure the manageability of the first-level supply-chain viability evaluation framework, technology and cost attributes pertaining to three broad categories (production, storage, transportation & distribution (T&D)) are considered. These parametric constraints for different timelines have been chosen considering the predominance or relative obsolescence of technological options and the trends from market analysis reports. Nuances such as efficiency levels, ease (or difficulty) of practical implementation, and cost reduction due to economies of scale have been imbibed in the evaluation framework.

Figure 4. Concatenation of chromosomes for HSC optimization

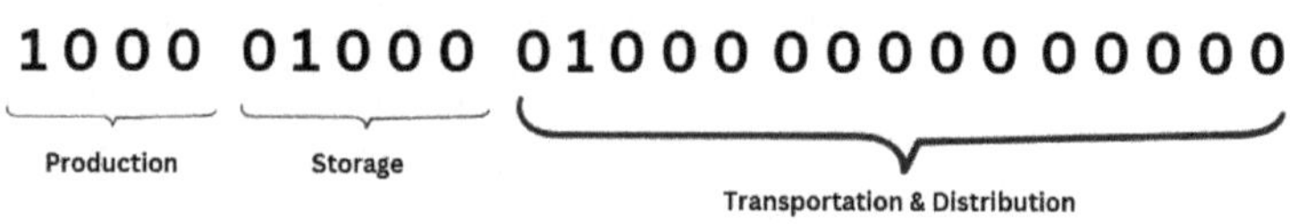

Figure 4 depicts a sample 24-gene chromosome that is used in our study of HSC optimization. The first four genes in the chromosome represent the production pathway, while the next five genes represent the storage mechanisms. The last fifteen genes represent the various T&D modes and pathways employed in HSC optimization. Here, the fragments 1000, 0100, and 010000000000000 are concatenated to represent the cost of hydrogen production through the PEM electrolyzer, the cost of storage in the liquid form, and the cost of T&D for the liquid hydrogen form as a complete (and composite) chromosomal illustration.

It is crucial to note that chromosomes are designed considering the specific constraints that are unique to the green HSC. The design ensures that the form of green hydrogen (compressed gas/liquid/metal hydride) is consistent with respect to both storage and T&D. Also, since the underground storage is not currently scalable for liquid and metal hydride forms, for this model, only the compressed gas form is considered for underground storage. This indicates that if the underground storage form is activated, only the compressed gas pathway will be activated in the T&D fragment.

3.2.1 Datasets on Green Hydrogen Production

While simulating the HSC network in the Indian context, the starting point is the indicative target production of green hydrogen in million tonnes at four chosen timelines - 2025, 2030, 2040, and 2050. The target production of green hydrogen (in million tonnes) currently stands at less than 1% of the total grey hydrogen produced annually in India (6 Mt). The National Green Hydrogen Mission (NGHM) envisages achieving 5 Mt of green hydrogen production by 2030. This study assumes a three-fold growth by 2040 to reach a production capacity of 15 Mt. Thereafter, an ambitious growth of another three times would take the production capacity to a gigantic 45 Mt by 2050.

Currently, Alkaline electrolyzers comprise the dominant technological pathway for green hydrogen production with a market share of ~38%. However, the global trends suggest that Proton Exchange Membrane (PEM) electrolyzers would become dominant with time, eventually acquiring an increased market share of ~50% compared to the current level of ~34% (Escobar-Yonoff et al., 2021). The Solid Oxide electrolyzer (SOE) would also grow marginally in market share at the expense of the receding market footprint of alkaline electrolyzers. All the technologies are expected to witness efficiency enhancement with time. Table 1 provides the market share and efficiency data pertinent to three dominant green hydrogen production pathways. Table 2 summarizes the target production and the 'net generation' under four pathways: 100% generation from PEM, 100% generation from Alkaline, 100% generation from SOE, and the mixed generation pathway comprising contributions from the three technological options. The relative shares of different production pathways in the base year (2025) are sourced from published literature (Patidar et al., 2024). It must be stated that the 'net generation' depends on the efficiency of production as well as the changing market shares of individual technologies at different timelines.

Table 1. Data pertinent to green hydrogen production pathways for the chosen timelines

Technology	2025		2030		2040		2050	
	Market Share (%)	Efficiency (%)	Market Share (%)	Efficiency (%)	Market Share (%)	Efficiency (%)	Market Share (%)	Efficiency (%)
PEM Electrolyzer	34	80	34	80	40	85	50	90
Alkaline Electrolyzer	38	45	38	50	28	60	15	70
Solid Oxide Electrolyzer	28	90	28	90	32	92	35	95

Table 2. Target and net production of green hydrogen under four different pathways at the chosen timelines

Production pathway	2025		2030		2040		2050	
	Target hydrogen production (Mt)	Net	Target hydrogen production (Mt)	Net	Target hydrogen production (Mt)	Net	Target hydrogen production (Mt)	Net
PEM Electrolyzer	0.06	0.048	5	4	15	12.75	45	40.5
Alkaline Electrolyzer	0.06	0.027	5	2.5	15	9	45	31.5
Solid Oxide Electrolyzer	0.06	0.054	5	4.5	15	13.8	45	42.75
Mixed production	PEM: 34%; Alkaline: 38%; SOE: 28%		PEM: 34%; Alkaline: 38%; SOE: 28%		PEM: 40%; Alkaline: 28%; SOE: 32%		PEM: 50%; Alkaline: 15%; SOE: 35%	
Production profile	0.06	0.042	5	3.57	15	12.04	45	39.94

Further, it is also important to take stock of the capital expenses involved in different hydrogen production pathways. Table 3 summarizes the CAPEX associated with the chosen GH2 production pathways at different timelines.

Table 3. CAPEX (USD/t) of the four different pathways at the chosen timelines

Production pathway	Cost of Hydrogen Production (USD/t of H2)			
	2025	2030	2040	2050
PEM	7000	6500	6000	5000
Alkaline	2880	2400	2000	1840
SOE	3000	3000	2500	2000
Mixed production	4314.4	3962	3760	3476

3.2.2 Datasets on Green Hydrogen Storage

The next important step following the production phase is the storage of hydrogen. Storage is crucial since the production and utilization of hydrogen may often witness a temporal mismatch attributable to the uncertainties of the real world. Based on the published literature, there are four different ways in which green hydrogen can be stored in different physical forms. These storage forms encompass Compressed gas storage, Liquid hydrogen storage, Metal hydride storage (solid chemical compound), and Underground storage (for scaled-up facilities, this storage stores hydrogen in the gaseous form under an appropriate pressurized condition). Since hydrogen production will be followed by on-site consumption as well as rapid disbursement, the sizing of the storage would be crucial in planning the HSC. Currently, liquid hydrogen storage boasts a market share of 40%, whereas the share of compressed gas storage stands at 25%. Global trends indicate that the market share of compressed gas will be captured progressively by solid metal hydride-based storage options since they offer superior volume efficiencies. In this study, it is assumed that in 2050, the relative shares of metal hydride, liquid, and compressed gas storage will be 40%, 30%, and 15%, respectively. The mixed storage scenario considers varying extents of contributions from different storage mechanisms at different timelines of interest. The relative shares of different storage mechanisms in the total mix are adopted from the literature (Stamatakis et al., 2018). Table 4 summarizes the envisaged hydrogen storage capacities (Mt) and the cost of storage per tonne of hydrogen for the chosen timelines.

The cost of storage is assumed to be reduced by 10% between successive timelines, irrespective of the mechanism, considering economies of scale.

Table 4. The envisaged storage capacities (Mt) and storage costs (USD/t) for the chosen timelines

Storage Mechanism	2025		2030		2040		2050	
	Storage capacity (Mt)	**Storage cost (USD/t of H2)**	**Storage capacity (Mt)**	**Storage cost (USD/t of H2)**	**Storage capacity (Mt)**	**Storage cost (USD/t of H2)**	**Storage capacity (Mt)**	**Storage cost (USD/t of H2)**
Compressed gas	0.012	210	2	189	7.5	170.1	27	153.09
Liquid	0.012	550	2	495	7.5	445.5	27	400.95
Metal Hydride (solid)	0.012	1160	2	1044	7.5	939.6	27	845.64
Underground (compressed gas)	0.012	99	2	89.1	7.5	80.19	27	72.17
Mixed storage	Compressed gas:25%; Liquid: 40%; Metal Hydride: 20%; Underground: 15%		Compressed gas:25%; Liquid: 35%; Metal Hydride: 25%; Underground: 15%		Compressed gas: 20%; Liquid: 35%; Metal Hydride: 30%; Underground: 15%		Compressed gas: 15%; Liquid: 30%; Metal Hydride: 40%; Underground:15%	
Storage profile	0.012	519.35	2	494.87	7.5	483.85	27	492.33

3.2.3 Datasets on Green Hydrogen Transportation & Distribution (T&D)

The T&D network forms a crucial part of the supply chain, ensuring reliable dispatch and disbursement of hydrogen to different end-users. The T&D design of the chapter assumes that pipelines are to be used for domestic transportation, while ships are used for international hydrogen trade. This assumption is consistentwith thecontemporary oil trade, wherein ships are preferred over pipelines owing to their route flexibility, which helps effectively meet the demand in dynamic conditions (Ansari & Sangwai, 2024).A major roadblock in the international trade of hydrogen via pipelines is the construction of specialized hydrogen pipelines that are made of advanced alloys or are polymer-lined. These specialized pipelines require a meticulous focus on strength, ductility, leakage testing, and welding procedures (Bannister et al., 2021; Gillette &Kolpa, 2008). Moreover, laying cross-country pipelines depends on two broad factors – geography (terrain, climate, etc.) and bilateral relations. Various treaties and agreements need to be signed between multiple countries, which could potentially invite further complexities and bottlenecks. Currently, there is no standardized offshore pipeline regulation covering hydrogen transmission, causing a major hurdle in the accessibility of international hydrogentrade via pipelines (Helgaker, n.d.). Therefore, very ambitious developments in this segment have been avoided in the current analysis.

India has launched the National Critical Mineral Mission (NCMM) toward securing a reasonable medium-to-long-term reserve for the priority materials through the acquisition of foreign reserves and by expanding the in-country resource base through progressive exploration and development of the mines. However, specific materials, intermediaries, and finished products may need to be imported at least for the next decade. To ensure an uninterrupted business scenario, demand-driven bottom-up analysis for critical energy industry value chains (e.g., green hydrogen supply chain) needs to be conducted. The demand for multipurpose fuel such as hydrogen will emerge from diverse end-users, and therefore, the downstream mapping would be crucial for establishing a resilient up and mid-stream value chain for green hydrogen in the country, which also includes the T&D segment.

Depending on the location of end-users with respect to the production facility, the hydrogen T&D network can be segregated into two broad categories: short-to-medium-distance transportation and long-haul transportation. In this study, four T&D configurations have been conceptualized, out of which two variants are tailor-made for short-to-medium distance hydrogen transport (TD1 and TD2), while the remaining two variants (TD3 and TD4) depict long-haul transportation and disbursement of green hydrogen. Notably, pipelines are quintessential for transporting and dispatching hydrogen in compressed gas and liquid forms. In contrast, trucks and other modes of transport, such as rail and ship, play a crucial role in transporting hydrogen stored in the form of solid metal hydride compounds. These distinct requirements at the system level affect the total cost attributable to T&D of green hydrogen. A total offive hydrogen T&D scenarios have been simulated in the present exercise. While four of them consider 100% contribution (share) from a single mode at a time from the aforesaid pool of four T&D modes (TD1, TD2, TD3, and TD4), the fifth scenario considers a balanced mix of all four modes to imbibe realism in conceptualizing the HSC.

Figure 5 exhibits the hydrogen T&D network for compressed gas and liquid forms (for the four modes described above), as evident from the presence of pipelines in the schematics. The schematics corresponding to the T&D network of hydrogen in solid metal hydride form are shown in Figure 6.

Figure 5. T&D network conceptualization in TD1, TD2, TD3, and TD4 modes, respectively, (from top to bottom) for compressed gas and liquid forms of hydrogen

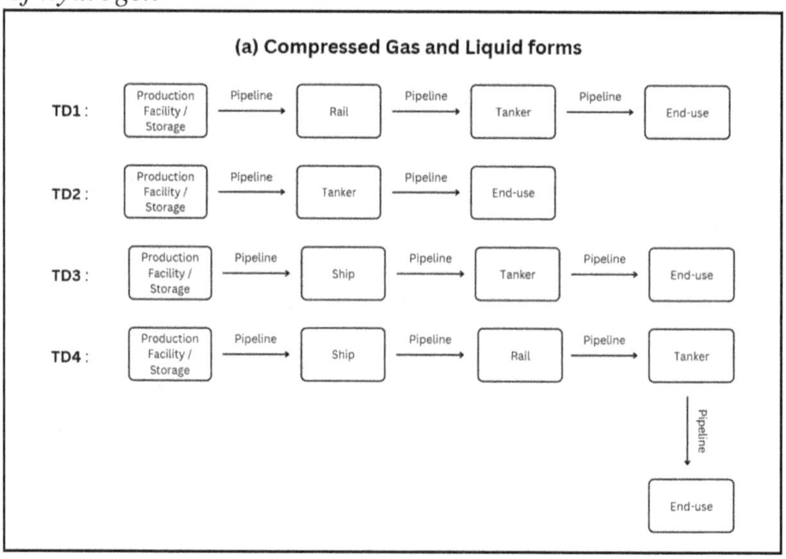

Figure 6. T&D network conceptualization in TD1, TD2, TD3, and TD4 modes, respectively, (from top to bottom) for metal hydride form (solid chemical compounds)

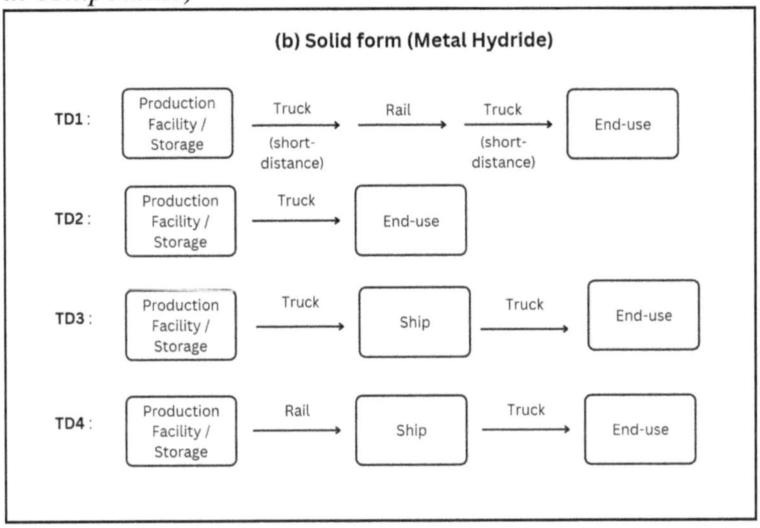

Table 5 summarizes the cost of transporting hydrogen in different physical forms under the four T&D modes for the chosen timelines. The cost of T&D for each mode has been assumed to be reduced by 10% between successive timelines, considering economies of scale.

Table 5. Cost of T&D (USD/t) in different physical forms under four modes for the chosen timelines

T&D configuration	2025		2030		2040		2050	
	Share (%)	Cost (USD/t of H2)	Share (%)	Cost (USD/t of H2)	Share (%)	Cost (USD/t of H2)	Share (%)	Cost (USD/t of H2)
TD1 Compressed gas	100	2286.5	100	2286.5	100	2057.85	100	1852.1
TD2 Compressed gas	100	858.5	100	858.5	100	772.65	100	695.39
TD3 Compressed gas	100	1827.5	100	1827.5	100	1644.75	100	1480.27
TD4 Compressed gas	100	3255.5	100	3255.5	100	2929.95	100	2636.96
TD1 Liquid	100	858.5	100	858.5	100	772.65	100	695.39

continued on following page

Table 5. Continued

T&D configuration	2025		2030		2040		2050	
	Share (%)	**Cost (USD/t of H2)**	**Share (%)**	**Cost (USD/t of H2)**	**Share (%)**	**Cost (USD/t of H2)**	**Share (%)**	**Cost (USD/t of H2)**
TD2 Liquid	100	531.25	100	531.25	100	478.13	100	430.32
TD3 Liquid	100	1500.25	100	1500.25	100	1350.23	100	1215.21
TD4 Liquid	100	1827.5	100	1827.5	100	1644.75	100	1480.28
TD1 Metal hydride	100	2460	100	2460	100	2214	100	1992.6
TD2 Metal hydride	100	360	100	360	100	324	100	291.6
TD3 Metal hydride	100	1560	100	1560	100	1404	100	1263.6
TD4 Metal hydride	100	3825	100	3825	100	3442.5	100	3098.25
Mixed T&D scenario	TD1: 20%; TD2: 30%; TD3: 25%; TD4: 25%							
Compressed gas	90	1985.6	80	1985.6	70	1792.4	60	1608.34
Liquid	90	1163.01	80	1163.01	70	1046.71	60	942.05
MH	90	1946.25	80	1946.25	70	1751.63	60	1576.46

4. RESULTS AND DISCUSSION

Since the main CAPEX for HSC is assumed to comprise thecost of production, thecost of storage,and thecost of T&D, the sum of these three components is considered the objective function to assess the viability of combinations emerging from the options considered in the production, storage, and T&D segments in this study. As depicted in Sections 3.2.1, 3.2.2, and 3.2.3, this study considers four hydrogen production pathways, five storage mechanisms, and fifteen different T&D pathways (depending on the physical form of hydrogen). In the simulations, only one option from each group is active at a time. Essentially, the problem statement of configuring the envisaged HSC in this case boils down to the concatenation of three chromosome fragments with 4, 5, and 15 genes, respectively. In each chromosome fragment, the gene corresponding to a particular option assumes a value of 1 when it is activated, while the others remain inactive (0). Therefore, at a particular instance, only three locations within the

24-bit chromosome assume a value of 1. A total of 140 scenarios were generated from the combinations of the aforementioned three chromosome fragments. Figure 7 delineates the functional steps executed through the *itertools* routine deployed for the supply-chain viability evaluation and screening exercise.

Figure 7. Flowchart of the key operations undertaken by the itertools routine

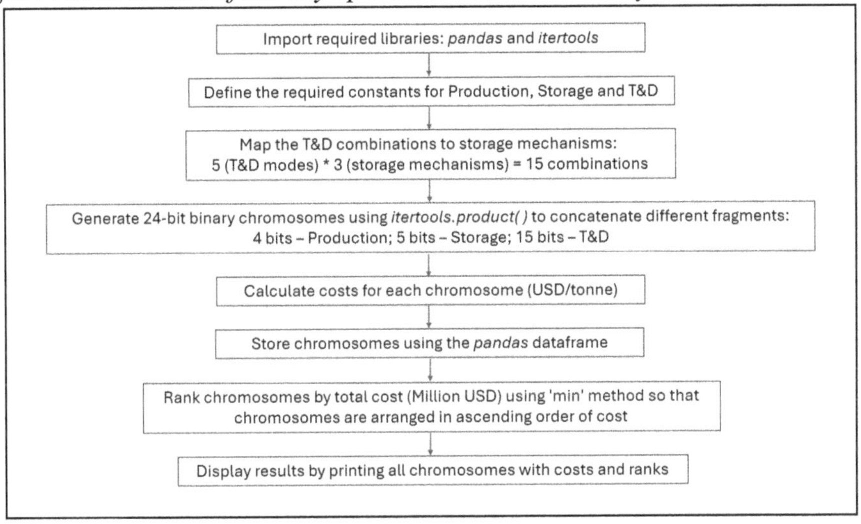

Since the objective of this exercise is to identify the viable HSC configurations based on broad CAPEX estimates, a ranking was performed to obtain the top five combinations of production, storage, and T&D for a meaningful evaluation. Figure 8 exhibits the top five scenarios for the chosen timelines (2025, 2030, 2040, and 2050). In the timelines of 2025, 2030,and 2040, the combination that yields the lowest CAPEX comprises production using an Alkaline electrolyzer accompanied by a mixed mode of hydrogen storage (see Table 4 for the description of mixed-mode storage for different timelines) and aided by TD2 transportation mode. However, the transportation cost is the least when only the metal hydride form of storage is ferried. Although theoretically, this scenario is thrown up as the most viable scenario by the algorithm based on the CAPEX alone, it does not serve as an effective HSC variant in real life. The main reason is that although the storage is of mixed type, only the solid form of hydrogen is touted as the most viable during disbursement. Therefore, a more realistic scenario comprising mixed solutions for all three segments (production, storage, and T&D) was investigated.

Figure 8. The top five scenarios for the chosen timelines (2025, 2030, 2040, and 2050)

All Chromosomes Ranked by Cost with Binary Representation:

Chromosome	COHP	COS	COTD	Total_Cost (USD/tonne)	Total_Cost (Million USD)	Rank
010000001000000000001000	COHP_Alk_2025	COS_Mixed_2025	COTD_TD2_MH_2025	3759.35	198.47	1
010000001001000000000000	COHP_Alk_2025	COS_UG_2025	COTD_TD2_Compgas_2025	3837.50	220.35	2
001000001000000000001000	COHP_SOE_2025	COS_Mixed_2025	COTD_TD2_MH_2025	3879.35	205.67	3
010000001000000100000000	COHP_Alk_2025	COS_Mixed_2025	COTD_TD2_Liq_2025	3930.60	207.72	4
010010000010000000000000	COHP_Alk_2025	COS_Compgas_2025	COTD_TD2_Compgas_2025	3948.50	221.68	5

All Chromosomes Ranked by Cost with Binary Representation:

Chromosome	COHP	COS	COTD	Total_Cost (USD/tonne)	Total_Cost (Million USD)	Rank
010000001000000000001000	COHP_Alk_2030	COS_Mixed_2030	COTD_TD2_MH_2030	3254.86	14429.73	1
010000001001000000000000	COHP_Alk_2030	COS_UG_2030	COTD_TD2_Compgas_2030	3347.60	15612.20	2
010000001000000100000000	COHP_Alk_2030	COS_Mixed_2030	COTD_TD2_Liq_2030	3426.11	15114.73	3
010001000000000100000000	COHP_Alk_2030	COS_Liq_2030	COTD_TD2_Liq_2030	3426.25	15115.00	4
010010000010000000000000	COHP_Alk_2030	COS_Compgas_2030	COTD_TD2_Compgas_2030	3447.50	15812.00	5

All Chromosomes Ranked by Cost with Binary Representation:

Chromosome	COHP	COS	COTD	Total_Cost (USD/tonne)	Total_Cost (Million USD)	Rank
010000001000000000001000	COHP_Alk_2040	COS_Mixed_2040	COTD_TD2_MH_2040	2807.83	37030.75	1
010000001001000000000000	COHP_Alk_2040	COS_UG_2040	COTD_TD2_Compgas_2040	2852.84	38714.25	2
010001000000000100000000	COHP_Alk_2040	COS_Liq_2040	COTD_TD2_Liq_2040	2923.63	38361.61	3
010010000010000000000000	COHP_Alk_2040	COS_Compgas_2040	COTD_TD2_Compgas_2040	2942.65	39387.82	4
010000001000000100000000	COHP_Alk_2040	COS_Mixed_2040	COTD_TD2_Liq_2040	2961.96	38649.12	5

All Chromosomes Ranked by Cost with Binary Representation:

Chromosome	COHP	COS	COTD	Total_Cost (USD/tonne)	Total_Cost (Million USD)	Rank
010000001001000000000000	COHP_Alk_2050	COS_UG_2050	COTD_TD2_Compgas_2050	2607.56	103524.12	1
010000001000000000001000	COHP_Alk_2050	COS_Mixed_2050	COTD_TD2_MH_2050	2623.93	103966.11	2
010001000000000100000000	COHP_Alk_2050	COS_Liq_2050	COTD_TD2_Liq_2050	2671.27	105244.29	3
010010000010000000000000	COHP_Alk_2050	COS_Compgas_2050	COTD_TD2_Compgas_2050	2688.48	105708.96	4
010000001000000100000000	COHP_Alk_2050	COS_Mixed_2050	COTD_TD2_Liq_2050	2762.65	107711.55	5

In 2025, the mixed scenario exhibited a total cost of USD 6780/tonne of hydrogen, and the total estimated CAPEX required for the main components of HSC was estimated at USD 370.2 million. The total cost for the mixed scenario is found to decrease with time. However, the monotonicity is lost in 2040 when the total cost per tonne of hydrogen is observed to increase slightly compared to the 2030 levels. In 2040, the higher cost of hydrogen emanates from the relatively higher share of PEM electrolyzers (40%) in the production technology mix. Table 3 shows that the cost of hydrogen production from PEM is almost three times that of Alkaline electrolyzers. Further, in 2040, the increased share of high-cost metal hydride storage form (30%) adds to the CAPEX estimates. From Table 4, one can observe that the cost of hydrogen storage in the metal hydride form is about 5.5 times that of compressed gas form and about 2.1 times that of liquid storage form. In 2050, the cost of hydrogen production will come down from the reduction in the cost attributable to the scale. These CAPEX trends are consistent with the observations from the other emerging sectors worldwide (Krishnan et al., 2023; Stamatakis et al., 2018).

The mixed scenario cost per tonne of hydrogen is estimated to be USD 5619.9, USD 5995.5, and USD 4910.4 in 2030, 2040, and 2050, respectively. However, as the system capacities for green hydrogen production, storage, and transportation & distribution are assumed to grow multi-fold with time, the total CAPEX witnessed a commensurate increase. The total estimated CAPEX for the mixed scenarios in 2030, 2040, and 2050 is ~ USD 25,452 million (USD 25.4 billion), ~ USD 78,421 million (USD 78.4 billion), and USD 1,95,148 million (USD 195.15 billion), respectively.

The results indicate that for the liquid and compressed gas storage mechanisms, the T&D costs will be on the higher side because of thepipelines. However, these two storage modes collectively would comprise 45% of the total storage capacity by 2050. Therefore, it is inevitable that a resilient HSC will come at a price. The CAPEX that goes into capacity creation for multiple technological options for a particular segment would ensure energy security as well as sustainability (through the low carbon footprint of GH2). The chapter establishes a preliminary understanding of the CAPEX variability that can emerge from the choice of technology for hydrogen production and storage, as well as the mode of hydrogen transmission & distribution. To explore this variability, 140 distinct scenarios were created. In conjunction with this primary screening, additional constraints need to be imposed to ascertain the optimal solutions specific to geographical regions and contexts.

To derive deeper insights from the simulated data, the scenarios with the first-time appearance of single modes in all three supply-chain segments were analyzed for the chosen timelines (2025, 2030, 2040, and 2050), as shown in Figure 9. As expected, alkaline electrolyzers and underground storage of hydrogen (in compressed gas form) lower the system costs. The underground storage mechanism reduces the material costs attributable to the specialized on-ground installations. From the transportation and distribution costs, it is evident that the end users should be located within short-to-medium distances (say, 200-300 km) for the best economic features. Compared to the mixed scenario (comprising mixed modes in all three supply-chain segments), the scenarios with single modes in all three supply-chain segments exhibit significantly lower CAPEX, since the use of single mode is devoid of the additional costs attributable to multiple pathways (modes). The estimated CAPEX for the most viable single-mode scenario is estimated to be USD 288.4 million, USD 15612.2 million (USD 15.6 billion), USD 38,714 million (USD 38.7 billion), and USD 1,03,524 million (USD 103.5 billion) in 2025, 2030, 2040, and 2050, respectively.

Figure 9. Simulated scenarios with first instances of the single modes in all three supply chain segments for the chosen timelines (2025, 2030, 2040, and 2050)

All Chromosomes Ranked by Cost with Binary Representation:

Chromosome	COHP	COS	COTD	Total_Cost (USD/tonne)	Total_Cost (Million USD)	Rank
0010000010000010000000000	COHP_SOE_2025	COS_UG_2025	COTD_Mixed_Compgas_2025	5084.60	288.41	35
0100000010010000000000000	COHP_Alk_2030	COS_UG_2030	COTD_TD2_Compgas_2030	3347.60	15612.20	2
0100000010010000000000000	COHP_Alk_2040	COS_UG_2040	COTD_TD2_Compgas_2040	2852.84	38714.25	2
0100000010010000000000000	COHP_Alk_2050	COS_UG_2050	COTD_TD2_Compgas_2050	2607.56	103524.12	1

Since Alkaline technology for production and a mix of different technologies for hydrogen storage exhibit favourable economics, there is a need to have a deeper look into the kind of critical materials and components they deploy.

As the green hydrogen infrastructure in India expands, the country aims to export a majority of its 5 Mt of green hydrogen at competitive prices by 2030. Green hydrogen production has received attractive financial stimulus in the coastal states of India (Odisha, Karnataka, Kerala, Andhra Pradesh, and Gujarat),which are at the forefront of investments, R&D, and engineering decisions to develop hydrogen valleys.

Beyond regional variations in solar and wind energy tariffs, several other factors influence the overall cost of green hydrogen projects. For instance, a recent tender by Indian Oil Corporation Limited (IOCL) in May 2025 for a 10,000 MTPA green hydrogen plant resulted in a cost of INR 397 per kg (~USD 4.6/kg). When considered alongside prevailing auction rates, preliminary estimates from this study suggest a likely range for the Levelized Cost of Hydrogen (LCOH). The market prices are expected to drop to ~INR 355 per kg (USD 4.1/kg) in the short term, driven by scale efficiencies and supportive policy frameworks. Nevertheless, sustained efforts to lower costs remain critical to ensuring widespread adoption and expanding end-use applications, especially if green hydrogen is to match the current global price of grey hydrogen (~USD 2.1/kg).Therefore, it is important to align energy policy with supply chain optimization to realize the full potential of green hydrogen in India (Chhabra et al., 2025).

5. FUTURE DIRECTIONS

According to the recent Statistical Review of World Energy, North America and the Asia Pacific produced about 2,091 kt and 1,929.7 kt of blue hydrogen in 2023, respectively. During the same period, their green hydrogen production was a mere 19.4 kt and 93.6 kt, respectively. These lopsided production statistics underscore the vast scope for appropriately mapping the global production potential of green hydrogen. Thus, an optimal configuration can lead to a proper balance between supply and demand in this capital-intensive emerging industry.

According to the Uppsala Conflict Data Program, state-based violence witnessed an upsurge by ~17% in 2023 compared to the 1991 figures, while non-state violence has increased by a whopping 240% over the same period (UCDP, n.d.). The dynamically changing regional stability patterns and geopolitical realities pose major disruption risks to the energy supply chains. Therefore, building resilient HSCs is crucial for ensuring energy security for several nations looking at climate-compatible long-term socio-economic prosperity. As part of innovation and optimization in the HSC, countries can consider having a distributed network, rather than a centralized hydrogen production. Although on-site hydrogen production may drive up capital costs, it can be potentially offset by reduced transportation costs and dependencies. Decentralized (captive) production can serve as pilot projects, which accentuate resilience from distant geopolitical tensions and drive down potential risks as supply chains are moved away from the hotspots of geopolitical conflict and tension(Medrano, 2021).

A recent report by Hydrogen Insight (20 March 2025)highlights the dire need for cost-effective renewable energy, without which clean initiatives like green steel and green ammonia will deteriorate to the status of a 'stranded asset' (Martin, 2025). Thus, AI-enabled optimization is critical in building resilient green hydrogen supply chains while also ensuring affordable energy at a global scale. As the models get more complex, genetic algorithms can be effectively employed to reduce dependencies on foreign supply of materials, technology, etc. This will help in projecting the global trends of green hydrogen so that the supply and infrastructure can be planned effectively to achieve economies of scale. Further, exploring multi-objective optimization in hydrogen systems will help address the competing interests of various stakeholders from production to end-users, apart from ensuring efficient RE-hydrogen coupling.

Policy considerations also play a massive role in kick-starting the scaling up of green hydrogen production. Governments may consider bringing forth a viability gap funding mechanism so that hydrogen manufacturers can procure electrolyzers at competitive prices. Reduced customs duties, allowing retrofitting of natural gas pipelines, easing right of way (ROW), developing hydrogen valleys (clusters), and developing transparent regulations can enable hydrogen blending at different points in the existing energy frameworks.

6. CONCLUSION

Green Hydrogen is an integral link in assimilating renewable energy sources into the energy mix. Integrating RE zones with hydrogen clusters can help optimize proximity and resource allocation, among other socio-economic advantages. Thus, it is an opportunity to gradually clean up hydrogen generation by leveraging RE sources. Among various challenges faced by the optimization of HSC, one of the most palpable ones is the geopolitical angle that impacts the possibility of transfer of technology, cooperation in research, development, and deployment, capacity building, financing, and industrial ecosystem preparedness for the different critical subsystems, parts, and components. The growing interest in green hydrogen as a mainstream clean energy carrier underscores the need for robust and secure supply chains in regions of high geopolitical risks, where certain hydrogen production facilities are located near border areas or regions susceptible to geopolitical tensions, ensuring uninterrupted production, safe storage, and demand-driven disbursement becomes crucial.

The progressive transition to green hydrogen will help drive local socio-economic development, thereby redistributing the benefits of clean energy across the globe. The inclusion of green hydrogen in the energy mix will also play a pivotal role in achieving some of the 2030 Sustainable Development Goals (SDGs), namely SDG 7 (Clean and Affordable Energy), SDG 9 (Industry, Innovation and Infrastructure), SDG 11 (Sustainable Cities and Communities), SDG 13 (Climate Action), etc.

The overarching spirit of this chapter revolves around demonstrating the utility of genetic simulation approaches toward enhancing the resilience of hydrogen supply chains by identifying robust and adaptive solutions. By leveraging evolutionary principles, genetic simulations enable efficient production, storage, and distribution strategies that minimize risks and improve energy security. The case study illustrates the need for data-driven optimization to address real-world challenges, ensuring a stable and efficient hydrogen supply network. Continued research and innovation are required in this emerging advanced technological field. Multidisciplinary collaborations among various stakeholders are required to plan decentralized clean hydrogen supply chains devoid of resource-based risks.

It is important to understand that since geopolitical conditions are dynamic, the simulations are only indicative. As technological solutions evolve (e.g., design and efficiency of electrolyzers improve), and systemic bottlenecks are eased (e.g., regulations associated with the right of way are simplified and streamlined), all scenario-building exercise requires periodic revisits. Although this chapter has considered the production, storage, and T&D costs, the inclusion of other parameters such as the indigenization potential of electrolyzers, the RE potential of a nation, and the sectoral demand for green hydrogen, etc., will enhance the efficacy of the model in simulating real-life scenarios. As investments in green hydrogen magnify, large-scale data arising from across the globe will help countries build resilient supply chains through AI-enabled optimization routines, aimed at affordable and accessible clean energy for all.

REFERENCES

Abad, A. V., & Dodds, P. E. (2020). Green hydrogen characterisation initiatives: Definitions, standards, guarantees of origin, and challenges. *Energy Policy*, *138*, 111300. DOI: 10.1016/j.enpol.2020.111300

Ansari, H. D., & Sangwai, J. S. (2024). Carbon transportation by pipelines and ships. In *Advances and Technology Development in Greenhouse Gases: Emission, Capture and Conversion* (pp. 137-162). Elsevier.

Arcos, J. M. M., & Santos, D. M. (2023). The hydrogen color spectrum: Techno-economic analysis of the available technologies for hydrogen production. *Gases*, *3*(1), 25–46. DOI: 10.3390/gases3010002

Ayodele, T. R., & Munda, J. L. (2019). The potential role of green hydrogen production in the South African energy mix. *Journal of Renewable and Sustainable Energy*, *11*(4), 044301. DOI: 10.1063/1.5089958

Banks, F. E. (2012). *Energy economics: a modern introduction*. Springer Science & Business Media.

Bannister, A., Chaplin, Z., Gant, S., Spriggs, C., & Thomson, N. (2021). *Approaches and Methods to Demonstrate Repurposing of the UK's Local Transmission System (LTS)*. Pipelines for Transportation of Hydrogen.

Barbosa-Póvoa, A. P., & Pinto, J. M. (2023). Resilient supply chains–robustness and dynamics in the context of industrial gas supply chains. *Computers & Chemical Engineering*, *179*, 108435. DOI: 10.1016/j.compchemeng.2023.108435

Bentley, P. J., & Wakefield, J. P. (1998). Finding acceptable solutions in the Pareto-optimal range using multi-objective genetic algorithms. In *Soft Computing in Engineering Design and Manufacturing* (pp. 231–240). Springer London. DOI: 10.1007/978-1-4471-0427-8_25

Bordoff, J., & O'Sullivan, M. L. (2022). Green upheaval: The new geopolitics of energy. *Foreign Affairs*, *101*, 68.

Castro, B., & Sen, R. (2022). Everyday adaptation: Theorizing climate change adaptation in daily life. *Global Environmental Change*, *75*, 102555. DOI: 10.1016/j.gloenvcha.2022.102555

Cheng, C. H. J., & Chiu, C. W. J. (2018). How important are global geopolitical risks to emerging countries? *Inter Economics*, *156*, 305–325. DOI: 10.1016/j.inteco.2018.05.002

Cherp, A., Jewell, J., & Goldthau, A. (2011). Governing global energy: Systems, transitions, complexity. *Global Policy*, *2*(1), 75–88. DOI: 10.1111/j.1758-5899.2010.00059.x

Chhabra, N., Majumdar, R., Ghosh, T., & Subramanyam, T. (June 13-14, 2025). Electricity Cost Sensitivity in Green Hydrogen Production: A Comparative Tariff Analysis Across Select Indian States. *Proceedings of the Energy & Carbon Management Conference: Case Studies, Progress & Future Directions (ECM 2025)*, IIT Guwahati, (Paper No. 18). DOI: 10.5281/zenodo.17009219

Dagnachew, A. G., Yalew, S. G., Tesfamichael, M., Okereke, C., & Abraham, E. (2025). A green hydrogen revolution in Africa remains elusive under current geopolitical realities. *Climate Policy*, *25*(2), 291–302. DOI: 10.1080/14693062.2024.2376740

Emiliozzi, S., Ferriani, F., & Gazzani, A. (2025). The European energy crisis and the consequences for the global natural gas market. *The Energy Journal (Cambridge, Mass.)*, *46*(1), 119–145. DOI: 10.1177/01956574241290640

Enumah, M. A. (2025). Analysis of Risk and Risk Management Strategies in Nigeria's Oil and Gas Industry.

Escobar-Yonoff, R., Maestre-Cambronel, D., Charry, S., Rincón-Montenegro, A., & Portnoy, I. (2021). Performance assessment and economic perspectives of integrated PEM fuel cell and PEM electrolyzer for electric power generation. *Heliyon*, *7*(3), e06506. DOI: 10.1016/j.heliyon.2021.e06506 PMID: 33817374

Fernandois, A., & Medel, C. (2020). Geopolitical tensions, OPEC news, and the oil price: A Granger causality analysis. *Revista de Análisis Económico*, *35*(2), 57–90. DOI: 10.4067/S0718-88702020000200057

Gillette, J. L., & Kolpa, R. L. (2008). *Overview of interstate hydrogen pipeline systems* (No. ANL/EVS/TM/08-2). Argonne National Laboratory (ANL), Argonne, IL (United States).

Gorji, S. A. (2023). Challenges and opportunities in the green hydrogen supply chain through metaheuristic optimization. *Journal of Computational Design and Engineering*, *10*(3), 1143–1157. DOI: 10.1093/jcde/qwad043

Helgaker, J. F.(n.d.). Transportation of hydrogen gas in offshore pipelines: H2Pipe.

Holland, J. H. (1992). Genetic algorithms. *Scientific American*, *267*(1), 66–73. DOI: 10.1038/scientificamerican0792-66

IEA. (2024). Global Hydrogen Review 2024, *IEA*, Paris https://www.iea.org/reports/global-hydrogen-review-2024, License: CC BY 4.0

Incer-Valverde, J., Korayem, A., Tsatsaronis, G., & Morosuk, T. (2023). "Colors" of hydrogen: Definitions and carbon intensity. *Energy Conversion and Management*, *291*, 117294. DOI: 10.1016/j.enconman.2023.117294

International Energy Agency. (2023). *World Energy Outlook*. https://www.iea.org/reports/world-energy-outlook-2023

International Energy Agency. (2024). *World Energy Outlook*. https://www.iea.org/reports/world-energy-outlook-2024

Iqbal, M. S., & Abdul Rahim, Z. (2025). Driving emerging technology adoption in Malaysian micro-, small, and medium-sized enterprises: A strategic intervention framework. *Journal of the International Council for Small Business*, 1-24.

IRENA and ILO. (2023). Renewable energy and jobs: Annual review 2023, *International Renewable Energy Agency*, Abu Dhabi, and International Labour Organization, Geneva.

Kaleem, A., Zaman, A., & Rajakaruna, S. (2024). Hydrogen at home: The current and future landscape of green hydrogen in residential settings. *Sustainable Energy Technologies and Assessments*, *72*, 104058. DOI: 10.1016/j.seta.2024.104058

Kamath, H. G., Majumdar, R., Krishnan, A. V., & Srikanth, R. (2022). Cost and environmental benefits of coal-concentrated solar power (CSP) hybridization in India. *Energy, 240*, 122805. DOI: 10.1016/j.energy.2021.122805

Krishnan, S., Koning, V., de Groot, M. T., de Groot, A., Mendoza, P. G., Junginger, M., & Kramer, G. J. (2023). Present and future cost of alkaline and PEM electrolyser stacks. *International Journal of Hydrogen Energy, 48*(83), 32313–32330. DOI: 10.1016/j.ijhydene.2023.05.031

Maka, A. O., & Mehmood, M. (2024). Green hydrogen energy production: Current status and potential. *Clean Energy*, *8*(2), 1–7. DOI: 10.1093/ce/zkae012

Marouani, I., Guesmi, T., Alshammari, B. M., Alqunun, K., Alzamil, A., Alturki, M., & Hadj Abdallah, H. (2023). Integration of Renewable-Energy-Based Green Hydrogen into the Energy Future. *Processes (Basel, Switzerland), 11*(9), 2685. DOI: 10.3390/pr11092685

Martin, P. (2025). "Stranded asset" | Thyssenkrupp's green steel plant not viable if supply of cheap renewable hydrogen never arrives. *Hydrogen Insight.*https://www.hydrogeninsight.com/industrial/stranded-asset-thyssenkrupps-green-steel-plant-not-viable-if-supply-of-cheap-renewable-hydrogen-never-arrives/2-1-1795325

Medrano, V. C. (2021). Metaheuristic and matheuristic approaches for multi-objective optimization problems in process engineering: application to the hydrogen supply chain design. Doctoral dissertation, Institut National Polytechnique de Toulouse-INPT.

Ministry of New and Renewable Energy. India. (2023). https://mnre.gov.in/en/hydrogen-overview/

Mitchell, M.(1998). An introduction to genetic algorithms. MIT Press. (DOI:) ISBN electronic:9780262280013DOI: 10.7551/mitpress/3927.001.0001

National Green Hydrogen Mission. (2023). Ministry of New and Renewable Energy, Government of India.

Ospanova, A. K., & Zakirova, D. I. (2020). Conditions and prospects of employment in the renewable energy sector. *Вестникуниверситета. Туран*, (2), 112–116.

Pandey, A., & Majumdar, R. (2023). Assessing End-of-Life Room Air Conditioner Recycling Potential for Sustainable Resource Utilization in India: A Case Study for Reducing Environmental Burden. In *Anthropogenic Environmental Hazards: Compensation and Mitigation* (pp. 41-69). Cham: Springer Nature Switzerland.(DOI:) ISBN 978-3-031-41012-3DOI: 10.1007/978-3-031-41013-0_3

Pandey, A., & Majumdar, R. (2025). Energy Efficiency and Circularity: Insights from Adoption Trends of Washing Machines, Critical Materials Demand and Responsible Use Strategies. In Osabohien, R. (Ed.), *Energy Efficiency in Critical Times: Security, Economics and Transition* (pp. 3–18). Elsevier., DOI: 10.1016/B978-0-443-28949-1.00001-1

Pandey, V., Sircar, A., Bist, N., Solanki, K., & Yadav, K. (2023). Accelerating the renewable energy sector through Industry 4.0: Optimization opportunities in the digital revolution. *International Journal of Innovation Studies*, *7*(2), 171–188. DOI: 10.1016/j.ijis.2023.03.003

Pascual, C., & Zambetakis, E. (2010). The geopolitics of energy. *Energy security: Economics, politics, strategies, and implications*, 9-35.

Patidar, R., Yadav, D., & Mallya, H. (2024). *How can Hydrogen Electrolysers be Made in India? A Bottom-up Cost Assessment to Quantify the Indigenisation Potential*. Council of Energy, Environment and Water.

Salomon, R. (1997, April). Raising theoretical questions about the utility of genetic algorithms. *International Conference on Evolutionary Programming* (pp. 275-284). Berlin, Heidelberg: Springer Berlin Heidelberg. DOI: 10.1007/BFb0014818

Saurabh, K., & Majumdar, R. (2022). Fuels for sustainable transport in India. In *Clean fuels for mobility* (pp. 27–55). Springer Singapore. DOI: 10.1007/978-981-16-8747-1_3

Saurabh, K., & Majumdar, R. (2023). Functional use-based positioning of conventional vehicles in conjunction with alternate low-emission fuels. In *Renewable fuels for sustainable mobility* (pp. 97–159). Springer Nature Singapore. DOI: 10.1007/978-981-99-1392-3_5

Shahzad, U. (2012). The need for renewable energy sources. *ITEE Journal.* 2(1), ISSN:2306-708X

Shakti Sustainable Energy Foundation. (2023). Energy Dialogues: Annual Report 2023. Shakti Foundation. https://shaktifoundation.in/wp-content/uploads/2024/05/shakti-annual-report-2023.pdf

Stamatakis, E., Zoulias, E., Tzamalis, G., Massina, Z., Analytis, V., Christodoulou, C., & Stubos, A. (2018). Metal hydride hydrogen compressors: Current developments & early markets. *Renewable Energy*, *127*, 850–862. DOI: 10.1016/j.renene.2018.04.073

Su, C. W., Khan, K., Umar, M., & Zhang, W. (2021). Does renewable energy redefine geopolitical risks? *Energy Policy*, *158*, 112566. DOI: 10.1016/j.enpol.2021.112566

UCDP. (n.d.). *Uppsala Conflict Data Program.*https://ucdp.uu.se/

Van de Graaf, T., Overland, I., Scholten, D., & Westphal, K. (2020). The new oil? The geopolitics and international governance of hydrogen. *Energy Research & Social Science*, *70*, 101667. DOI: 10.1016/j.erss.2020.101667 PMID: 32835007

Wijaya, C. Y. (2024). Python's itertools for memory-efficient iteration – NBD Lite #23. *Non-Brand Data.* https://www.nb-data.com/p/pythons-itertools-for-memory-efficient

Yang, M., Hunger, R., Berrettoni, S., Sprecher, B., & Wang, B. (2023). A review of hydrogen storage and transport technologies. *Clean Energy*, *7*(1), 190–216. DOI: 10.1093/ce/zkad021

Zakaria, Z., & Kamarudin, S. K. (2021). A review of alkaline solid polymer membrane in the application of AEM electrolyzer: Materials and characterization. *International Journal of Energy Research*, *45*(13), 18337–18354. DOI: 10.1002/er.6983

Zhou, Y., Li, R., Lv, Z., Liu, J., Zhou, H., & Xu, C. (2022). Green hydrogen: A promising way to a carbon-free society. *Chinese Journal of Chemical Engineering*, *43*, 2–13. Advance online publication. DOI: 10.1016/j.cjche.2022.02.001

KEY TERMS AND DEFINITIONS

AI-Enabled Supply Chain Optimization: This optimization method employs artificial intelligence tools such as machine learning, predictive analytics, etc., to improve the efficiency and resilience of supply chains based on learning from a diverse set of case studies with large datasets.

Genetic Simulation: It refers to the modeling of evolutionary processes. Solutions are generated by mimicking natural selection to produce potentially evolved 'offspring'.

Geopolitical Vulnerability: It refers to a nation's susceptibility to negative impacts arising from its dependence on international resources, trade relations, etc. It can potentially harm a nation's security and stability.

Green Hydrogen: It refers to the hydrogen produced by the process of renewable-powered electrolysis. Since the process does not emit any greenhouse gases, green hydrogen offers a sustainable solution by being a clean energy carrier.

Metal Hydride: This is a promising mechanism for storing hydrogen in a solid form. The method involves hydrogen forming chemical bonds with metals or metal alloys, which can absorb or release hydrogen under controlled pressure and temperature conditions.

Resource Availability: It refers to the pool of resources (financial, human, natural, artificial, etc.) available for a country to achieve a specific goal.

Underground Storage of Hydrogen: To effectively balance supply and demand at a large scale, hydrogen can be stored in natural (salt caverns, aquifers, depleted oil reservoirs, etc.) or artificial (engineered caverns, etc.) underground reservoirs.

APPENDIX

Additional Resources

For a comprehensive understanding of the *itertools* module and its functions, the Python documentation https://docs.python.org/3/library/itertools.html can be referred to.

Abbreviations

AEM- Alkaline Exchange Membrane
AI - Artificial Intelligence
CAPEX- Capital Expenditure
CO2- Carbon Dioxide
EJ- Exajoule (1 EJ = 1018 Joules)
EU- European Union
FY- Financial Year
GA- Genetic Algorithm
GH2- Green Hydrogen
GHG- Greenhouse Gas
HSC- Hydrogen Supply Chain
IEA- International Energy Agency
IRENA- International Renewable Energy Agency
ISA- International Solar Alliance
kt- Kilo tonne
MOO- Multi-Objective Optimization
Mt- Million Tonnes
MTPA- Million Tonnes Per Annum
MW- Megawatt
NDC- Nationally Determined Contribution
NGHM- National Green Hydrogen Mission

NGO- Non-Governmental Organization
OPEC- Oil and Petroleum Exporting Countries
OPEX- Operating Expenditure
OSOWOG- One Sun-One World-One Grid
P2H2P- Power to Hydrogen to Power
PPP- Public-Private Partnership
PEM- Proton Exchange Membrane
R&D- Research and Development
RE- Renewable Energy
SDG- Sustainable Development Goal
SMR- Steam Methane Reforming
T&D- Transportation & Distribution
UNFCCC- United Nations Framework Convention on Climate Change
USD/t- US Dollars Per Tonne

Nomenclature

Alk- Alkaline Electrolyzer
COHP- Cost of Hydrogen Production
Compgas- Compressed Gas
COS- Cost of Storage
COTD- Cost of Transportation & Distribution
Liq- Liquid
MH- Metal Hydride
PEM- Proton Exchange Membrane Electrolyzer
SOE- Solid Oxide Electrolyzer
TD1, TD2, TD3, TD4- Different Modes of T&D

Chapter 6
Sustainable AI Technologies:
Challenges and Opportunities

Mohammad A. Al Khaldy
https://orcid.org/0009-0009-7502-4668
Department of Business Intelligence and Data Analytics, University of Petra, Jordan

Mohammad Alauthman
https://orcid.org/0000-0003-0319-1968
Department of Information Security, University of Petra, Amman, Jordan

Amjad Aldweesh
https://orcid.org/0000-0001-9358-1323
College of Computing and Information Technology, Shaqra University, Shaqra, Saudi Arabia

Ammar Almomani
https://orcid.org/0000-0002-8808-6114
Department of Computer Information Science, Higher Colleges of Technology, Sharjah, UAE

Ahmad Al-Qerem
https://orcid.org/0000-0003-2187-6194
Computer Science Department, Faculty of Information Technology, Zarqa University, Zarqa, Jordan

Mouhammd Alkasassbeh
https://orcid.org/0000-0001-8396-7441
Princess Sumaya University for Technology, Jordan

ABSTRACT

Sustainable AI merges artificial intelligence (AI) development with ecological, social, and economic resilience. It addresses energy consumption,

DOI: 10.4018/979-8-3373-1077-0.ch006

resource management, ethical implications, and policy integration. This chapter explores current practices, identifies challenges, and uncovers opportunities for developing systems that align with sustainable goals. It reviews existing research on carbon footprints, data governance, ethical frameworks, public policy, and cross-sector collaboration. It also analyzes potential methods to measure and mitigate AI's environmental impact, with illustrative tables and diagrams spread throughout. Finally, the chapter offers an outlook on integrating these findings into a cohesive vision for sustainable AI, bridging academic and industry efforts, and enhancing practical governance frameworks.

INTRODUCTION

AI has expanded rapidly. It influences transportation, finance, healthcare, and other crucial domains. While AI research focuses on model accuracy, data availability, and computational capabilities, awareness of ecological and social implications is growing (van Wynsberghe, 2021). The rise of energy-hungry models, concerns about e-waste, and the need for fair and transparent AI set the stage for rethinking how these systems evolve.

Sustainability in AI refers to practices that limit resource exhaustion, align with social good, and maintain economic viability (Nishant et al., 2020). This approach ensures that while models progress, they remain sensitive to environmental footprints and social justice (Bossert & Hagendorff, 2023). This chapter provides an extensive analysis of sustainable AI, addressing carbon emissions, ethical design, data governance, technical innovations, and policy frameworks.

Discussion begins with the conceptual foundations of sustainable AI. It then explores environmental impacts, social responsibilities, and potential regulatory measures. The chapter also includes integrated tables and figures to illustrate key mechanisms, frameworks, and concepts in the sustainability domain. This holistic presentation aims to supply a robust reference for students, researchers, policy experts, and technology leaders considering or implementing AI solutions that balance efficiency with responsibility.

LITERATURE REVIEW AND CONCEPTUAL FOUNDATIONS OF SUSTAINABLE AI

Evolving Definitions of Sustainable AI

Researchers have sought to define sustainable AI as more than just carbon-aware computation. It involves environmental awareness, fairness, societal wellbeing, and intergenerational justice (Halsband, 2022). Van Wynsberghe (2021) proposed a framework that combines AI for sustainability with sustainability of AI, urging that systems developed to support sustainability goals themselves should have minimal environmental costs. Nishant et al. (2020) observed that sustainability in AI must align with the triple bottom line of economic, social, and environmental factors, while also advocating robust governance to address unintended consequences.

Sustainable AI overlaps with "Green AI," a concept popularized by Schwartz et al. (2020) in their call for efficiency in computation. Green AI includes energy-awareness, transparency in reporting computational resources, and eco-friendly data centers (Henderson et al., 2020). However, Green AI sometimes focuses on operational efficiency, such as limiting carbon footprints from training large models (Strubell et al., 2020). Sustainable AI broadens that scope by including fairness in data collection, biodiversity impacts of hardware sourcing, and distribution of benefits across communities (Bossert & Hagendorff, 2023).

This expanded viewpoint extends the lens beyond single AI applications. Some scholars argue that sustainable AI includes frameworks for entire product lifecycles, from design to disposal (Gupta et al., 2022). AI hardware can harm landfills if e-waste is not managed well. AI algorithms can create social divides if data curation is inadequate. These concerns highlight a multi-dimensional approach to sustainability, going beyond immediate carbon emissions to embrace holistic principles of responsible innovation (Goel et al., 2024).

Historical Perspective and Motivations

AI research dates back decades. Early AI systems were comparatively small. Energy consumption and data scale were modest, so environmental ramifications were less urgent. As specialized hardware improved and data sets became massive, training deep networks demanded significant electricity (Rolnick et al., 2022). This shift prompted researchers to scrutinize the carbon footprints of advanced models. Lannelongue et al. (2021) quantified the carbon usage of computational tasks and emphasized transparency to allow better optimization strategies.

Parallel concerns emerged around social justice (Bender et al., 2021). AI models with poor data governance can replicate biases that harm marginalized communities. Sustainable AI encourages equitable data representation and inclusive innovation to ensure that AI serves global populations without reinforcing existing inequalities (Cowls et al., 2021). The motivation is to coordinate environmental stewardship and social equity, ensuring that AI's benefits do not come at an ecological or ethical cost (Năstasă & Dumitra, 2024).

Government bodies and global institutions also recognized the significance of sustainable AI (Vinuesa et al., 2020). The United Nations (UN) introduced the Sustainable Development Goals (SDGs), urging technology developers to align innovations with objectives such as poverty eradication, climate action, and responsible consumption (Vinuesa et al., 2020). AI can facilitate progress toward many SDGs by optimizing transportation and analyzing climate data, but it can also conflict with certain SDGs if it accelerates environmental harm (Kaack et al., 2022). This tension underscores the necessity of carefully balancing AI advancement with ecological and social constraints.

Key Pillars of Sustainable AI

Sustainable AI rests on specific core pillars: energy efficiency, ethical design, resource allocation, transparency, and social impact (van Wynsberghe, 2021). Energy efficiency addresses how model training and inference can reduce carbon emissions. Ethical design ensures fairness, accountability, and respect for data privacy. Resource allocation explores how hardware and materials are sourced, maintained, and disposed. Transparency includes robust reporting of data and computational costs, and social impact evaluates who gains from AI, and at whose expense.

Interdisciplinary studies combine computer science, ethics, and social sciences to shape these pillars. For example, Schütze (2024) critiques oversimplified discourses on AI's environmental footprint and suggests deeper engagement with social contexts. This approach recognizes that energy-efficient AI is not automatically socially just if, for instance, the data used reflect demographic imbalances (Bender et al., 2021). Similarly, resource allocation ties into fair trade concerns, such as sourcing rare minerals in conflict regions. The pillars link to each other, forming a network of considerations that define sustainable AI in practice.

The Environmental Footprint of AI

AI's environmental concerns center on training large neural networks. Studies measured how developing advanced language models can emit carbon dioxide at levels comparable to large passenger cars across their entire lifecycles (Henderson et al., 2020; Strubell et al., 2020). Data centers, often powered by non-renewable energy sources, exacerbate the carbon burden (Gupta et al., 2022). This impact extends beyond carbon footprints to water usage for cooling and e-waste generation when hardware becomes obsolete (Patterson et al., 2022). Table 1 presents key parameters influencing AI's environmental load.

Table 1. Main parameters influencing AI's environmental impact

Parameter	Description	Example	Mitigation Strategy
Computation Scale	Total FLOPs used for training or inference	Large neural networks with billions of parameters	Model pruning, efficient architectures
Energy Source	Source of electricity (renewable vs. fossil)	Coal-powered data centers vs. solar-powered facilities	Renewable energy adoption
Hardware Lifespan	Frequency of hardware replacement and disposal	Upgrading GPUs yearly	Refurbishment, recycling, modular designs
Cooling Requirements	Energy needed to cool data centers or hardware clusters	Air conditioning in server farms in warm climates	Free cooling, water cooling, HVDC design
Model Development Cycle	Number of experiments and hyperparameter searches	Automated hyperparameter tuning that tries many configurations	Early stopping, advanced search strategies

In addition to training, inference can pose substantial energy demands if deployed at scale (Schwartz et al., 2020). Edge computing solutions can mitigate some overhead by processing data locally on devices, thus reducing server load. This approach, however, requires hardware optimization to keep devices energy-efficient. Early design choices, such as model architecture and training methods, significantly affect downstream inference costs (Verdecchia et al., 2023).

Concurrently, measurement challenges hamper objective evaluations. Researchers proposed standard metrics for reporting energy use and carbon emissions to allow meaningful comparisons across algorithms (Henderson et al., 2020). Efforts to label AI models with "energy consumption tags" or "green certification" aim to encourage responsible practices in the AI community (Schwartz et al., 2020). Despite these advancements, universal standards remain a work in progress, reflecting the broader complexity of attributing carbon footprints within a global supply chain.

THE SCOPE AND DIMENSIONS OF SUSTAINABLE AI

Environmental Dimension

The environmental dimension focuses on air, water, and biodiversity. AI consumes resources such as electricity and raw materials, and these resources connect to greenhouse gas emissions, pollution, and habitat destruction (Van Wynsberghe et al., 2022). Gupta et al. (2022) identified data center cooling as a major contributor to water usage in areas that may already face shortages. The environmental dimension thus encompasses all direct and indirect burdens AI can place on ecosystems. Tools for evaluating these burdens include lifecycle analyses, which examine the extraction of minerals for hardware, manufacturing and operational phases, distribution, and disposal processes (Cugurullo, 2021).

AI can also contribute to environmental solutions. Many climate modeling techniques rely on machine learning for better predictions, optimizing renewable energy grids, and managing resources (Rolnick et al., 2022). The tension between AI's resource demand and its potential for environmental remediation is a core theme in the sustainability discourse (Kaack et al., 2022). Tools that automate satellite imagery analysis detect deforestation, track illegal fishing, or monitor pollution (Vinuesa et al., 2020). These solutions demonstrate AI's capacity for ecological benefits if developed thoughtfully.

Social Dimension

Sustainable AI must address social impacts. This includes data bias, job displacement, and cultural shifts caused by automation. When large-scale AI systems reinforce biases, disadvantaged groups may face discrimination (Bender et al., 2021). Sustainable AI places emphasis on inclusive data sets, transparency in model decisions, and equitable access to AI-driven resources (Nishant et al., 2020).

Intergenerational equity is another consideration. Long-term decisions around resource use and technology design affect future generations. Algorithms that degrade biodiversity or intensify climate hazards risk shifting burdens to those not yet born (Halsband, 2022). Ethical frameworks for sustainable AI must consider this time horizon. Government initiatives can encourage robust regulation, requiring that companies disclose AI's societal effects and adopt mitigation strategies (Wilson & van der Velden, 2022).

Economic Dimension

Economic factors also shape sustainable AI. Training advanced models is expensive, raising concerns about large corporations monopolizing AI resources. Smaller organizations may lack the capital to adopt cutting-edge, energy-efficient hardware (Schoormann et al., 2023). This imbalance can limit competition and hamper innovation. Conversely, adopting sustainable AI methods can cut operational costs through energy savings (Dhiman et al., 2024). Over time, best practices in model efficiency become mainstream, leading to new economic opportunities such as specialized hardware for low-power AI or carbon credit markets that reward green computing (Mazzi & Floridi, 2023).

Equally significant is the economic opportunity AI presents for boosting productivity in agriculture, manufacturing, and logistics (Goel et al., 2024). Automated systems that reduce waste can enhance the supply chain's resilience. Such gains translate into stable, more sustainable economic models if properly implemented. Yet, equitable distribution of these gains remains crucial because an unchecked approach can widen socio-economic gaps (Nishant et al., 2020). Balanced public policies that incentivize sustainable AI solutions while preventing market concentration can support a more inclusive innovation environment (Crawford, 2021).

TECHNICAL APPROACHES FOR SUSTAINABLE AI

Efficient Model Architectures

Model complexity drives resource usage. Traditional deep networks rely on substantial layers, large parameter counts, and extensive training cycles (Schwartz et al., 2020). Researchers now experiment with more compact architectures, leveraging techniques such as pruning, quantization, knowledge distillation, and low-rank factorization to reduce computational overhead (Patterson et al., 2022). Pruning removes weights deemed unimportant, while quantization reduces the precision of model parameters. Both strategies diminish memory footprints and energy consumption with limited effects on accuracy (Strubell et al., 2020).

Distillation involves training a smaller "student model" using the outputs or intermediate representations of a larger "teacher model." The student model then performs nearly as well as the teacher but with fewer parameters (Schwartz et al., 2020). Low-rank factorization decomposes large matrices into factors with smaller dimensions, reducing multiplication operations. Each approach contributes to resource-efficient AI systems without undermining performance objectives.

Renewable Energy Integration

Shifting data center power sources from fossil fuels to renewables is crucial to reducing AI's carbon footprint (Gupta et al., 2022). Cloud providers have begun to adopt solar, wind, and hydroelectric power to run servers. Overcoming intermittent supply from renewables is possible with load balancing and local battery storage. AI-driven solutions can schedule tasks when renewable energy supply peaks, further lowering carbon intensity (Verdecchia et al., 2023). Energy scheduling frameworks incorporate predictive analytics to forecast wind or solar availability and optimize job distribution accordingly.

Beyond large data centers, smaller facilities and local computations can also harness renewable energy. Edge devices might rely on solar panels or energy harvesting techniques in remote settings, particularly in rural communities where infrastructure is minimal (Rolnick et al., 2022). Integrating AI with microgrids can make local systems more resilient and sustainable, but this approach requires robust design that accounts for hardware constraints, environmental factors, and maintenance challenges (Kaack et al., 2022).

Adaptive Computation and Early Stopping

Adaptive computational strategies reduce unnecessary resource consumption. They reallocate computing resources based on an algorithm's current stage of training or inference. For instance, once a model converges to a stable accuracy threshold, continued fine-tuning might yield negligible benefits at the cost of extra energy (Strubell et al., 2020). Early stopping detects such plateauing, halting training to save energy and time.

Some approaches dynamically change network size or precision based on real-time performance metrics (Năstasă & Dumitra, 2024). For example, if a model runs on a mobile device, it could switch to a more compact architecture. Similarly, large data center workloads can scale down at off-peak hours, preserving resources. These adaptive methods require careful monitoring of usage patterns and performance metrics, but they align AI with broader sustainability goals.

Below is a flowchart representation of a typical sustainable AI lifecycle, highlighting core processes from data collection to eventual hardware recycling.

Figure 1. Basic flowchart of a sustainable AI lifecycle

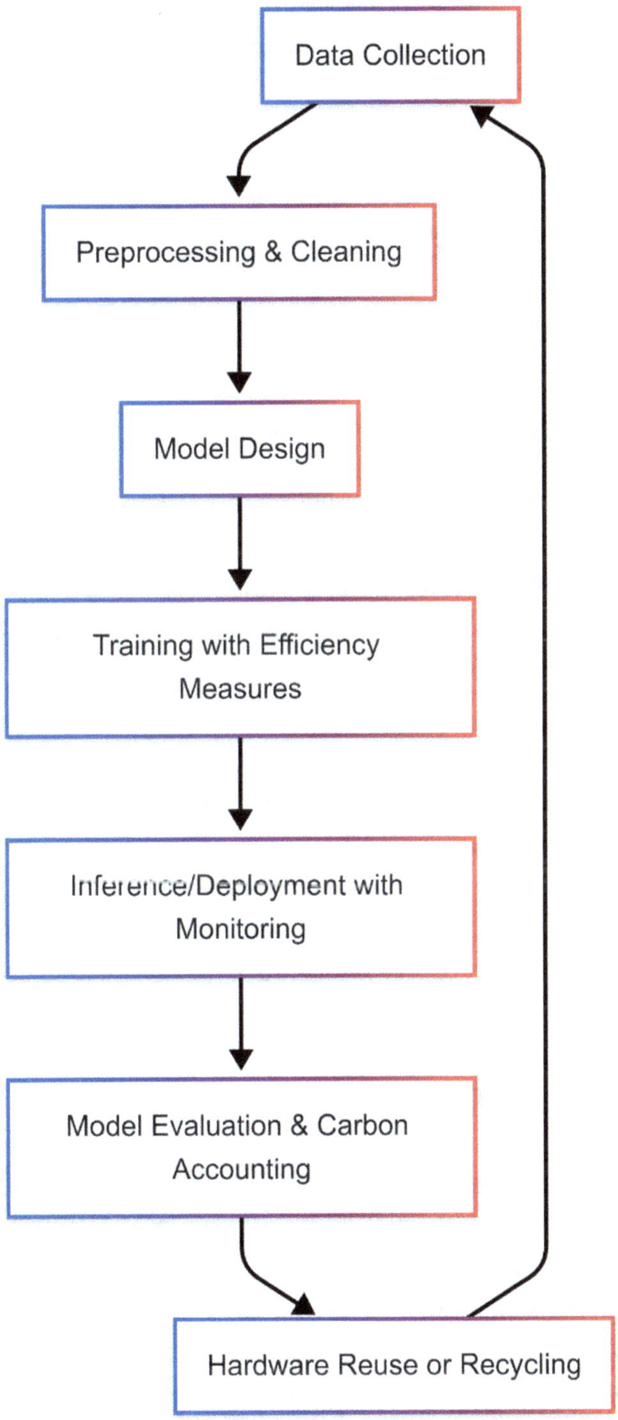

This loop emphasizes a continuous evaluation of environmental and social factors at each stage. After the model's functional life, hardware disposal or recycling feeds back into data collection for improved design in a subsequent cycle. Such iterative processes underscore the dynamic nature of sustainable AI development.

POLICY AND GOVERNANCE FOR SUSTAINABLE AI

Emerging Regulatory Frameworks

National and international bodies have started to form guidelines and regulations for AI that incorporate sustainability concerns (Wilson & van der Velden, 2022). The European Union (EU) introduced legislative proposals for AI governance focusing on safety, transparency, and accountability. While environmental sustainability is not the centerpiece, it overlaps with risk management strategies when systems can significantly harm ecological stability (Gupta et al., 2022).

Policy instruments can encourage or mandate the reporting of energy consumption and carbon footprint. They might promote "Green AI" labels for products meeting certain efficiency thresholds (Schwartz et al., 2020). Other proposals target corporate disclosure of resource usage and ethical compliance in AI supply chains, similar to existing frameworks for conflict minerals (Crawford, 2021). Cooperation between governments, academia, and industry fosters inclusive, balanced approaches that avoid placing excessive burdens on start-ups while ensuring minimal ecological harm.

Standards and Certifications

Voluntary industry standards and certifications can motivate sustainable AI practices. Organizations such as the Institute of Electrical and Electronics Engineers (IEEE) develop codes of conduct and best practices. They recommend systematic reporting on energy usage, interpretability, and potential biases (Nishant et al., 2020). Some green computing standards, like the ISO 14000 series, might extend to AI by focusing on product lifecycle management. The synergy between such standards and local laws drives more consistent compliance, bridging the gap between self-regulation and formal regulation (Brevini, 2021).

Measuring compliance requires consistent metrics. As Henderson et al. (2020) noted, standardizing the measurement of power usage effectiveness (PUE) or carbon usage effectiveness (CUE) can clarify AI's environmental performance. Industry groups can certify data centers or AI applications that meet or surpass these thresholds. The competitive advantage gained from green certifications can incentivize firms to adopt sustainable methods. Over time, consumer demand for ethical technology may further spur standard adoption.

International Collaboration

Sustainability challenges transcend borders, requiring cooperation and knowledge exchange among governments. Collaborative forums like the G20 or the UN specialized agencies can host dialogues on best practices for sustainable AI (Vinuesa et al., 2020). These dialogues address legal and infrastructural disparities. High-income countries with advanced AI resources might share green data center technology or sponsor sustainable AI initiatives in lower-income regions. Meanwhile, local communities can highlight contexts where AI exacerbates climate or social vulnerabilities (Dauvergne, 2020).

Global initiatives can harmonize efforts to reduce repetitive regulatory processes, align on universal frameworks, and accelerate technology transfer. Joint projects in climate modeling or pandemic response illustrate how AI can serve global interests (Năstasă & Dumitra, 2024). Sustained international collaboration ensures that while AI matures, it remains cognizant of collective human and environmental needs.

The following diagram outlines key stakeholders in the regulatory ecosystem, their interactions, and the flow of policies.

Figure 2. Regulatory ecosystem in sustainable AI

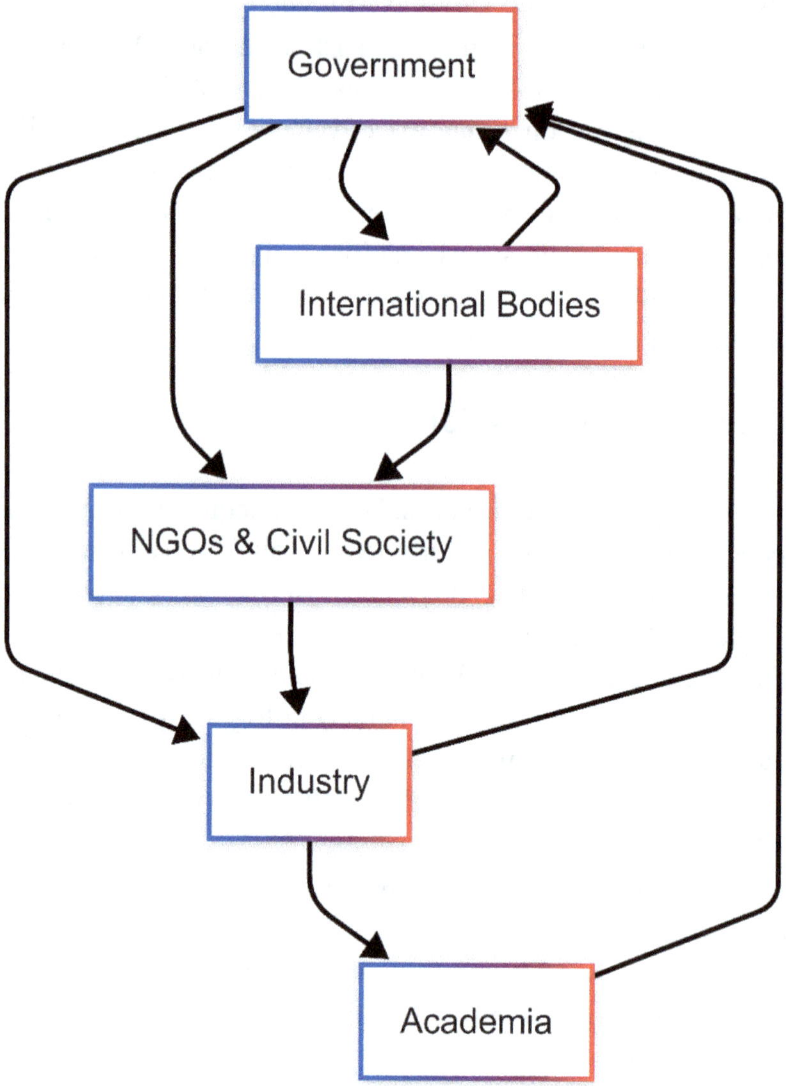

Each stakeholder shapes AI's policy environment. Governments set legal requirements, industry innovates solutions, academia offers research and best practices, NGOs advocate for ethical and sustainable standards, and international bodies coordinate global frameworks. Their interconnections facilitate checks and balances, encouraging a holistic approach to sustainable AI.

SOCIAL AND ETHICAL CONSIDERATIONS IN SUSTAINABLE AI

Data Governance and Fairness

A system is only as ethical as its data. Imbalanced data sets might intensify discrimination or produce skewed outcomes (Cowls et al., 2021). Responsible data governance includes representative sampling, privacy protections, and transparent labeling (Bender et al., 2021). Sustainable AI encourages the building of inclusive data sets, often requiring collaboration among different communities to capture diverse perspectives. This inclusive approach is vital because AI that aims to serve social good must avoid exacerbating existing inequalities (Cowls et al., 2023).

Accountability and Transparency

Sustainability relies on accountability structures. Engineers should be able to trace an AI model's energy consumption and verify its decision-making rationale (Mazzi & Floridi, 2023). Transparent AI fosters trust among users and stakeholders. Explainable models offer insights into potential biases or reasons behind specific predictions, reducing the risk of hidden environmental or social harms (Bossert & Hagendorff, 2023). If an AI-powered system for resource allocation fails, accountability mechanisms should clarify whether flaws occurred in data preprocessing, algorithm selection, or deployment processes.

Community Engagement

Sustainable AI initiatives benefit from community participation. Locals can articulate relevant problems, ensuring that AI solutions align with actual needs (Dauvergne, 2020). For instance, in a region facing water shortages, using machine learning to optimize irrigation systems might yield tangible benefits. Engaging local stakeholders early builds trust, fosters adoption, and enhances the solution's cultural appropriateness. Without such engagement, top-down AI deployments may fail to address specific socioeconomic contexts (Crawford, 2021).

OPPORTUNITIES AND USE CASES

Climate Modeling and Forecasting

One prominent use of AI is climate modeling. Traditional climate models are computationally heavy, but AI-driven approaches can process large-scale atmospheric and oceanic data to refine predictions (Kaack et al., 2022). Machine learning techniques reduce the complexity of numerical models while maintaining accuracy, enabling faster climate simulations. Early identification of extreme weather events can support disaster planning, saving lives and resources (Rolnick et al., 2022). Such applications illustrate how AI can be deployed responsibly to tackle pressing planetary challenges.

Smart Grids and Energy Management

AI can optimize electricity grids by balancing generation and consumption in real-time. Such systems integrate renewable energy sources while minimizing reliance on fossil fuels (Himeur et al., 2021). Predictive algorithms anticipate surges in power demand or fluctuations in solar and wind output. The system then redistributes energy or triggers storage solutions. This agility stabilizes grids and lowers carbon emissions (Dhiman et al., 2024). Machine learning can also detect anomalies in consumption, reducing waste and pointing to efficiency upgrades (Himeur et al., 2021).

Sustainable Agriculture

AI helps farmers monitor soil conditions, predict pest infestations, and schedule irrigation precisely (Vinuesa et al., 2020). By analyzing satellite imagery, sensors, and weather data, AI detects patterns that lead to better resource allocation. This reduces fertilizer and water overuse, lessening environmental harm (Goel et al., 2024). Farmers can also benefit from AI's predictive maintenance to keep machinery in optimal condition (Cowls et al., 2023). These techniques exemplify how advanced analytics can reshape agriculture, sustaining yields with fewer inputs.

Circular Economy and Waste Management

The circular economy strives to extend product lifecycles, reduce waste, and promote recycling. AI supports this goal by analyzing supply chains to identify inefficiencies, matching waste outputs with industries that can use recycled materials (Rolnick et al., 2022). Automated vision systems at recycling facilities distinguish materials, improving sorting accuracy (Nishant et al., 2020). AI-driven platforms can also match used goods to potential buyers, advancing reuse markets (van Wynsberghe, 2021). These methods help realize a closed-loop system where fewer raw materials enter production, mitigating ecological strain.

Table 2. Selected sustainable AI use cases and their benefits

Use Case	Description	Potential Impact	Reference
Climate Modeling	AI-powered climate simulations, detection of extreme weather patterns	Early disaster prevention, targeted climate policy	Kaack et al., 2022; Rolnick et al., 2022
Smart Grids & Energy Management	Real-time balancing of renewable and fossil sources, anomaly detection	Reduced carbon emissions, grid stability	Himeur et al., 2021; Dhiman et al., 2024
Sustainable Agriculture	Precision farming and resource optimization	Decreased water and fertilizer usage, improved yield	Vinuesa et al., 2020; Goel et al., 2024
Circular Economy & Waste Management	Automated material sorting and recycling optimization	Resource conservation, minimized landfill usage	Nishant et al., 2020; van Wynsberghe, 2021

These use cases offer a glimpse into AI's potential to address sustainability challenges. However, each example also demands careful consideration of data ethics, model transparency, and potential inequalities in technology access.

CHALLENGES AND BARRIERS

Computational Barriers

High-performance computing clusters are expensive. They also consume significant energy, creating a paradox where advanced AI that might help identify energy efficiencies could itself be resource-intensive (Henderson et al., 2020). Smaller organizations and lower-income countries often face barriers in accessing these computational resources, perpetuating inequities in AI development and use (Schoormann et al., 2023). Shared infrastructure and open-source collaborations can address this imbalance, yet large-scale adoption of such solutions remains limited.

Data Quality and Availability

AI models rely on large, high-quality data sets. Gathering and cleaning this data poses a challenge, especially for sustainability-related tasks that require domain-specific or localized information (Bender et al., 2021). Bias in data collection leads to biased outcomes, eroding trust in AI (Cowls et al., 2021). Data privacy laws can further limit data sharing, restricting the capacity to develop robust models (Crawford, 2021). Balancing data utility and privacy remains an active area of research and policy debate (Wilson & van der Velden, 2022).

Ethical and Regulatory Uncertainties

Regulators struggle to keep pace with rapid AI innovation. Ethical dilemmas arise around AI's role in shaping public discourse, displacing jobs, and affecting human autonomy (Brevini, 2021). These ethical and regulatory uncertainties can create a volatile environment for investors and innovators. Clear policies that prioritize sustainability can guide responsible AI growth, but forging international consensus around the specifics is complex (Cugurullo, 2021). Varied socio-political contexts compound these difficulties, leading to patchwork regulations that limit cohesive strategies.

Cultural and Social Resistance

Even when sustainable AI solutions are available, local communities may resist adoption if they lack trust in technology or fear job displacement (Dauvergne, 2020). Overcoming such resistance requires transparent engagement and capacity building. Misinformation or misunderstandings about AI's nature can also create friction. Addressing these issues demands outreach that respects local values, languages, and customs, ensuring that AI solutions enhance, rather than disrupt, daily life (Crawford, 2021).

Below is a conceptual sequence diagram showing how various sustainable AI use cases can integrate within a larger framework, from data gathering to policy implementation.

Figure 3. Use case integration in sustainable AI

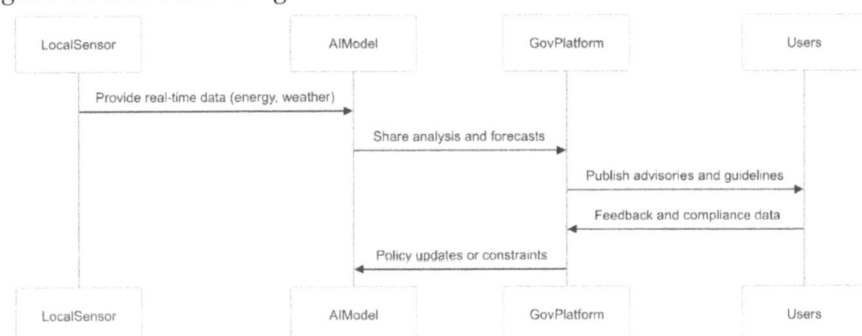

In this sequence, local sensors gather data for AI models focused on sustainability. Analyses are passed to government platforms, which then inform citizens or industries through advisories. Citizens provide feedback, and the government refines policies, which in turn shape AI's parameters, ensuring a participatory and adaptive cycle.

Table 3. Challenges and associated mitigation strategies

Challenge	Description	Mitigation Strategies	References
Computational Demand	Large-scale models require vast energy and hardware	Adopt efficient architectures, shift to renewables	Strubell et al., 2020; Henderson et al., 2020
Data Bias	Skewed datasets lead to unfair outcomes	Inclusive data collection, bias audits	Bender et al., 2021; Cowls et al., 2021
Regulatory Gaps	Lack of standardized policies for sustainable AI	Lobby for AI-specific legislation, create global standards	Wilson & van der Velden, 2022; Crawford, 2021
Cultural Resistance	Communities may distrust or reject new technologies	Community engagement, transparent communication	Dauvergne, 2020; Nishant et al., 2020

The table highlights that while each challenge is significant, it can be moderated by proactive strategies. These strategies include designing efficient models, working toward inclusive data, advocating policy reforms, and involving local communities early.

FUTURE DIRECTIONS FOR SUSTAINABLE AI

Interdisciplinary Collaborations

Sustainable AI is inherently interdisciplinary. It merges technical knowledge with environmental science, ethics, law, and social sciences. Collaborative research that unites these fields can generate holistic solutions. For instance, ecologists can guide the data needs for biodiversity modeling, while social scientists measure cultural acceptance of proposed AI solutions (Cowls et al., 2023). As collaboration grows, the AI community can refine best practices and form integrated teams that consider multiple angles from concept to deployment (van Wynsberghe et al., 2022).

Quantum Computing and New Paradigms

Emerging fields like quantum computing promise computational leaps with potentially different energy profiles (Verdecchia et al., 2023). While quantum hardware remains nascent, it offers a glimpse into future paradigms. If these systems can solve certain optimization problems more efficiently, it may reduce the resources demanded by classical supercomputers. Still, quantum computing development requires substantial energy for cooling. Research is ongoing to determine how quantum AI could align with sustainability goals (Patterson et al., 2022).

AI-Assisted Resource Discovery

Beyond optimizing existing systems, AI can discover new resources or methods for sustainability. Machine learning can identify efficient chemical reactions that reduce waste in manufacturing (Goel et al., 2024). In renewable energy research, AI identifies better photovoltaic materials by screening large chemical databases. Similar techniques can be extended to biofuels or novel battery technologies (Rolnick et al., 2022). These breakthroughs illustrate how AI can catalyze green innovations, bridging scientific research and industrial application.

Strengthening Ethical Guidelines

Ethical AI frameworks continue to evolve. Future guidelines may expand to set explicit environmental targets. For example, an AI system might be required to operate within a certain carbon budget or demonstrate positive social outcomes (Bossert & Hagendorff, 2023). Audits and oversight committees can scrutinize both the development and application phases of AI systems, ensuring compliance and accountability (Schütze, 2024). As these ethical frameworks mature, they influence grant allocations, industry investment, and public perception, driving the AI field toward more sustainable norms.

Community-Led Innovation

In many regions, local communities innovate with AI to address specific sustainability needs. These grassroots efforts often reflect practical constraints, using inexpensive hardware and open-source software to solve urgent problems such as wastewater treatment or reforestation monitoring (Năstasă & Dumitra, 2024). Supporting this bottom-up approach can diversify the AI landscape, preventing the concentration of knowledge and power in large tech hubs. Fostering local innovation aligns with the broader movement for democratizing AI, ensuring that sustainability does not become an abstract principle but a tangible reality for communities worldwide (Cowls et al., 2021).

Table 4. Emerging trends and potential research directions

Trend	Description	Potential Impact	References
Quantum-Assisted AI	Harnessing quantum computing for optimization	Possible lower energy usage for complex tasks	Patterson et al., 2022; Verdecchia et al., 2023
Community-Led AI	Bottom-up solutions by local stakeholders	More inclusive development and deployment	Năstasă & Dumitra, 2024; Cowls et al., 2021
AI for Novel Materials Discovery	Machine learning to accelerate green tech R&D	Faster creation of sustainable solutions	Goel et al., 2024; Rolnick et al., 2022
Expanded Ethical Frameworks	Integrated metrics for social and environmental justice	Greater accountability and transparency	Bossert & Hagendorff, 2023; Schütze, 2024

These trends highlight directions that blend scientific research, engineering, ethics, and policy. The shift toward novel paradigms, collaboration, community-based initiatives, and stronger ethical rules may define the future shape of sustainable AI.

CONCLUSION AND RECOMMENDATIONS

Sustainable AI embodies a holistic philosophy that aligns advanced computational methods with ecological balance and social well-being. Early approaches highlighted the importance of resource efficiency, coining the term "Green AI" to capture the necessity of cutting carbon footprints (Schwartz et al., 2020). Subsequent research broadened the perspective by recognizing the interconnectedness of environmental, social, and economic dimensions (Nishant et al., 2020). While energy consumption remains a critical concern, issues of data bias, resource sourcing, regulatory frameworks, and cultural acceptance are equally pivotal (Crawford, 2021).

This chapter outlined how sustainable AI can address real-world needs—climate modeling, smart grids, agriculture, and circular economies—while remaining conscious of ethical standards and community contexts (Rolnick et al., 2022; Goel et al., 2024). To make these opportunities a reality, researchers must continue refining model architectures, adopt renewable energy solutions, and implement adaptive computation strategies (Strubell et al., 2020; Henderson et al., 2020). Policymakers, meanwhile, can encourage better reporting, set regulatory baselines, and facilitate cross-border collaborations (Wilson & van der Velden, 2022). Civil society and local communities must also have a voice in shaping AI's direction to ensure equitable access and trust (Dauvergne, 2020).

The sustainability journey does not end with partial solutions. The field requires continual innovation, stronger ethical guidelines, and interdisciplinary cooperation (van Wynsberghe et al., 2022). Future research can investigate quantum computing's role, expand community-led initiatives, explore AI-driven materials discovery, and refine frameworks to ensure environmental footprints remain within planetary boundaries (Verdecchia et al., 2023). By focusing on synergy between technology, ecology, and society, sustainable AI holds the promise of harnessing computational power responsibly. It can mitigate climate challenges, promote social equity, and enrich economies without depleting the resources on which future generations depend. The vision for a sustainable AI future is within reach, provided that researchers, policymakers, industry leaders, and communities collaboratively steer this transformative technology in a direction that respects and preserves our shared planet.

REFERENCES

Bender, E. M., Gebru, T., McMillan-Major, A., & Mitchell, S. (2021). On the dangers of stochastic parrots: Can language models be too big? In *Proceedings of the 2021 ACM Conference on Fairness, Accountability, and Transparency (FAccT '21)* (pp. 610–623). ACM. DOI: 10.1145/3442188.3445922

Bossert, L. N., & Hagendorff, T. (2023). The ethics of sustainable AI: Why animals (should) matter for a sustainable use of AI. *Sustainable Development (Bradford)*, *31*(5), 3459–3467. DOI: 10.1002/sd.2596

Brevini, B. (2021). *Is AI good for the planet?* Polity Press.

Cowls, J., Tsamados, A., Taddeo, M., & Floridi, L. (2021). A definition, benchmark and database of AI for social good initiatives. *Nature Machine Intelligence*, *3*(2), 111–115. DOI: 10.1038/s42256-021-00296-0

Cowls, J., Tsamados, A., Taddeo, M., & Floridi, L. (2023). The AI gambit: Leveraging artificial intelligence to combat climate change—Opportunities, challenges, and recommendations. *AI & Society*, *38*(1), 283–307. DOI: 10.1007/s00146-021-01294-x

Crawford, K. (2021). *Atlas of AI: Power, politics, and the planetary costs of artificial intelligence*. Yale University Press.

Cugurullo, F. (2021). *Frankenstein Urbanism: Eco, smart and autonomous cities, artificial intelligence and the end of the city*. Routledge. DOI: 10.4324/9781315652627

Dauvergne, P. (2020). *AI in the Wild: Sustainability in the age of artificial intelligence*. MIT Press. DOI: 10.7551/mitpress/12350.001.0001

Dhiman, R., Miteff, S., Wang, Y., Ma, S.-C., Amirikas, R., & Fabian, B. (2024). Artificial intelligence and sustainability—A review. *Analytics*, *3*(1), 140–164. DOI: 10.3390/analytics3010008

Goel, A., Raut, G., Sharma, A., & Taneja, U. (2024). Artificial intelligence and sustainable business: A review and future research directions. *South Asian Journal of Business and Management Cases*, *13*(3), 340–365. DOI: 10.1177/22779779241302146

Gupta, A., Ott, M., Melnikov, A., Candido, S., Brooks, D., Chauhan, G., & Hazelwood, K. (2022). Sustainable AI: Environmental implications, challenges and opportunities. In *Proceedings of the 5th MLSys Conference (MLSys 2022)*. (Preprint available on arXiv)

Halsband, A. (2022). Sustainable AI and intergenerational justice. *Sustainability (Basel)*, *14*(7), 3922. DOI: 10.3390/su14073922

Henderson, P., Hu, J., Romoff, J., Brunskill, E., Jurafsky, D., & Pineau, J. (2020). Towards the systematic reporting of the energy and carbon footprints of machine learning. *Journal of Machine Learning Research*, *21*, 1–43.

Himeur, Y., Ghanem, K., Alsalemi, A., Bensaali, F., & Amira, A. (2021). Artificial intelligence based anomaly detection of energy consumption in buildings: A review, current trends and new perspectives. *Applied Energy*, *287*, 116601. DOI: 10.1016/j.apenergy.2021.116601

Kaack, L. H., Donti, P. L., Strubell, E., Dai, A. M., & Kolter, J. Z. (2022). Aligning artificial intelligence with climate change mitigation. *Nature Climate Change*, *12*(6), 518–524. DOI: 10.1038/s41558-022-01377-7

Lannelongue, L., Grealey, J., & Inouye, M. (2021). Green algorithms: Quantifying the carbon footprint of computation. *Nature Computational Science*, *1*(3), 172–180. DOI: 10.1038/s43588-021-00056-9

Mazzi, F., & Floridi, L. (Eds.). (2023). *The ethics of artificial intelligence for the Sustainable Development Goals*. Springer. DOI: 10.1007/978-3-031-21147-8

Năstasă, A., & Dumitra, T.-C. (2024). Artificial intelligence and sustainable development during the pandemic: An overview of the scientific debates. *Heliyon*, *10*(1), e030412. DOI: 10.1016/j.heliyon.2023.e030412

Nishant, R., Kennedy, M., & Corbett, J. (2020). Artificial intelligence for sustainability: Challenges, opportunities, and a research agenda. *International Journal of Information Management*, *53*, 102104. DOI: 10.1016/j.ijinfomgt.2020.102104

Patterson, D., Gonzalez, J., Hölzle, U., Le, Q., Liang, C., Munguia, L.-M., . . . Dean, J. (2022). The carbon footprint of machine learning training will plateau, then shrink. *arXiv Preprint arXiv:2204.05149*. https://doi.org//arXiv.2204.05149DOI: 10.48550

Rolnick, D., Donti, P. L., Kaack, L. H., Kochanski, K., Lacoste, A., Sankaran, K., Ross, A. S., Milojevic-Dupont, N., Jaques, N., Waldman-Brown, A., Luccioni, A. S., Maharaj, T., Sherwin, E. D., Mukkavilli, S. K., Kording, K. P., Gomes, C. P., Ng, A. Y., Hassabis, D., Platt, J. C., & Bengio, Y. (2022). Tackling climate change with machine learning. *ACM Computing Surveys*, *55*(2), 42. Advance online publication. DOI: 10.1145/3485128

Schwartz, R., Dodge, J., Smith, N. A., & Etzioni, O. (2020). Green AI. *Communications of the ACM*, *63*(12), 54–63. DOI: 10.1145/3381831

Schoormann, T., Strobel, G., Möller, F., Petrik, D., & Zschech, P. (2023). Artificial intelligence for sustainability: A systematic review of information systems literature. *Communications of the Association for Information Systems*, *52*(1), 199–237. DOI: 10.17705/1CAIS.05209

Schütze, P. (2024). The problem of sustainable AI: A critical assessment of an emerging phenomenon. *Weizenbaum Journal of the Digital Society*, *4*(1), 1–21.

Strubell, E., Ganesh, A., & McCallum, A. (2020). Energy and policy considerations for deep learning in NLP. In *Proceedings of the 58th Annual Meeting of the Association for Computational Linguistics (ACL)* (pp. 3645–3650). ACL. DOI: 10.18653/v1/2020.acl-main.345

van Wynsberghe, A. (2021). Sustainable AI: AI for sustainability and the sustainability of AI. *AI and Ethics*, *1*(3), 213–218. DOI: 10.1007/s43681-021-00043-6 van Wynsberghe, A., Vandemeulebroucke, T., Bolte, L., & Nachid, J. (2022). Towards the sustainability of AI: Multi-disciplinary approaches to investigate the hidden costs of AI [Editorial]. *Sustainability (Basel), 14*(24), 16352. DOI: 10.3390/su142416352

Verdecchia, R., Sallou, J., & Cruz, L. (2023). A systematic review of Green AI. *Wiley Interdisciplinary Reviews. Data Mining and Knowledge Discovery, 13*(1), e1507. DOI: 10.1002/widm.1507

Vinuesa, R., Azizpour, H., Leite, I., Balaam, M., Dignum, V., Domisch, S., & Nerini, F. F. (2020). The role of artificial intelligence in achieving the Sustainable Development Goals. *Nature Communications, 11*(1), 233. DOI: 10.1038/s41467-019-14108-y

Wilson, C., & van der Velden, M. (2022). Sustainable AI: An integrated model to guide public sector decision-making. *Technology in Society, 68*, 101926. DOI: 10.1016/j.techsoc.2022.101926

Chapter 7
The Green Finance:
AI's Contribution to Environmental Sustainability

Chedlia Farhat
https://orcid.org/0009-0002-2451-3858
Faculty of Economic Sciences and Management of Tunis, Tunisia

Mouna Mouelhi
Faculty of Economic Sciences and Management of Tunis, Tunisia

ABSTRACT

This study examines the interplay between artificial intelligence, sustainable finance, and environmental sustainability in four OECD countries from 2007 to 2023. Using the panel ARDL method, our analysis shows that AI reduces carbon emissions, particularly in the long run. Initially, AI investments lead to a temporary rise in emissions due to implementation costs, but this trend reverses over time, aiding carbon neutrality and supporting SDGs, especially SDG 7 and SDG 13. The findings stress the need for short-term fiscal incentives and long-term regulatory frameworks integrating AI into sustainable finance. This research enriches the literature by addressing AI's overlooked role in sustainability and providing policy insights. Future studies could expand the geographic scope and examine AI's specific contributions to sustainable finance.

DOI: 10.4018/979-8-3373-1077-0.ch007

INTRODUCTION

Artificial Intelligence (AI) is emerging as a driving force in advancing urban sustainable development. By simulating human behavior and cognitive processes, AI can provide decision-making recommendations based on specific human instructions and prompts (Babina et al., 2023). In addition, AI has the potential to enhance production technology, optimize layouts of industrial structures, and improve energy efficiency; ultimately, this leads to urban sustainable development.

Finance and technology are increasingly recognized as key components in the global effort to reduce greenhouse gas emissions by 40% by 2030. The escalating impacts of climate change pose a serious threat to global security. Rising sea levels and extreme weather conditions are alarming consequences of environmental degradation. This underscores the urgent need to take robust measures to protect the environment. Environmental protection includes all activities and actions that aim at preventing, reducing, and eliminating environmental degradation.

In addressing these environmental challenges, AI offers numerous opportunities. It plays a key role in transforming financial systems to promote environmental sustainability. In this vein, the concept of green finance has been hailed as an indispensable tool in the fight against global warming. Financial institutions, alongside international organizations and data providers, have a responsibility to align the financial sector with ambitious and timely climate objectives. The shift towards green and environmentally-friendly finance represents a proactive response by the financial markets to the climate crisis.

Previous research on green finance has focused on aspects such as the pricing of green bonds (Hachenberg & Schiereck, 2018), the practical aspect for the issuer (Gianfrate & Peri, 2019), the importance of the green bond premium and the market reaction to the issuance of green bonds (Tang & Zhang, 2020; Flammer, 2021). However, relatively few studies have investigated the role of green bonds in reducing the carbon footprint of non-financial companies (Fatica & Panzica, 2021; Flammer, 2021).

In the broader context of the zealous fight against global warming, the financial sector's role is crucial. In this regard, Article 21c of the Paris

Agreements highlights that realigning the financial sector with climate objectives requires not only the mobilization of financial institutions, but also the rigorous efforts of international organizations and data providers. Expanding ecological finance is essential both for funding the ecological transition and for addressing ethical considerations, as well as for mitigating risks associated with a potential 'climate bubble' and stranded assets i.e., which are vulnerable to devaluation due to environmental liabilities.

In this vein, questions about the profitability of more ecological assets seem justified. For example, research by Koundouri, Pittis and Plataniotis (2021) evaluated company performance based on the adoption of Environmental, Social, and Governance (ESG) criteria. Their results seem to be conclusive. They suggested that companies with strong ESG performance not only face lower risks but also enjoy higher profit margins and returns on equity. This conclusion is reinforced by additional studies (Berg et al., 2019; Busch et al., 2011), which indicate a positive correlation between environmental performance and financial performance.

Green finance is inextricably linked to multiple Sustainable Development Goals (SDGs). These goals can be achieved, in part, through active engagement of the private sector in green investments. Purcel (2020) contends that achieving the objectives set forth by the Paris Agreement and the SDGs can only be realized by promoting green financing and fostering technological innovations. However, Nabavi-Pelesaraei et al. (2022a, 2022b) advocate for an environmental life cycle assessment approach to bolster the SDGs, providing insights into more sustainable practices for biodiesel production and medical waste management.

The shortcomings of previous research open a new avenue for investigating the interplay between these critical elements. Accordingly, this study addresses the following research questions:

H1: Does AI play a crucial role in sustainable finance by reducing the carbon footprint?
H2: Does AI contribute to achieving SDG objectives by optimizing sustainable investment management?

The paper is structured into three sections. Section 1 reviews the existing literature, while Section 2 outlines the empirical methodology. Section 3 reports and analyzes the empirical results. The final section presents the main conclusions along with policy implications.

1. LITERATURE REVIEW

1.1 AI, Green Finance and Environment

The integration of AI and sustainable investments is emerging as a pivotal strategy for ensuring a prosperous future for both humanity and the natural environment. Al Mamun et al. (2022) conducted an investigation across 46 countries and their results demonstrated that green bonds exert a significant impact on reducing carbon emissions over both short and long time horizons. This particular finding can perhaps be attributed to green bonds' inherent environmental commitments, which make it challenging for conventional financial instruments to adequately support waste management, pollution abatement, and improvements in energy efficiency. AI offers substantial promise in addressing these societal challenges, particularly in the realm of sustainability. With the dual pressures of climate change and environmental degradation, innovative and advanced technological solutions are required; AI serves as a crucial tool not only in reducing pollution and poverty but also for curbing resource depletion and enhancing environmental and social governance (Chayjan et al., 2020; Alonso & Marqués, 2019). Machine learning algorithms are adept at detecting complex patterns, thereby enabling investors to extract business insights that align closely with their sustainability objectives.

Existing research has mainly focused on the role of green finance in driving technological progress (Zhang et al., 2022), with comparably little attention to its impact on and interplay with AI (Chen et al., 2024). Numerous surveys have consistently highlighted the positive influence of green finance on technological progress and promotion. For example, Xu et al. (2023) used China's green finance pilot policies to illustrate how green finance can foster technology exchange and collaboration among businesses. Moreover, the observed strong correlation between environmental performance and growing global climate concerns has spurred the increased adoption of green finance. Studies by Khan et al. (2022) and Murshed et al. (2022) report a diminished influence of renewable energy on the ecological footprint, while Sharif et al. (2022) document that green financing not only reduces emissions but also promotes broader environmental sustainability and sustainable development. Zhang et al. (2022) used quarterly data from 1998 to 2020. They demonstrated that the impact of green finance on carbon emissions efficiency exhibits a double threshold effect; one that is dependent on the level of regional economic development. Furthermore, regional innovation appears to serve as a vital conduit through which green finance enhances carbon emission efficiency (Wu et al., 2024).

1.2. Literature Review: Relationship between AI, sustainable finance, and SDGs

AI has increasingly become an essential tool in advancing sustainable finance and fostering ecological transitions. Its growing influence on financial decision-making and resource allocation plays a central role in optimizing investments that are aligned with the SDGs. Drawing on the related literature, this review examines the interaction between AI and sustainable finance, with a particular focus on its role in achieving the SDGs.

1.2.1. Relationship Between AI, sustainable Finance and SDG Goals

This literature review examines the complex and interplay between AI, green finance, and the SDGs, with a particular focus on the structural transition from fossil fuel consumption to renewable energy. The integration of new technologies, such as AI, alongside sustainable financial policies aimed at decarbonization, has become a key theme in recent research due to their efficiency and effectiveness in promoting sustainability.

Recent studies underscore the potential of AI and sustainable finance to support the SDGs during periods of crisis. Chishti et al. (2024) employed a CAViaR-TVP-VAR model to demonstrate that AI can stabilize economic cycles in both the short and long term, thereby enhancing sustainability outcomes. Complementary research by Zhou et al. (2024) and Ahmad and Zheng (2023) confirm the role of AI in ensuring economic sustainability. Furthermore, Chishti et al. (2024) emphasize that green finance is instrumental in mitigating long-term economic fluctuations, directly contributing to achieving SDG 13 and SDG 7. Such sustainable financial policy facilitates the transition toward a low-carbon economy aligned with the SDGs. Additionally, green technological innovations further augment AI' sability to lower carbon emissions and ensure sustainability (Zhou et al., 2024). AI's role extends beyond emission reductions; it also improves access to financing, thereby facilitating sustainable development (Xu et al., 2023).

Raihan (2024) emphasizes AI's transformative potential in optimizing financial technologies and its contributions to the SDGs. His findings suggest that AI not only enhances financial inclusion and reduces poverty but also stimulates economic growth by revolutionizing financial services through advanced applications such as natural language processing and computer vision. Despite these promising developments, challenges such as algorithmic bias and the digital divide must be addressed to ensure that AI is deployed ethically and equitably. Musleh Al-Sartawi et al. (2022) further stress AI's transformative role in sustainable finance, noting that the convergence of advanced data analytics and sustainability principles can tackle global challenges while opening new avenues for responsible investments. However, it remains imperative to intensify efforts to promote the ethical and transparent use of AI in this context.

The International Monetary Fund (IMF) has recognized AI as a key driver for increasing global growth rates, wage levels, and output per capita (Pavot, D., 2021). In addition, Chui and Francisco (2017) project that by 2030, AI could generate an additional $13 trillion to global economic activity. These perspectives imply that AI has the potential to substantially stimulate international economic development by enhancing economic models based on sustainable finance. Supporting this view, Chang et al. (2023) employed a static panel model to link AI to total factor productivity in green sectors, thereby assessing AI's impact on green economic development. They further provided a bidirectional analysis of AI's influence on the natural resource market in China, revealing that AI's effect on carbon intensity varies across different sectors and phases of development.

Zhao et al. (2024) corroborate these findings by demonstrating that AI is pivotal for renewable energy development, particularly in less-developed countries, thereby bolstering several SDGs, including SDG 7, SDG 9, and SDG 13. Finally, climate finance mechanisms further amplify the positive impacts of AI, underscoring the necessity of integrated policy approaches to maximize the benefits of AI and climate finance in the energy transition and the achievement of the SDGs.

1.2.2. The Impact of Artificial Intelligence on Sustainable Finance

AI serves as a transformative catalyst for sustainablefinancial innovation, contributing to betterresource allocation and effective ESG riskassessment. Mele et al. (2022) provided evidence that AI stimulateseconomicgrowth-whileimprovingenvironmentalquality. In a similar vein, Magazzino et al. (2021) indicatethat AI enhancesenvironmentalefficiency by optimizingenergyconsumption and reducingcarbonemissions.Moreover, AI's capacity to automate the collection and analysis of ESG data equips investors with critical insights that facilitate the integration of ESG criteria into their decision-making processes. Solarin et al. (2022) further affirm that AI significantly boosts renewable energy production in emerging economies, particularly within the BRICS nations, where sustainable energy solutions are urgently needed. Complementarily, Sharma et al. (2021) show that AI enhances asset management for renewable energy investments.

1.2.3. The Role of AI in Achieving SDG

AI plays a central role in achieving SDGs by streamlining the energy transition, promoting financial inclusion, and optimizing sustainable investments. According to Zhao et al. (2024), AI contributes to the expansion of renewable energy and the reduction of carbon emissions, reinforcing SDG 7 and SDG 13. Moreover, Raihan (2024) highlights that AI promotesfinancial inclusion, reducing poverty and supporting SDG 1.Xu et al. (2023) alsoassertthat AI facilitates access to financing for sustainable projects; thereby, stimulating SDG 9. By combining predictive algorithms and big data analysis, AI improves risk management in sustainable investments (Musleh Al-Sartawi et al., 2022). Finally, Chang et al. (2023) demonstrate that AI not only enhances energy efficiency but also fosters environmentally friendly economic growth, enabling simultaneous advancement across multiple SDGs.

2. METHODOLOGY AND DATA

The methodology adopted for the treatment of our problem is the Autoregressive Distributed lag (ARDL) model developed by Pesaran and Shin (1999), then extended by Pesaran et al. (2001). On the one hand, this test can be used in the case of non-stationary time series without the constraint of the same order of integration, contrary to other tests. On the other hand, this model allows to treat simultaneously the short-term effect and the long term dynamics and can be categorized as an error correction model.

Considering the dependent variable " " and the independent variable " ", we note:

- Autoregressive (AR) models: these are dynamic models where among the explanatory variables (), the lagged dependent variable (its past values) is found. In general, they are as follows (implicit form):

Yt = (, Yt-p) ... (1a)

- The term "autoregressive" reflects the regression of a variable on itself, i.e., on its own lagged values.

Models with staggered or distributed lag (DL): these are dynamic models whose explanatory variables are Xt and its past or lagged values. In general, their form is:

Yt = (, Xt-q) ... (1b)

The term "staggered lags" shows that the short-term effects of Xt on Yt are different from the long-term effects. From one time point to another, the scales of response of Yt to the change in Xt differ.

Autoregressive lagged models (ARDL): these models combine the features of two previous ones; they include, among the explanatory variables (Xt), the lagged dependent variable (Yt-) and the past values of the independent variable ($Xt\text{-}q$). They have the following general form:

$$Yt = (, Yt\text{-}p, Xt\text{-}q) \ldots (1c)$$

These dynamic models generally suffer from problems of error autocorrelation, with the presence of the lagged endogenous variable as an explanatory variable (AR and ARDL models), and of multi-linearity (DL and ARDL models), which complicates the estimation of the parameters by Ordinary Least Squares/OLS. Here, it is important to use robust estimation techniques (SUR method, etc.) to overcome these problems. Also, it should be noted that the variables considered in these models must be stationary to avoid spurious regressions. In its general (explicit) form, an ARDL model is written as follows: (Kuma, 2018)

$$Yt = \varphi + a1Yt\text{-}1 + apYt\text{-}p + b0Xt + \ldots + bqXq\text{-}t + \varepsilon t \ldots (1d) \text{ or}$$

$$Yt = \varphi + \sum p\, aiYt\text{-}\imath + \sum q\, bjXj\text{-}t + \varepsilon t$$

With $\varepsilon t \sim (0, \sigma)$: error term; "$b0$ " reflects the short-run effect of Xt on YtIf we consider the following long-run or equilibrium relationship "$Yt = k + \varnothing Xt + u$ ", the long-run effect of on (i.e., "$\varnothing$") can be calculated as follows:

$$\varnothing = \sum bj/(1 - \sum ai)$$

As with any dynamic model, the information criteria (AIC, SIC and HQ) will be used to determine the optimal lag (p* or q*); an optimal lag is the one whose model the estimated model offers the minimum value of one of the stated criteria: Akaike's (AIC), Schwarz's (SIC) and Hannover's (HQ)

(SIC) and Hannan and Quinn (HQ). Their values are calculated as follows:

$(p) = log| \sum| +2\ n2p\ T$

$(p) = log| \sum|+\ LogT\ n2p\ T$

$HQ(p) = log| \sum|+\ 2LogT\ n2p\ T$

With: $\sum$ = variance-covariance matrix of estimated residuals; T = number of observations; p = lag of the estimated model; and n = number of regressors.

All these dynamic models can help capture the short-term dynamics and long-term effects of one or more explanatory variables on a variable to be explained. This will only be possible if the time series under study are cointegrated, thus allowing the estimation of an error correction model/ MCE. In fact, two series are said to be "cointegrated

In fact, two series are said to be "cointegrated" if they are integrated of the same order; and a series will be said to be "integrated of order d" if it has to be differentiated "d" times to make it stationary. A stationary series is stationary in mean and variance if its mean (() =) remains invariant or constant over time and its variance does not increase over time (*Var* (*Yt*) = σ), and likewise for its covariances ($E\ (Yt\ -\ c)(Yt\text{-}p\ -\ c) = \gamma p$).

To test the stationarity of a time series (absence of unit root), several tests are available in most software: Augmented Dickey-Fuller/ADF test, Phillippe-Perron/PP test, Andrews and Zivot/AZ test, Ng-Perron, Kwiatkowski, Phillips, Schmidt, and Shin/KPSS test, Ouliaris-Park-Perron, Eliott-Rothenberg-Stock, etc. The first three tests are easy to apply and are commonly used. It is noteworthy to mention that the ADF test is effective in the presence of autocorrelation of errors, the PP test is recommended in the presence of heteroscedastic errors, the AZ test is suitable for series that are victims of a change of regime (break in trend) identified endogenously, and the KPSS test decomposes a series into three components (deterministic part, random part, white noise) with the null hypothesis of stationarity. The ARDL model, being part of the family of dynamic models, can be used to estimate short-term dynamics and long-term effects for cointegrated or even integrated series of different orders, as it will be seen with the bounds test approach of Pesaran et al. (1996), Pesaran and Shin (1995), and Pesaran et al. (2001). However, the way how to apply an ARDL model for integrated series at orders that exceed 1 is not figured out yet.

This paper follows the methodology of recent studies on the "economic growth - environmental pollution" nexus (Ang, 2007; Soytas et al, 2007; Ang, 2008) by also including green investment and high technology as explanatory variables. In order to test the long-run relationship, also called cointegration, between CO2 emissions, green investment and high technology, the following linear logarithmic form is proposed:

$$\text{Carbon emission}_{it} = \beta_0 + \beta_1 (\text{GDP per capita})_{it} + \beta_2 (\text{invenergy})_{it} + \beta_3 ht_{it} + U_{it} \ldots. \quad (1)$$

Where Carbon emission is measured by carbon dioxide (CO_2) emissions (total), excluding LULUCF (% change from 1990), and represents the dependent variable. GDP per capita denotes the level of economic growth, ht (High Technology) is used as a proxy for artificial intelligence, and invenergy, which stands for investment in energy, serves as an indicator of sustainable finance. These three explanatory variables are considered control variables in the model.

- i refers to the countries in the panel (1 to 4),
- t denotes the time period (2007–2023),
- β represents the coefficients for the lagged and contemporaneous variables,
- and u is the error term.

The data on carbon emissions, sustainable finance, GDP per capita, and artificial intelligence are obtained from the World Development Indicators (WDI) database.

3. RESULTS AND DISCUSSION

3.1 Estimation Results

The estimation approach of our research is based on a panel ARDL model to evaluate the impact of artificial intelligence (AI) on sustainable finance and environmental sustainability. Before applying the model estimation, we first conduct an analysis of descriptive statistics, followed by a cross-sectional dependence test, and finally a second-generation stationarity test of the variables.

Table 1. Descriptive statistics

Variable	Obs	Mean	Std. Dev.	Min	Max
CO2	68	1.9476	0.286	1.1167	2.2942
GDPPC	68	4.2604	0.1377	3.996	4.6255
INVENERGY	68	8.6948	0.7418	7.1658	10.1333
HT	68	9.5909	0.7596	8.5567	10.96

The results of the descriptive statistics presented in Table I highlight a moderate variability in CO_2 emissions, indicating a homogeneous trend among the countries. However, energy investment and artificial intelligence (HT) show greater dispersion, reflecting substantial differences in commitment to the energy transition and green digitalization. Finally, GDP per capita exhibits low dispersion, indicating economic stability within the sample.

Table 2. Cross-Sectional Dependence (CD): Test Pesaran (2004)

Variable	CD-test	p-value	corr	abs(corr)
Residus	-1.34	0.182	-0.132	0.287

The validity of the model under study may be affected by the presence of cross-sectional dependence, which violates the assumption of independence among observations. The results presented in Table II reject the null hypothesis of no cross-sectional dependence among the countries in the panel. This confirms that economic or environmental shocks do not appear to spread directly from one country to another, thereby justifying a country-by-country modeling approach.

Table 3. Second-Generation Stationarity Test (CIPS)

Variable	CIPS Statistic	10% Critical Value	5% Critical Value	1% Critical Value	Stationarity
CO2	-1.32	-2.21	-2.34	-2.6	I(1)
D.CO2	-3.944	-2.21	-2.34	-2.6	I(0)
GDPPC	-1.789	-2.21	-2.34	-2.6	I(1)
D.GDPPC	-3.615	-2.21	-2.34	-2.6	I(0)
INVENERGY	-2.304	-2.21	-2.34	-2.6	I(1)
D.INVENERGY	-3.973	-2.21	-2.34	-2.6	I(0)
HT	-2.107	-2.21	-2.34	-2.6	I(1)
D.HT	-3.611	-2.21	-2.34	-2.6	I(0)

In order to account for the integrating properties of the variables and cross-sectional dependence, we use a second-generation stationarity test, the CIPS (Cross-sectionally Augmented IPS test). The CIPS test results are presented in Table 3. These results indicate that all variables are integrated of order one, meaning they are non-stationary at level but become stationary after first differencing. This validates the use of the ARDL estimation approach, which is particularly suitable for series integrated of mixed orders (I(0) and I(1)).

The results of the panel ARDL estimation of our model are presented in Tables 4 and 5, showing respectively the long-term and short-term effects.

Table 4. Long-run ARDL estimates

Variables	MG Coef.	MG Std. Err.	MG P>lzl	PMG Coef.	PMG Std. Err.	PMG P>lzl	DFE Coef.	DFE Std. Err.	DFE P>lzl
gdppc	1.456 ***	0.469	0.002	1.408 ***	0.389	0.001	1.362 ***	0.347	0.0
invenergy	-0.083 ***	0.021	0.0	-0.071 ***	0.019	0.0	-0.065 ***	0.016	0.0
ht	-0.512 ***	0.182	0.005	-0.476 ***	0.159	0.003	-0.438 ***	0.141	0.002

(***, **, * significant at 1%, 5%, 10%)

Table 4 presents the long-term effects of the variables GDP per capita, invenergy, and ht on carbon emissions, as specified in our model to assess the influence of AI on CO_2 emissions through the sustainable finance channel. These estimations were carried out using three distinct estimators: MG, PMG, and DFE. The Mean Group (MG) method estimates the coefficients separately for each country and takes the average of these coefficients. In contrast, the Pooled Mean Group (PMG) method accounts for individual specificities while constraining certain coefficients to be identical. As for the Dynamic Fixed Effects (DFE) method, it is a dynamic panel technique that considers both individual fixed effects and time fixed effects.

This long-term analysis highlights strong structural relationships between the variables. The results show that GDP per capita has a positive and significant impact on CO_2 emissions (MG = 1.456***; PMG = 1.408***; DFE = 1.362***), supporting the classical effect of rapid economic growth, often observed in emerging countries. This finding is consistent with the Environmental Kuznets Curve hypothesis, which suggests that pollution tends to increase as countries develop economically.

On the other hand, sustainable finance—measured by investment in renewable energy (INVENERGY)—shows a significant and negative effect on carbon emissions (MG = -0.083***; PMG = -0.071***; DFE = -0.065***). This result empirically validates hypothesis H1 and confirms that the mobilization of green finance can play a decisive role in the energy transition by reducing emissions while promoting energy efficiency. This finding aligns with the conclusions of Al Mamun et al. (2022) and Murshed et al. (2022), who also highlighted the mitigating effect of green investments on environmental degradation. The empirical outcomes emphasize that this mitigating effect of sustainable finance is further strengthened by the indirect contribution of artificial intelligence.

Regarding the HT variable, representing the indicator of artificial intelligence, it has a negative and significant impact on CO_2 emissions (MG = -0.512***; PMG = -0.476***; DFE = -0.438***). This result is crucial, as it demonstrates that AI constitutes a strategic lever for sustainable finance and is not limited to being a mere technological tool. This lever of sustainable investment facilitates the optimization of green and sustainable portfolios as well as the assessment of ESG risks. Consequently, AI enables the identification of low-carbon footprint investments and directly contributes to the achievement of the Sustainable Development Goals (SDGs), particularly SDG 13 and SDG 9.

Finally, the empirical findings revealed a significant negative impact of GDP per capita and AI on carbon emissions, indicating that sustainable finance mitigates environmental degradation through the integration of new technologies as decision-support tools in sustainable investments. Consequently, OECD economies should promote the use of artificial intelligence in the assessment of green and sustainable investments and encourage research and innovation in this field to enhance the effectiveness and efficiency of AI. This could involve the development of new financial technologies and the design of innovative green and sustainable financial products. Furthermore, governments should aim to balance economic growth with environmental protection by adopting AI as a strategic decision-making tool for evaluating sustainable investments, thereby supporting both economic and environmental sustainability.

Table 5. Short-run ARDL estimates

Variables	MG Coef.	MG Std. Err.	MG P>|z|	PMG Coef.	PMG Std. Err.	PMG P>|z|	DFE Coef.	DFE Std. Err.	DFE P>|z|
ec	-0.512 ***	0.081	0.0	-0.438 ***	0.077	0.0	-0.389 ***	0.072	0.0
gdppc	0.722 **	0.296	0.014	0.612 **	0.268	0.022	0.578 **	0.253	0.02
invenergy	-0.021 **	0.009	0.023	-0.019 **	0.007	0.016	-0.017 **	0.006	0.012
ht	0.109 ***	0.044	0.008	0.093 **	0.041	0.011	0.086 ***	0.038	0.009
_cons	0.214	0.147	0.145	-0.071 ***	0.024	0.003	0.002	0.007	0.775

(***, **, * significant at 1%, 5%, 10%)

Regarding short-term effects, economic growth (GDP per capita) is positively associated with emissions (MG = 0.722**; PMG = 0.612**; DFE = 0.578**), highlighting that the impacts of economic expansion are immediate and require swift compensatory policies. In contrast, the results show that sustainable finance maintains its negative and significant effect (MG = -0.021**; PMG = -0.019**; DFE = -0.017**), emphasizing the prompt effectiveness of green finance policies in mitigating emissions, even within a limited time frame.

Moreover, the results reveal a contradictory short-term behavior of AI, showing a positive but moderate effect on carbon emissions (MG = 0.109***; PMG = 0.093**; DFE = 0.086***). This trend may be explained by the initial costs of technological integration, the increased energy consumption of digital infrastructures, and, above all, the still imperfect adoption of green technologies. However, the benefits become evident in the long term, which calls for supportive policies and incentives to promote the adoption of environmentally responsible AI.

These empirical findings confirm that artificial intelligence can be a driving force in transforming sustainable finance. By combining technological innovations with sustainable investments, the four OECD countries have a powerful lever to reconcile economic growth with decarbonization. Our ARDL model proved particularly relevant in capturing the differentiated dynamics between the short and long term, thereby enhancing the credibility and robustness of our empirical findings. The results support the idea that public strategies such as promoting green AI, incentivizing sustainable investment, and strengthening digital infrastructure are essential to achieving carbon neutrality goals by 2030 and 2050.

3.2 Discussion

To evaluate the efficiency and consistency of the estimators, we employed the Hausman test, which assesses the null hypothesis that the MG, PMG, and DFE estimators fulfill the criteria of both efficiency and consistency. The empirical results derived from our panel ARDL model reveal complex and statistically significant interactions between artificial intelligence (AI), sustainable finance, and environmental sustainability across four OECD countries over the period 2007–2023.

In the short term, the findings indicate a significant positive association between economic growth and CO_2 emissions, suggesting that a surge in economic activity is immediately accompanied by a rise in environmental degradation. This observation aligns with the empirical evidence provided by Alonso and Marqués (2019) and Khan et al. (2022). Conversely, investment in renewable energy used here as a proxy for sustainable finance exhibits immediate and statistically significant effectiveness in reducing carbon emissions. This underscores the financial viability of employing innovative technologies in assessing the sustainability of investment decisions. These insights are corroborated by the work of Md Al Mamun et al. (2022), which emphasizes the short-term impact of green bonds in mitigating pollutant emissions.

Interestingly, the short-term effect of AI on emissions appears slightly positive (MG = 0.109***; PMG = 0.093**; DFE = 0.086***), potentially reflecting the initial phase of technological integration, increased energy consumption of digital infrastructure, and the learning curve associated with adopting green technologies. However, this initial cost is counterbalanced by the longer-term ecological gains of AI, as noted by Garcia et al. (2021) and Raihan (2024).

This short-term dynamic implies several essential strategic and policy recommendations. First, it is necessary to strengthen immediate financial incentives to encourage companies to accelerate the adoption of AI technologies specifically dedicated to energy efficiency and sustainable finance. Moreover, public policies should include compensatory mechanisms to support the significant initial investment in AI, thereby facilitating a faster transition toward a sustainable economic model. In this context, the integration of clean technologies can be considered a catalytic mechanism that promotes decarbonization, including in energy-intensive sectors. Thus, the adoption of artificial intelligence within a clean ecological system enhances the environmental profitability of investments. Therefore, it would be wise to create dedicated funds for green technological innovation, facilitating a faster adoption of AI in key sectors of OECD countries.

This short-term dynamic gives rise to several key strategic and policy recommendations. First and foremost, it is crucial to strengthen immediate financial incentives that encourage businesses to adopt artificial intelligence (AI) technologies tailored to improving energy efficiency and advancing sustainable finance. Additionally, public authorities should implement supportive mechanisms to ease the high initial costs associated with AI deployment, thereby accelerating the shift toward a greener and more resilient economic model.

In this context, the integration of clean technologies can serve as a catalyst for decarbonization, especially in sectors with high energy intensity. The deployment of AI within environmentally conscious systems enhances the ecological return on investment by promoting more efficient resource allocation and sustainable practices. Consequently, it is advisable to establish dedicated funding mechanisms that support green technological innovation, facilitating the broader and more rapid adoption of AI in key strategic sectors across OECD economies. In the long run, the ARDL estimation results reveal a clear reversal of the short-term trend. Artificial intelligence (AI) exhibits a strongly significant effect in reducing CO_2 emissions. More specifically, the tangible environmental benefits of AI become evident over an extended time horizon, as a result of improved industrial process optimization and more efficient resource management. These empirical findings provide robust validation of Hypothesis H1, which posits that AI plays a crucial role in sustainable finance by contributing to the reduction of the carbon footprint. This outcome is consistent with the findings of Chishti et al. (2024) and Zhao et al. (2024), who demonstrate through advanced algorithms and continuous optimization processes that AI is capable of sustainably lowering pollutant emissions and enhancing energy efficiency.

Furthermore, sustainable finance continues to exert a highly significant long-term impact. Investment in sustainable energy retains its effectiveness over time, resulting in a durable reduction of emissions. These findings align with the conclusions of Wu et al. (2024), who emphasize the pivotal role of green finance in facilitating the transition toward a low-carbon economy.

With regard to achieving the Sustainable Development Goals (SDGs), artificial intelligence (AI) plays a pivotal role by optimizing the management of financial flows directed toward sustainable investments. By enabling more efficient resource allocation, AI maximizes the positive impact of green investments, thereby facilitating a more rapid and lasting reduction in CO_2 emissions. Our empirical findings clearly indicate that the combined use of sustainable finance and AI is essential for achieving long-term carbon neutrality. In this regard, the work of Sharif et al. (2022) strongly supports our conclusions, highlighting sustainable finance as a key instrument for meeting the climate targets established by the United Nations' SDGs, particularly SDG 7 (Affordable and Clean Energy) and SDG 13 (Climate Action).

AI reinforces this driving role of sustainable investment by channeling funds toward low-carbon projects and directly contributing to the achievement of both SDG 13 and SDG 9 (Industry, Innovation, and Infrastructure). This long-term dynamic also provides strong empirical support for our second hypothesis (H2), which emphasizes the role of AI in advancing the SDGs through the enhanced optimization of sustainable investment management.

These robust findings underscore the importance of pursuing ambitious long-term policy strategies. Policymakers are therefore encouraged to prioritize the development of strong regulatory frameworks that ensure the lasting benefits of AI and green finance. Promoting international technological cooperation, particularly among OECD member countries, could further accelerate the dissemination of best practices in AI and sustainable finance, thereby reducing the regional disparities observed in environmental impacts (Xu et al., 2023; Lee & Lee, 2022).

The empirical robustness of our model is reinforced by the rigorous statistical tests employed, including the second-generation unit root test (CIPS), cross-sectional dependence diagnostics, and ARDL estimations in both the short and long term. These modern econometric techniques ensure the reliability of our results and address methodological gaps identified in prior research (Musleh Al-Sartawi et al., 2022).

Furthermore, a comparison between the short- and long-term effects of artificial intelligence reveals a clear transition from an initially positive to a strongly negative impact on carbon emissions, highlighting the importance of adopting a long-term temporal perspective in the design of environmental policies. This conclusion also underscores the need for policymakers to implement forward-looking strategies, such as strengthening the regulatory framework surrounding AI applications in sustainable finance and increasing support for research and development in the technological sector.

Finally, this study makes a significant contribution to the growing body of literature by addressing a critical gap: the complex interaction between artificial intelligence, sustainable finance, and environmental sustainability within the context of emerging OECD economies. It provides robust empirical evidence and advances current understanding of the mechanisms through which AI can effectively catalyze a successful ecological transition. In doing so, it strengthens both the theoretical and methodological frameworks of the field. The findings of this research thus offer a sound scientific basis upon which policymakers can build to guide their short- and long-term strategies toward a more sustainable and technologically advanced economy.

CONCLUSION

This study set out to explore the impact of artificial intelligence (AI) on sustainable finance and environmental sustainability within a sample of four OECD countries over the period 2007–2023. By addressing gaps in the existing literature, our research validated the initial research question concerning the complex and relatively underexplored interactions between these three critical dimensions of sustainable development.

Our empirical findings, based on the ARDL model, confirm both of our proposed hypotheses. First, AI plays a crucial role in sustainable finance by significantly contributing to the reduction of the carbon footprint (H1). Second, AI actively supports the achievement of the Sustainable Development Goals (SDGs) notably SDG 7 and SDG 13 by enhancing the management and efficiency of green investments (H2). In the short term, the initially positive impact of AI on emissions can be attributed to the upfront costs associated with technological adoption and investment. However, over the long term, this effect reverses and becomes strongly negative, clearly demonstrating AI's potential to support a sustained reduction in environmental pollution.

Our research also demonstrated the robustness of the ARDL model employed, as evidenced by the highly significant error correction terms and the preliminary diagnostic tests conducted namely, second-generation stationarity tests and the absence of cross-sectional dependence. These results suggest that the proposed model provides a reliable analytical framework to guide both environmental and financial policymaking toward carbon neutrality.

From a practical perspective, this study recommends that policymakers implement short-term incentive measures to ease the burden of initial technological and clean energy investments, while simultaneously designing long-term strategies that fully integrate AI into sustainable finance policies. Despite its meaningful contribution to the literature, this study is not without limitations. Chief among them is the relatively small sample size and the restricted number of countries included in the analysis. Future research could expand the dataset to incorporate additional countries or regions and further investigate the specific mechanisms through which AI interacts with sustainable finance and climate objectives.

REFERENCES

Ahmad, M., & Zheng, J. (2023). The Cyclical and Nonlinear Impact of R&D and Innovation Activities on Economic Growth in OECD Economies: A New Perspective. *Journal of the Knowledge Economy*, *14*(1), 544–593. DOI: 10.1007/s13132-021-00887-7

Al Mamun, M., Boubaker, S., & Nguyen, D. K. (2022). Green finance and decarbonization: Evidence from around the world. *Finance Research Letters*, *46*, 102807. DOI: 10.1016/j.frl.2022.102807

Alonso, A., & Marqués, J. M. (2019). Financial innovation for a sustainable economy. *Banco de España Occasional Paper*, (1916).

Ang, J. B. (2007). CO2 emissions, energy consumption, and output in France. *Energy Policy*, *35*(10), 4772–4778. DOI: 10.1016/j.enpol.2007.03.032

Ang, J. B. (2008). A survey of recent developments in the literature of finance and growth. *Journal of Economic Surveys*, *22*(3), 536–576. DOI: 10.1111/j.1467-6419.2007.00542.x

Babina, T., Fedyk, A., He, A. X., & Hodson, J. (2023). Artificial Intelligence and Firms' Systematic Risk. *Available at SSRN* 4868770.

Berg, S., Kutra, D., Kroeger, T., Straehle, C. N., Kausler, B. X., Haubold, C., Schiegg, M., Ales, J., Beier, T., Rudy, M., Eren, K., Cervantes, J. I., Xu, B., Beuttenmueller, F., Wolny, A., Zhang, C., Koethe, U., Hamprecht, F. A., & Kreshuk, A. (2019). Ilastik: Interactive machine learning for (bio) image analysis. *Nature Methods*, *16*(12), 1226–1232. DOI: 10.1038/s41592-019-0582-9 PMID: 31570887

Busch, T., Christensen, B. J., & Nielsen, M. Ø. (2011). The role of implied volatility in forecasting future realized volatility and jumps in foreign exchange, stock, and bond markets. *Journal of Econometrics*, *160*(1), 48–57. DOI: 10.1016/j.jeconom.2010.03.014

Chang, L.. (2023). Rôle de l'intelligence artificielle dans le développement économique vert: Déterminants conjoints des ressources naturelles et de la productivité totale des facteurs verts. *Resources Policy*.

Chayjan, M. R., Bagheri, T., Kianian, A., & Someh, N. G. (2020). Using data mining for prediction of retail banking customer's churn behaviour. *International Journal of Electronic Banking*, *2*(4), 303–320. DOI: 10.1504/IJEBANK.2020.114770

Chishti, M. Z., Dogan, E., & Binsaeed, R. H. (2024). Can artificial intelligence and green finance affect economic cycles? *Technological Forecasting and Social Change*, *209*, 123740. DOI: 10.1016/j.techfore.2024.123740

Chui, M., & Francisco, S. (2017). Artificial intelligence: The next digital frontier. McKinsey and Company Global Institute, 47(3.6), 6–8.

Fatica, S., & Panzica, R. (2021). Green bonds as a tool against climate change? *Business Strategy and the Environment*, *30*(5), 2688–2701. DOI: 10.1002/bse.2771

Flammer, C. (2021). Corporate green bonds. *Journal of Financial Economics*, *142*(2), 499–516. DOI: 10.1016/j.jfineco.2021.01.010

Gianfrate, G., & Peri, M. (2019). The green advantage: Exploring the convenience of issuing green bonds. *Journal of Cleaner Production*, *219*, 127–135. DOI: 10.1016/j.jclepro.2019.02.022

Hachenberg, B., & Schiereck, D. (2018). Are green bonds priced differently from conventional bonds? *Journal of Asset Management*, *19*(6), 371–383. DOI: 10.1057/s41260-018-0088-5

Khan, K., Su, C. W., Rehman, A. U., & Ullah, R. (2022). Is technological innovation a driver of renewable energy? *Technology in Society*, *70*, 102044. DOI: 10.1016/j.techsoc.2022.102044

Magazzino, C., Alola, A. A., & Schneider, N. (2021). The trilemma of innovation, logistics performance, and environmental quality in 25 topmost logistics countries: A quantile regression evidence. *Journal of Cleaner Production*, *322*, 129050. DOI: 10.1016/j.jclepro.2021.129050 PMID: 36567950

Mele, M., Magazzino, C., Schneider, N., Gurrieri, A. R., & Golpira, H. (2022). Innovation, income, and waste disposal operations in Korea: Evidence from a spectral granger causality analysis and artificial neural networks experiments. *Economics and Politics*, *39*(2), 427–459.

Murshed, M., Apergis, N., Alam, M. S., Khan, U., & Mahmud, S. (2022). The impacts of renewable energy, financial inclusivity, globalization, economic growth, and urbanization on carbon productivity: Evidence from net moderation and mediation effects of energy efficiency gains. *Renewable Energy*, *196*, 824–838. DOI: 10.1016/j.renene.2022.07.012

Musleh Al-Sartawi, A. M., Hussainey, K., & Razzaque, A. (2022). The role of artificial intelligence in sustainable finance. *Journal of Sustainable Finance & Investment*, •••, 1–6. DOI: 10.1080/20430795.2022.2057405

Pavot, D. (2021). Le Fonds monétaire international. Revue québécoise de droit international, 283–302.

Pesaran, M. H., & Shin, Y. (1995). *An autoregressive distributed lag modelling approach to cointegration analysis* (Vol. 9514). Department of Applied Economics, University of Cambridge.

Pesaran, M. H., Shin, Y., & Smith, R. J. (1996). *Testing for the'Existence of a Long-run Relationship'* (No. 9622). Faculty of Economics, University of Cambridge.

Pesaran, M. H., Shin, Y., & Smith, R. J. (2001). Bounds testing approaches to the analysis of level relationships. *Journal of Applied Econometrics*, *16*(3), 289–326. DOI: 10.1002/jae.616

Purcel, A. A. (2020). *Economic development and environmental quality nexus in developing and transition economies* (Doctoral dissertation, Université Clermont Auvergne [2017-2020]; Universitatea Babe -Bolyai (Cluj-Napoca, Roumanie; 1945-....)).

Raihan, A. (2024). A review of the potential opportunities and challenges of the digital economy for sustainability. *Innovation and Green Development*, *3*(4), 100174. DOI: 10.1016/j.igd.2024.100174

Sharif, A., Saqib, N., Dong, K., & Khan, S. A. R. (2022). Nexus between green technology innovation, green financing, and CO2 emissions in the G7 countries: The moderating role of social globalisation. *Sustainable Development (Bradford)*, *30*(6), 1934–1946. DOI: 10.1002/sd.2360

Sharma, R., Shahbaz, M., Kautish, P., & Vo, X. V. (2021). Analyzing the impact of export diversification and technological innovation on renewable energy consumption: Evidences from BRICS nations. *Renewable Energy*, *178*, 1034–1045. DOI: 10.1016/j.renene.2021.06.125

Solarin, S. A., Bello, M. O., & Tiwari, A. K. (2022). The impact of technological innovation on renewable energy production: Accounting for the roles of economic and environmental factors using a method of moments quantile regression. *Heliyon*, *8*(7), e09913. DOI: 10.1016/j.heliyon.2022.e09913 PMID: 35855992

Soytas, U., Sari, R., & Ewing, B. T. (2007). Energy consumption, income, and carbon emissions in the United States. *Ecological Economics*, *62*(3-4), 482–489. DOI: 10.1016/j.ecolecon.2006.07.009

Tang, D. Y., & Zhang, Y. (2020). Do shareholders benefit from green bonds? *Journal of Corporate Finance*, *61*, 101427. DOI: 10.1016/j.jcorpfin.2018.12.001

Wu, C., Yang, Y., Zhang, Y., Xu, H., He, X., Wu, X., & Chou, S. (2024). Hard carbon for sodium-ion batteries: Progress, strategies and future perspective. *Chemical Science (Cambridge)*, *15*(17), 6244–6268. DOI: 10.1039/D4SC00734D PMID: 38699270

Xu, A., Zhu, Y., & Wang, W. (2023). Micro green technology innovation effects of green finance pilot policy—From the perspectives of action points and green value. *Journal of Business Research*, *159*, 113724. DOI: 10.1016/j.jbusres.2023.113724

Zhang, D., Zheng, M., Feng, G. F., & Chang, C. P. (2022). Does an environmental policy bring green innovation in renewable energy? *Renewable Energy*, *195*, 1113–1124. DOI: 10.1016/j.renene.2022.06.074

Zhao, Q., Su, C. W., & Guo, J. M. (2024). Does technological innovation promote renewable energy investment? *SAGE Open*, *14*(1), 21582440241227760. DOI: 10.1177/21582440241227760

Zhou, W., Zhang, Y., & Li, X. (2024). Artificial intelligence, green technological progress, energy conservation, and carbon emission reduction in China: An examination based on dynamic spatial Durbin modeling. *Journal of Cleaner Production*, *446*, 141142. DOI: 10.1016/j.jclepro.2024.141142

Compilation of References

Abad, A. V., & Dodds, P. E. (2020). Green hydrogen characterisation initiatives: Definitions, standards, guarantees of origin, and challenges. *Energy Policy*, *138*, 111300. DOI: 10.1016/j.enpol.2020.111300

Abbass, K., Qasim, M. Z., Song, H., Murshed, M., Mahmood, H., & Younis, I. (2022). A review of the global climate change impacts, adaptation, and sustainable mitigation measures. *Environmental Science and Pollution Research International*, *29*(28), 42539–42559. DOI: 10.1007/s11356-022-19718-6

Ahmad, M., & Zheng, J. (2023). The Cyclical and Nonlinear Impact of R&D and Innovation Activities on Economic Growth in OECD Economies: A New Perspective. *Journal of the Knowledge Economy*, *14*(1), 544–593. DOI: 10.1007/s13132-021-00887-7

Ahmed, A. A., Sayed, S., Abdoulhalik, A., Moutari, S., & Oyedele, L. (2024). Applications of machine learning to water resources management: A review of present status and future opportunities. *Journal of Cleaner Production*, *441*, 140715. DOI: 10.1016/j.jclepro.2024.140715

Akaike, H. (1979). A Bayesian extension of the minimum AIC procedure of autoregressive model fitting. *Biometrika*, *66*(2), 237–242. DOI: 10.1093/biomet/66.2.237

Akhyar, A., Zulkifley, M. A., Lee, J., Song, T., Han, J., Cho, C., Hyun, S., Son, Y., & Hong, B.-W. (2024). Deep artificial intelligence applications for natural disaster management systems: *A methodological review. Ecological Indicators*, *163*, 112067. DOI: 10.1016/j.ecolind.2024.112067

Al Mamun, M., Boubaker, S., & Nguyen, D. K. (2022). Green finance and decarbonization: Evidence from around the world. *Finance Research Letters*, *46*, 102807. DOI: 10.1016/j.frl.2022.102807

Albahri, A. S., Khaleel, Y. L., Habeeb, M. A., Ismael, R. D., Hameed, Q. A., Deveci, M., Homod, R. Z., Albahri, O. S., Alamoodi, A. H., & Alzubaidi, L. (2024). A systematic review of trustworthy artificial intelligence applications in natural disasters. *Computers and Electrical Engineering*, 118(Part B), 109409.DOI: 10.1016/j.compeleceng.2024.109409

Al-Falahi, A. H., Saddique, N., Spank, U., & Bernhofer, C. (2024). Building high-resolution projections of temperature potential changes using statistical downscaling for the future period 2026–2100 in the highland region of Yemen – A supportive approach for empowering environmental planning and decision-making. *Environmental and Sustainability Indicators*, *24*, 100490. DOI: 10.1016/j.indic.2024.100490

Alijoyo, F. A. (2024). AI-powered deep learning for sustainable Industry 4.0 and Internet of Things: Enhancing energy management in smart buildings. *Alexandria Engineering Journal*, *104*, 409–422. DOI: 10.1016/j.aej.2024.07.110

Ali, Z., Muhammad, A., Lee, N., Waqar, M., & Lee, S. W. (2025). Artificial Intelligence for Sustainable Agriculture: A Comprehensive Review of AI-Driven Technologies in Crop Production. *Sustainability (Basel)*, *17*(5), 2281. DOI: 10.3390/su17052281

Alonso, A., & Marqués, J. M. (2019). Financial innovation for a sustainable economy. *Banco de España Occasional Paper*, (1916).

Alotaibi, E., & Nassif, N. (2024). Artificial intelligence in environmental monitoring: In-depth analysis. *Discover Artificial Intelligence*, *4*(1), 84. DOI: 10.1007/s44163-024-00198-1

Al-Sartawi, A., Hussainey, K., & Razzaque, A. (2022). The role of artificial intelligence in sustainable finance. *Journal of Sustainable Finance & Investment*, *11*(3), 213–229. DOI: 10.1080/20430795.2022.2057405

Altın, H. (2024). The impact of energy efficiency and renewable energy consumption on carbon emissions in G7 countries. *International Journal of Sustainable Engineering*, *17*(1), 134–142. DOI: 10.1080/19397038.2024.2319648

Alzoubi, Y. I., & Mishra, A. (2024). Green artificial intelligence initiatives: Potentials and challenges. *Journal of Cleaner Production*, *468*, 143090. DOI: 10.1016/j.jclepro.2024.143090

Amazon. (2022). The Climate Pledge Fund. Amazon Sustainability. https://sustainability.aboutamazon.com/climate-solutions

Aminzadegan, S., Shahriari, M., Mehranfar, F., & Abramović, B. (2022). Factors affecting the emission of pollutants in different types of transportation: *A literature review. Energy Reports*, *8*, 2508–2529. DOI: 10.1016/j.egyr.2022.01.161

Andersson-Sköld, Y., Thorsson, S., Rayner, D., Lindberg, F., Janhäll, S., Jonsson, A., Moback, U., Bergman, R., & Granberg, M. (2015). An integrated method for assessing climate-related risks and adaptation alternatives in urban areas. *Climate Risk Management*, *7*, 31–50. DOI: 10.1016/j.crm.2015.01.003

Ang, J. B. (2007). CO2 emissions, energy consumption, and output in France. *Energy Policy*, *35*(10), 4772–4778. DOI: 10.1016/j.enpol.2007.03.032

Ang, J. B. (2008). A survey of recent developments in the literature of finance and growth. *Journal of Economic Surveys*, *22*(3), 536–576. DOI: 10.1111/j.1467-6419.2007.00542.x

Ansari, H. D., & Sangwai, J. S. (2024). Carbon transportation by pipelines and ships. In *Advances and Technology Development in Greenhouse Gases: Emission, Capture and Conversion* (pp. 137-162). Elsevier.

Arcos, J. M. M., & Santos, D. M. (2023). The hydrogen color spectrum: Techno-economic analysis of the available technologies for hydrogen production. *Gases*, *3*(1), 25–46. DOI: 10.3390/gases3010002

Attaran, M., & Celik, B. G. (2023). Digital Twin: Benefits, use cases, challenges, and opportunities. *Decision Analytics Journal, 6*, 100165. DOI: 10.1016/j.dajour.2023.100165

Ayodele, T. R., & Munda, J. L. (2019). The potential role of green hydrogen production in the South African energy mix. *Journal of Renewable and Sustainable Energy, 11*(4), 044301. DOI: 10.1063/1.5089958

Babina, T., Fedyk, A., He, A. X., & Hodson, J. (2023). Artificial Intelligence and Firms' Systematic Risk. *Available at SSRN* 4868770.

Bamisile, O., Cai, D., Adun, H., Dagbasi, M., Ukwuoma, C. C., Huang, Q., Johnson, N., & Bamisile, O. (2024). Towards renewables development: Review optimization techniques for energy storage and hybrid renewable energy systems. *Heliyon, 10*(19), e37482. DOI: 10.1016/j.heliyon.2024.e37482

Banks, F. E. (2012). *Energy economics: a modern introduction.* Springer Science & Business Media.

Bannister, A., Chaplin, Z., Gant, S., Spriggs, C., & Thomson, N. (2021). *Approaches and Methods to Demonstrate Repurposing of the UK's Local Transmission System (LTS).* Pipelines for Transportation of Hydrogen.

Barbosa-Póvoa, A. P., & Pinto, J. M. (2023). Resilient supply chains–robustness and dynamics in the context of industrial gas supply chains. *Computers & Chemical Engineering, 179*, 108435. DOI: 10.1016/j.compchemeng.2023.108435

Bender, E. M., Gebru, T., McMillan-Major, A., & Mitchell, S. (2021). On the dangers of stochastic parrots: Can language models be too big? In *Proceedings of the 2021 ACM Conference on Fairness, Accountability, and Transparency (FAccT '21)* (pp. 610–623). ACM. DOI: 10.1145/3442188.3445922

Bentley, P. J., & Wakefield, J. P. (1998). Finding acceptable solutions in the Pareto-optimal range using multi-objective genetic algorithms. In *Soft Computing in Engineering Design and Manufacturing* (pp. 231–240). Springer London. DOI: 10.1007/978-1-4471-0427-8_25

Berg, S., Kutra, D., Kroeger, T., Straehle, C. N., Kausler, B. X., Haubold, C., Schiegg, M., Ales, J., Beier, T., Rudy, M., Eren, K., Cervantes, J. I., Xu, B., Beuttenmueller, F., Wolny, A., Zhang, C., Koethe, U., Hamprecht, F. A., & Kreshuk, A. (2019). Ilastik: Interactive machine learning for (bio) image analysis. *Nature Methods*, *16*(12), 1226–1232. DOI: 10.1038/s41592-019-0582-9 PMID: 31570887

Bibri, S. E., Huang, J., Jagatheesaperumal, S. K., & Krogstie, J. (2024a). The synergistic interplay of artificial intelligence and digital twin in environmentally planning sustainable smart cities: A comprehensive systematic review. *Environmental Science and Ecotechnology*, *20*, 100433. DOI: 10.1016/j.ese.2024.100433

Bibri, S. E., Krogstie, J., Kaboli, A., & Alahi, A. (2024b). Smarter eco-cities and their leading-edge artificial intelligence of things solutions for environmental sustainability: A comprehensive systematic review. *Environmental Science and Ecotechnology*, *19*, 100330. DOI: 10.1016/j.ese.2023.100330

Bokhari, A. A., & Myeong, S. (2022). Use of artificial intelligence in smart cities for smart decision-making: A social innovation perspective. *Sustainability (Basel)*, *14*(2), 620. DOI: 10.3390/su14020620

Bolan, S., Padhye, L. P., Jasemizad, T., Govarthanan, M., Karmegam, N., Wijesekara, H., Amarasiri, D., Hou, D., Zhou, P., Biswal, B. K., Balasubramanian, R., Wang, H., Siddique, K. H. M., Rinklebe, J., Kirkham, M. B., & Bolan, N. (2024). Impacts of climate change on the fate of contaminants through extreme weather events. *The Science of the Total Environment*, *909*, 168388. DOI: 10.1016/j.scitotenv.2023.168388

Bolón-Canedo, V., Morán-Fernández, L., Cancela, B., & Alonso-Betanzos, A. (2024b). A review of green artificial intelligence: Towards a more sustainable future. *Neurocomputing*, *599*, 128096. DOI: 10.1016/j.neucom.2024.128096

Bordoff, J., & O'Sullivan, M. L. (2022). Green upheaval: The new geopolitics of energy. *Foreign Affairs*, *101*, 68.

Bossert, L. N., & Hagendorff, T. (2023). The ethics of sustainable AI: Why animals (should) matter for a sustainable use of AI. *Sustainable Development (Bradford)*, *31*(5), 3459–3467. DOI: 10.1002/sd.2596

Boumaiza, A., & Maher, K. (2024). Leveraging blockchain technology to enhance transparency and efficiency in carbon trading markets. *International Journal of Electrical Power & Energy Systems*, *162*, 110225. DOI: 10.1016/j.ijepes.2024.110225

Bragazzi, N. L., Dai, H., Damiani, G., Behzadifar, M., Martini, M., & Wu, J. (2020). How big data and artificial intelligence can help better manage the COVID-19 pandemic. *International Journal of Environmental Research and Public Health*, *17*(9), 3176. DOI: 10.3390/ijerph17093176 PMID: 32370204

Brevini, B. (2021). *Is AI good for the planet?* Polity Press.

Brown, R. L., Durbin, J., & Evans, J. M. (1975). Techniques for testing the constancy of regression relationships over time. *Journal of the Royal Statistical Society. Series B, Statistical Methodology*, *37*(2), 149–192. DOI: 10.1111/j.2517-6161.1975.tb01532.x

Brundtland, G. H. (1987). Our Common Future: Report of the World Commission on Environment and Development (UN Document A/42/427). United Nations.

Buckton, S. J., Fazey, I., Sharpe, B., Om, E. S., Doherty, B., Ball, P., Denby, K., Bryant, M., Lait, R., Bridle, S., Cain, M., Carmen, E., Collins, L., Nixon, N., Yap, C., Connolly, A., Fletcher, B., Frankowska, A., Gardner, G., & Sinclair, M. (2023). The regenerative lens: A conceptual framework for regenerative social-ecological systems. *One Earth*, *6*(7), 824–842. DOI: 10.1016/j.oneear.2023.06.006

Bullock, J., Luccioni, A., Pham, K. H., Lam, C. S. N., & Luengo-Oroz, M. (2020). Mapping the landscape of artificial intelligence applications against COVID-19. *Journal of Artificial Intelligence Research*, *69*, 807–845. DOI: 10.1613/jair.1.12162

Busch, T., Christensen, B. J., & Nielsen, M. Ø. (2011). The role of implied volatility in forecasting future realized volatility and jumps in foreign exchange, stock, and bond markets. *Journal of Econometrics*, *160*(1), 48–57. DOI: 10.1016/j.jeconom.2010.03.014

Castro, B., & Sen, R. (2022). Everyday adaptation: Theorizing climate change adaptation in daily life. *Global Environmental Change*, *75*, 102555. DOI: 10.1016/j.gloenvcha.2022.102555

Cath, C. (2018). Governing artificial intelligence: Ethical, legal and technical opportunities and challenges. *Philosophical Transactions. Series A, Mathematical, Physical, and Engineering Sciences*, *376*(2133), 20180080. DOI: 10.1098/rsta.2018.0080 PMID: 30322996

Ceballos, G., Ehrlich, P. R., & Raven, P. H. (2020). Vertebrates on the brink as indicators of biological annihilation and the sixth mass extinction. *Proceedings of the National Academy of Sciences of the United States of America*, *117*(24), 13596–13602. DOI: 10.1073/pnas.1922686117 PMID: 32482862

Chang, L.. (2023). Rôle de l'intelligence artificielle dans le développement économique vert: Déterminants conjoints des ressources naturelles et de la productivité totale des facteurs verts. *Resources Policy*.

Chayjan, M. R., Bagheri, T., Kianian, A., & Someh, N. G. (2020). Using data mining for prediction of retail banking customer's churn behaviour. *International Journal of Electronic Banking*, *2*(4), 303–320. DOI: 10.1504/IJEBANK.2020.114770

Cheng, C. H. J., & Chiu, C. W. J. (2018). How important are global geopolitical risks to emerging countries? *Inter Economics*, *156*, 305–325. DOI: 10.1016/j.inteco.2018.05.002

Chen, L., Chen, Z., Zhang, Y., Liu, Y., Osman, A. I., Farghali, M., Hua, J., Al-Fatesh, A., Ihara, I., Rooney, D. W., & Yap, P.-S. (2023). Artificial intelligence-based solutions for climate change: *A review. Environmental Chemistry Letters*, *21*(5), 2525–2557. DOI: 10.1007/s10311-023-01617-y

Chen, W., & Hu, M. (2020). The impact of AI-driven technologies on accessibility in the hospitality industry. *Journal of Hospitality and Tourism Technology, 11*(3), 397–415. DOI: 10.1108/JHTT-08-2019-0105

Chen, X., & Hu, Y. (2020). The Role of AI-Driven Translation Tools in Hospitality. *Tourism and Hospitality Study, 21*(2), 190–204. DOI: 10.1177/1467358420974316

Cherp, A., Jewell, J., & Goldthau, A. (2011). Governing global energy: Systems, transitions, complexity. *Global Policy, 2*(1), 75–88. DOI: 10.1111/j.1758-5899.2010.00059.x

Chhabra, N., Majumdar, R., Ghosh, T., & Subramanyam, T. (June 13-14, 2025). Electricity Cost Sensitivity in Green Hydrogen Production: A Comparative Tariff Analysis Across Select Indian States. *Proceedings of the Energy & Carbon Management Conference: Case Studies, Progress & Future Directions (ECM 2025)*, IIT Guwahati, (Paper No. 18). DOI: 10.5281/zenodo.17009219

Chishti, M. Z., Dogan, E., & Binsaeed, R. H. (2024). Can artificial intelligence and green finance affect economic cycles? *Technological Forecasting and Social Change, 209*, 123740. DOI: 10.1016/j.techfore.2024.123740

Choudhary, B., Dhar, V., & Pawase, A. S. (2024). Blue carbon and the role of mangroves in carbon sequestration: Its mechanisms, estimation, human impacts, and conservation strategies for economic incentives. *Journal of Sea Research, 199*, 102504. DOI: 10.1016/j.seares.2024.102504

Chui, M., & Francisco, S. (2017). Artificial intelligence: The next digital frontier. McKinsey and Company Global Institute, 47(3.6), 6–8.

Collins, C., Dennehy, D., Conboy, K., & Mikalef, P. (2021). Artificial intelligence in information systems research: A systematic literature review and research agenda. *International Journal of Information Management, 60*, 102383. DOI: 10.1016/j.ijinfomgt.2021.102383

Cowls, J., Tsamados, A., Taddeo, M., & Floridi, L. (2021). A definition, benchmark and database of AI for social good initiatives. *Nature Machine Intelligence, 3*(2), 111–115. DOI: 10.1038/s42256-021-00296-0

Cowls, J., Tsamados, A., Taddeo, M., & Floridi, L. (2023). The AI gambit: Leveraging artificial intelligence to combat climate change—Opportunities, challenges, and recommendations. *AI & Society, 38*(1), 283–307. DOI: 10.1007/s00146-021-01294-x

Crawford, K. (2021). *Atlas of AI: Power, politics, and the planetary costs of artificial intelligence*. Yale University Press.

Crawford, K. (2021). *The atlas of AI: Power, politics, and the planetary costs of artificial intelligence*. Yale University Press.

Cugurullo, F. (2021). *Frankenstein Urbanism: Eco, smart and autonomous cities, artificial intelligence and the end of the city*. Routledge. DOI: 10.4324/9781315652627

Dagnachew, A. G., Yalew, S. G., Tesfamichael, M., Okereke, C., & Abraham, E. (2025). A green hydrogen revolution in Africa remains elusive under current geopolitical realities. *Climate Policy, 25*(2), 291–302. DOI: 10.1080/14693062.2024.2376740

Das, A., & Swain, P. K. (2024). Navigating the sea level rise: Exploring the interplay of climate change, sea level rise, and coastal communities in India. *Environmental Monitoring and Assessment, 196*(11), 1010. DOI: 10.1007/s10661-024-13191-z

Das, S., Choudhury, M. R., Chatterjee, B., Das, P., Bagri, S., Paul, D., Bera, M., & Dutta, S. (2024). Unravelling the urban climate crisis: Exploring the nexus of urbanization, climate change, and their impacts on the environment and human wellbeing – *A global perspective. AIMS Public Health, 11*(3), 963–1001. DOI: 10.3934/publichealth.2024050

Dastin, J. (2018). "Amazon Scraps Secret AI Recruiting Tool That Showed Bias Against Women." Reuters, Retrieved from https://www.reuters.com

Dauvergne, P. (2020). *AI in the Wild: Sustainability in the age of artificial intelligence*. MIT Press. DOI: 10.7551/mitpress/12350.001.0001

Davison, A. M., de Koning, K., Taubert, F., & Schakel, J.-K. (2025). Automated near real-time monitoring in ecology: Status quo and ways forward. *Ecological Informatics, 103157*, 103157. Advance online publication. DOI: 10.1016/j.ecoinf.2025.103157

Dhiman, R., Miteff, S., Wang, Y., Ma, S.-C., Amirikas, R., & Fabian, B. (2024). Artificial intelligence and sustainability—A review. *Analytics, 3*(1), 140–164. DOI: 10.3390/analytics3010008

Dickey, D. A., & Fuller, W. A. (1979). Distribution of the estimators for autoregressive time series with a unit root. *Journal of the American Statistical Association, 74*(366), 427–431. DOI: 10.2307/2286348

Dinda, S. (2004). Environmental Kuznets Curve hypothesis: A survey. *Ecological Economics, 49*(4), 431–455. DOI: 10.1016/j.ecolecon.2004.02.011

Ding, N., Xi, Y., Jiang, W., Li, H., Su, J., Yang, S., & Lie, T. T. (2025). State-of-the-art carbon metering: Continuous emission monitoring systems for industrial applications. *Heliyon, 11*(3), e42308. DOI: 10.1016/j.heliyon.2025.e42308

Dritsas, E., & Trigka, M. (2025). Exploring the intersection of machine learning and big data: A survey. *Machine Learning and Knowledge Extraction, 7*(1), 13. DOI: 10.3390/make7010013

Du, L., Zuo, J., Vanzo, J., Chang, R., & Zillante, G. (2023). Assessing and predicting the risks of illegal dumping based on road characteristics. *Waste Management (New York, N.Y.), 169*, 332–341. DOI: 10.1016/j.wasman.2023.07.031

Durgun, Y. (2024). Real-time water quality monitoring using AI-enabled sensors: Detection of contaminants and UV disinfection analysis in smart urban water systems. *Journal of King Saud University. Science, 36*(9), 103409. DOI: 10.1016/j.jksus.2024.103409

El Geneidy, S., Baumeister, S., Marini Govigli, V., Orfanidou, T., & Wallius, V. (2021). The carbon footprint of a knowledge organization and emission scenarios for a post-COVID-19 world. *Environmental Impact Assessment Review, 91*, 106645. DOI: 10.1016/j.eiar.2021.106645

Emiliozzi, S., Ferriani, F., & Gazzani, A. (2025). The European energy crisis and the consequences for the global natural gas market. *The Energy Journal (Cambridge, Mass.)*, *46*(1), 119–145. DOI: 10.1177/01956574241290640

Enders, W., & Lee, J. (2012). The flexible Fourier form and Dickey–Fuller type unit root tests. *Economics Letters*, *117*(1), 196–199. DOI: 10.1016/j.econlet.2012.04.081

Enumah, M. A. (2025). Analysis of Risk and Risk Management Strategies in Nigeria's Oil and Gas Industry.

Escobar-Yonoff, R., Maestre-Cambroncl, D., Charry, S., Rincón-Montenegro, A., & Portnoy, I. (2021). Performance assessment and economic perspectives of integrated PEM fuel cell and PEM electrolyzer for electric power generation. *Heliyon*, *7*(3), e06506. DOI: 10.1016/j.heliyon.2021.e06506 PMID: 33817374

European Commission. (2015). *SmartNet: Smart TSO-DSO interaction schemes, market architectures, and ICT solutions for the integration of ancillary services from demand-side management and distributed generation.* https://cordis.europa.eu/project/id/691405

European Commission. (2021). *Proposal for a regulation laying down harmonised rules on artificial intelligence (AI Act).* https://eur-lex.europa.eu/legal-content/EN/TXT/?uri=CELEX%3A52021PC0206

Evans, R., & Gao, J. (2016, July 20). DeepMind AI reduces Google data centre cooling bill by 40%. *DeepMind.* https://deepmind.com/discover/blog/deepmind-ai-reduces-google-data-centre-cooling-bill-by-40/

Fan, Y.. (2020). Multilingual Chatbots in Hospitality: Addressing Language Accessibility. *Service Industries Journal*, *40*(7-8), 620–634. DOI: 10.1080/02642069.2020.1718845

Fartmann, T., Kämpfer, S., Brüggeshemke, J., Juchem, M., Klauer, F., Weking, S., & Löffler, F. (2018). Landscape scale effects of Christmas tree plantations in an intensively used low mountain landscape – Applying breeding bird assemblages as indicators. *Ecological Indicators*, *94*, 409–419. DOI: 10.1016/j.ecolind.2018.07.006

Fatica, S., & Panzica, R. (2021). Green bonds as a tool against climate change? *Business Strategy and the Environment*, *30*(5), 2688–2701. DOI: 10.1002/bse.2771

Feng, T., Xiong, R., & Huan, P. (2023). Productive use of natural resources in agriculture: The main policy lessons. *Resources Policy,* 85(Part A), 103793.DOI: 10.1016/j.resourpol.2023.103793

Fernandois, A., & Medel, C. (2020). Geopolitical tensions, OPEC news, and the oil price: A Granger causality analysis. *Revista de Análisis Económico*, *35*(2), 57–90. DOI: 10.4067/S0718-88702020000200057

Figenbaum, E. (2017). Perspectives on Norway's supercharged electric vehicle policy. *Environmental Innovation and Societal Transitions*, *25*, 14–34. DOI: 10.1016/j.eist.2016.11.002

Flammer, C. (2021). Corporate green bonds. *Journal of Financial Economics*, *142*(2), 499–516. DOI: 10.1016/j.jfineco.2021.01.010

Floridi, L., Cowls, J., Beltrametti, M., Chatila, R., Chazerand, P., Dignum, V., Luetge, C., Madelin, R., Pagallo, U., Rossi, F., Schafer, B., Valcke, P., & Vayena, E. (2018). AI4People—An ethical framework for a good AI society: Opportunities, risks, principles, and recommendations. *Minds and Machines*, *28*(4), 689–707. DOI: 10.1007/s11023-018-9482-5 PMID: 30930541

Friedman, N., & Ormiston, J. (2022). Blockchain as a sustainability-oriented innovation? Opportunities for and resistance to Blockchain technology as a driver of sustainability in global food supply chains. *Technological Forecasting and Social Change*, *175*, 121403. DOI: 10.1016/j.techfore.2021.121403

Furtak, K., & Wolińska, A. (2023). The impact of extreme weather events as a consequence of climate change on the soil moisture and on the quality of the soil environment and agriculture – *A review. Catena*, *231*, 107378. DOI: 10.1016/j.catena.2023.107378

Futa, B., Gmitrowicz-Iwan, J., Skersienė, A., Šlepetienė, A., & Parašotas, I. (2024). Innovative soil management strategies for sustainable agriculture. *Sustainability (Basel)*, *16*(21), 9481. DOI: 10.3390/su16219481

Gbadeyan, O. J., Muthivhi, J., Linganiso, L. Z., & Deenadayalu, N. (2024). Decoupling economic growth from carbon emissions: A transition toward low-carbon energy systems—A critical review. *Cleanroom Technology*, *6*(3), 1076–1113. DOI: 10.3390/cleantechnol6030054

Geissdoerfer, M., Vladimirova, D., & Evans, S. (2018). Sustainable business model innovation: A review. *Journal of Cleaner Production*, *198*, 401–416. DOI: 10.1016/j.jclepro.2018.06.240

Georgescu, I. A., Oprea, S. V., & Bâra, A. (2025). An analysis of the geopolitical and economics influence on tourist arrivals in Russia using a nonlinear autoregressive distributed lag model. *Kybernetes*, *54*(9), 5080–5105. DOI: 10.1108/K-01-2024-0265

Ghaffarian, S., Taghikhah, F. R., & Maier, H. R. (2023). Explainable artificial intelligence in disaster risk management: Achievements and prospective futures. *International Journal of Disaster Risk Reduction*, *98*, 104123. DOI: 10.1016/j.ijdrr.2023.104123

Gianfrate, G., & Peri, M. (2019). The green advantage: Exploring the convenience of issuing green bonds. *Journal of Cleaner Production*, *219*, 127–135. DOI: 10.1016/j.jclepro.2019.02.022

Gikunda, K. (2024). "Harnessing Artificial Intelligence for Sustainable Agricultural Development in Africa: Opportunities, Challenges, and Impact. arxiv. https://doi.org//arXiv.2401.06171DOI: 10.48550

Gillette, J. L., & Kolpa, R. L. (2008). *Overview of interstate hydrogen pipeline systems* (No. ANL/EVS/TM/08-2). Argonne National Laboratory (ANL), Argonne, IL (United States).

Global Partnership on Artificial Intelligence. (2022). *Annual report 2022*. https://gpai.ai/annual-report-2022

Goel, A., Raut, G., Sharma, A., & Taneja, U. (2024). Artificial intelligence and sustainable business: A review and future research directions. *South Asian Journal of Business and Management Cases, 13*(3), 340–365. DOI: 10.1177/22779779241302146

Goh, S. K., Sam, C. Y., & McNown, R. (2017). Re-examining foreign direct investment, exports, and economic growth in Asian economies using a bootstrap ARDL approach. *Journal of Asian Economics, 51*, 12–22. DOI: 10.1016/j.asieco.2017.06.001

Google Research. (2024, March 20). How Google uses AI to improve global flood forecasting. https://blog.google/technology/ai/google-ai-global-flood-forecasting

Gorji, S. A. (2023). Challenges and opportunities in the green hydrogen supply chain through metaheuristic optimization. *Journal of Computational Design and Engineering, 10*(3), 1143–1157. DOI: 10.1093/jcde/qwad043

Grahn, R., Qian, S., & Hendrickson, C. (2021). Improving the performance of first- and last-mile mobility services through transit coordination, real-time demand prediction, advanced reservations, and trip prioritization. *Transportation Research Part C, Emerging Technologies, 133*, 103430. DOI: 10.1016/j.trc.2021.103430

Greif, L., Kimmig, A., El Bobbou, S., Jurisch, P., & Ovtcharova, J. (2024). Strategic view on the current role of AI in advancing environmental sustainability: A SWOT analysis. *Discover Artificial Intelligence, 4*(1), 45. DOI: 10.1007/s44163-024-00146-z

Gretzel, U.. (2021). Big Data and Artificial Intelligence in Tourism and Hospitality. *Journal of Hospitality Marketing & Management, 30*(3), 289–309. DOI: 10.1080/19368623.2021.1841100

Grossman, G. M., & Krueger, A. B. (1995). Economic growth and the environment. *The Quarterly Journal of Economics, 110*(2), 353–377. DOI: 10.2307/2118443

Gupta, A., Ott, M., Melnikov, A., Candido, S., Brooks, D., Chauhan, G., & Hazelwood, K. (2022). Sustainable AI: Environmental implications, challenges and opportunities. In *Proceedings of the 5th MLSys Conference (MLSys 2022)*. (Preprint available on arXiv)

Gupta, M., Abdelsalam, M., Khorsandroo, S., & Mittal, S. (2020). Security and privacy in smart farming: Challenges and opportunities. *IEEE Access : Practical Innovations, Open Solutions*, *8*, 34564–34584. DOI: 10.1109/ACCESS.2020.2975142

Gyongyosi, L., & Imre, S. (2019). A survey on quantum computing technology. *Computer Science Review*, *31*, 51–71. DOI: 10.1016/j.cosrev.2018.11.002

Hachenberg, B., & Schiereck, D. (2018). Are green bonds priced differently from conventional bonds? *Journal of Asset Management*, *19*(6), 371–383. DOI: 10.1057/s41260-018-0088-5

Halsband, A. (2022). Sustainable AI and intergenerational justice. *Sustainability (Basel)*, *14*(7), 3922. DOI: 10.3390/su14073922

Hariyani, D., Hariyani, P., Mishra, S., & Sharma, M. K. (2024). Leveraging digital technologies for advancing circular economy practices and enhancing life cycle analysis: A systematic literature review. *Waste Management Bulletin*, *2*(3), 69–83. DOI: 10.1016/j.wmb.2024.06.007

Helgaker, J. F.(n.d.). Transportation of hydrogen gas in offshore pipelines: H2Pipe.

Henderson, P., Hu, J., Romoff, J., Brunskill, E., Jurafsky, D., & Pineau, J. (2020). Towards the systematic reporting of the energy and carbon footprints of machine learning. *Journal of Machine Learning Research*, *21*, 1–43.

Himeur, Y., Ghanem, K., Alsalemi, A., Bensaali, F., & Amira, A. (2021). Artificial intelligence based anomaly detection of energy consumption in buildings: A review, current trends and new perspectives. *Applied Energy*, *287*, 116601. DOI: 10.1016/j.apenergy.2021.116601

Hojnik, J., & Ruzzier, M. (2016). What drives eco-innovation? A review of an emerging literature. *Environmental Innovation and Societal Transitions*, *19*, 31–41. DOI: 10.1016/j.eist.2015.09.006

Holland, J. H. (1992). Genetic algorithms. *Scientific American*, *267*(1), 66–73. DOI: 10.1038/scientificamerican0792-66

Holmes, W., Bialik, M., & Fadel, C. (2019). *Artificial intelligence in education: Promises and implications for teaching and learning*. Center for Curriculum Redesign. https://curriculumredesign.org/wp-content/uploads/AIED-Book-Excerpt-CCR.pdf

Huang, A., & Back, K. (2020). Using AI for Diversity Training in Hospitality. *Journal of Hospitality & Tourism Study*, *45*(5), 1062–1079. DOI: 10.1177/1096348020965701

Huang, J., Bibri, S. E., & Keel, P. (2025). Generative spatial artificial intelligence for sustainable smart cities: A pioneering large flow model for urban digital twin. *Environmental Science and Ecotechnology*, *24*, 100526. DOI: 10.1016/j.ese.2025.100526

Hussain, I., Elomri, A., Kerbache, L., & El Omri, A. (2024). Smart city solutions: Comparative analysis of waste management models in IoT-enabled environments using multi-agent simulation. *Sustainable Cities and Society*, *103*, 105247. DOI: 10.1016/j.scs.2024.105247

IEA. (2024). Global Hydrogen Review 2024, *IEA*, Paris https://www.iea.org/reports/global-hydrogen-review-2024, License: CC BY 4.0

Incer-Valverde, J., Korayem, A., Tsatsaronis, G., & Morosuk, T. (2023). "Colors" of hydrogen: Definitions and carbon intensity. *Energy Conversion and Management*, *291*, 117294. DOI: 10.1016/j.enconman.2023.117294

Ingrao, C., Strippoli, R., Lagioia, G., & Huisingh, D. (2023). Water scarcity in agriculture: An overview of causes, impacts, and approaches for reducing the risks. *Heliyon,* 9(8), e18507.doi: . 2023.e18507.DOI: 10.1016/j.heliyon

International Energy Agency (IEA). (2021). *World Energy Outlook 2021*. Paris: IEA. https://www.iea.org/reports/world-energy-outlook-2021

International Energy Agency. (2023). *World Energy Outlook*. https://www.iea.org/reports/world-energy-outlook-2023

International Energy Agency. (2024). *World Energy Outlook*. https://www.iea.org/reports/world-energy-outlook-2024

International Renewable Energy Agency. (2020). *Renewable energy statistics 2020*. Abu Dhabi: IRENA. https://www.irena.org/publications/2020/Jul/Renewable-energy-statistics-2020

Iqbal, M. S., & Abdul Rahim, Z. (2025). Driving emerging technology adoption in Malaysian micro-, small, and medium-sized enterprises: A strategic intervention framework. *Journal of the International Council for Small Business*, 1-24.

IRENA and ILO. (2023). Renewable energy and jobs: Annual review 2023, *International Renewable Energy Agency*, Abu Dhabi, and International Labour Organization, Geneva.

Islam, B. S., Valles, D., Hibbitts, T. J., Ryberg, W. A., Walkup, D. K., & Forstner, M. R. J. (2023). Animal species recognition with deep convolutional neural networks from ecological camera trap images. *Animals (Basel)*, *13*(9), 1526. DOI: 10.3390/ani13091526

Ivanov, S., & Webster, C. (2019). Adoption of robots, artificial intelligence, and service automation by travel, tourism, and hospitality companies – A cost-benefit analysis. *International Journal of Contemporary Hospitality Management*, *31*(9), 3875–3896. DOI: 10.1108/IJCHM-07-2018-0580

Ivanov, S., & Webster, C. (2019). *Robots, Artificial Intelligence, and Service Automation in Travel, Tourism, and Hospitality*. Emerald Publishing., DOI: 10.1108/9781787566873

Jakhar, R., Samek, L., & Styszko, K. (2023). A comprehensive study of the impact of waste fires on the environment and health. *Sustainability (Basel)*, *15*(19), 14241. DOI: 10.3390/su151914241

Janga, B., Asamani, G. P., Sun, Z., & Cristea, N. (2023). A review of practical AI for remote sensing in Earth sciences. *Remote Sensing (Basel), 15*(16), 4112. DOI: 10.3390/rs15164112

Javaid, M., Haleem, A., Singh, R. P., & Suman, R. (2022). Enhancing smart farming through the applications of Agriculture 4.0 technologies. *International Journal of Intelligent Networks, 3*, 150–164. DOI: 10.1016/j.ijin.2022.09.004

Javanmardi, E., Liu, S., & Xie, N. (2023). Exploring the challenges to sustainable development from the perspective of grey systems theory. *Systems, 11*(2), 70. DOI: 10.3390/systems11020070

Javed, A., Rapposelli, A., Khan, F., Javed, A., & Abid, N. (2024). Do green technology innovation, environmental policy, and the transition to renewable energy matter in times of ecological crises? A step towards ecological sustainability. *Technological Forecasting and Social Change, 207*, 123638. Advance online publication. DOI: 10.1016/j.techfore.2024.123638

Jeantet, L., & Dufourq, E. (2023). Improving deep learning acoustic classifiers with contextual information for wildlife monitoring. *Ecological Informatics, 77*, 102256. DOI: 10.1016/j.ecoinf.2023.102256

Jobin, A., Ienca, M., & Vayena, E. (2019). The global landscape of AI ethics guidelines. *Nature Machine Intelligence, 1*(9), 389–399. DOI: 10.1038/s42256-019-0088-2

Kaack, L. H., Donti, P. L., Strubell, E., Dai, A. M., & Kolter, J. Z. (2022). Aligning artificial intelligence with climate change mitigation. *Nature Climate Change, 12*(6), 518–524. DOI: 10.1038/s41558-022-01377-7

Kaleem, A., Zaman, A., & Rajakaruna, S. (2024). Hydrogen at home: The current and future landscape of green hydrogen in residential settings. *Sustainable Energy Technologies and Assessments, 72*, 104058. DOI: 10.1016/j.seta.2024.104058

Kamath, H. G., Majumdar, R., Krishnan, A. V., & Srikanth, R. (2022). Cost and environmental benefits of coal-concentrated solar power (CSP) hybridization in India. *Energy, 240*, 122805. DOI: 10.1016/j.energy.2021.122805

Kamminga, J., Ayele, E., Meratnia, N., & Havinga, P. (2018). Poaching Detection Technologies—*A Survey. Sensors (Basel)*, *18*(5), 1474. DOI: 10.3390/s18051474

Kartal, M. T., Taşkın, D., Shahbaz, M., Depren, S. K., & Pata, U. K. (2024). Effects of environment, social, and governance (ESG) disclosures on ESG scores: Investigating the role of corporate governance for publicly traded Turkish companies. *Journal of Environmental Management*, *368*, 122205. DOI: 10.1016/j.jenvman.2024.122205

Khan, K., Su, C. W., Rehman, A. U., & Ullah, R. (2022). Is technological innovation a driver of renewable energy? *Technology in Society*, *70*, 102044. DOI: 10.1016/j.techsoc.2022.102044

Kirikkaleli, D., Güngör, H., & Adebayo, T. S. (2023). Renewable energy consumption, technological innovation, and CO_2 emissions in Norway: Evidence from advanced econometric techniques. *Energy Reports*, *9*, 1135–1147. DOI: 10.1016/j.egyr.2023.01.087

Korah, A., Koch, J. A. M., & Wimberly, M. C. (2024). Understanding urban growth modeling in Africa: Dynamics, drivers, and challenges. *Cities (London, England)*, *146*, 104734. DOI: 10.1016/j.cities.2023.104734

Krishnan, S., Koning, V., de Groot, M. T., de Groot, A., Mendoza, P. G., Junginger, M., & Kramer, G. J. (2023). Present and future cost of alkaline and PEM electrolyser stacks. *International Journal of Hydrogen Energy*, *48*(83), 32313–32330. DOI: 10.1016/j.ijhydene.2023.05.031

Kumar, R., Singh, P., & Sharma, L. (2022). AI-driven Personalization in Hospitality: A Cultural Sensitivity Perspective. *Journal of Service Study*, *29*(2), 145–160.

Kumar, S., Tiwari, P., & Zymbler, M. (2019). Internet of Things is a revolutionary approach for future technology enhancement: *A review. Journal of Big Data*, *6*(1), 111. DOI: 10.1186/s40537-019-0268-2

Kuschel, K., & Sanders, M. (2020). AI Personalization Strategies in Hospitality: Enhancing Guest Experience while Maintaining Privacy. *Journal of Hospitality Marketing & Management*, *31*(3), 210–223.

Lannelongue, L., Grealey, J., & Inouye, M. (2021). Green algorithms: Quantifying the carbon footprint of computation. *Nature Computational Science*, *1*(3), 172–180. DOI: 10.1038/s43588-021-00056-9

Li, J., Chen, W., & Wu, L. (2021). Reducing bias in AI-powered recruitment processes: A study in the hospitality industry. *Tourism Management Perspectives*, *40*, 100873. DOI: 10.1016/j.tmp.2021.100873

Li, P., Yang, H., Wu, H., Wang, Y., Su, H., Zheng, T., Zhu, F., Zhang, G., & Han, Y. (2024). Deep learning model for solar and wind energy forecasting considering Northwest China as an example. *Results in Engineering*, *24*, 102939. DOI: 10.1016/j.rineng.2024.102939

Longoni, C., Bonezzi, A., & Morewedge, C. K. (2019). Resistance to medical artificial intelligence. *The Journal of Consumer Research*, *46*(4), 629–650. DOI: 10.1093/jcr/ucz013

Ludlow, J., & Enders, W. (2000). Estimating non-linear ARMA models using Fourier series. *International Journal of Forecasting*, *16*(3), 333–347. DOI: 10.1016/S0169-2070(00)00048-0

Lu, Y.. (2020). Artificial Intelligence in Hospitality: The Innovative Role of Chatbots. *Journal of Hospitality and Tourism Management*, *45*, 89–98. DOI: 10.1016/j.jhtm.2020.08.008

Magazzino, C., Alola, A. A., & Schneider, N. (2021). The trilemma of innovation, logistics performance, and environmental quality in 25 topmost logistics countries: A quantile regression evidence. *Journal of Cleaner Production*, *322*, 129050. DOI: 10.1016/j.jclepro.2021.129050 PMID: 36567950

Mahdi, N. M., Jassim, A. H., Abulqasim, S. A., Basem, A., Ogaili, A. A. F., & Al-Haddad, L. A. (2024). Leak detection and localization in water distribution systems using advanced feature analysis and an Artificial Neural Network. *Desalination and Water Treatment*, *320*, 100685. DOI: 10.1016/j.dwt.2024.100685

Mahmood, M., Chowdhury, P., Yeassin, R., Hasan, M., Ahmad, T., & Chowdhury, N.-U.-R. (2024). Impacts of digitalization on smart grids, renewable energy, and demand response: An updated review of current applications. *Energy Conversion and Management*: X, 24, 100790.DOI: 10.1016/j.ecmx.2024.100790

Maka, A. O., & Mehmood, M. (2024). Green hydrogen energy production: Current status and potential. *Clean Energy*, *8*(2), 1–7. DOI: 10.1093/ce/zkae012

Mana, A. A., Allouhi, A., Hamrani, A., Rehman, S., el Jamaoui, I., & Jayachandran, K. (2024). Sustainable AI-based production agriculture: Exploring AI applications and implications in agricultural practices. *Smart Agricultural Technology*, *7*, 100416. DOI: 10.1016/j.atech.2024.100416

Mao, Z., & Zhang, L. (2021). The Role of AI in Personalized Guest Experiences. *Tourism Review*, *76*(4), 827–839. DOI: 10.1108/TR-03-2021-0135

Marouani, I., Guesmi, T., Alshammari, B. M., Alqunun, K., Alzamil, A., Alturki, M., & Hadj Abdallah, H. (2023). Integration of Renewable-Energy-Based Green Hydrogen into the Energy Future. *Processes (Basel, Switzerland)*, *11*(9), 2685. DOI: 10.3390/pr11092685

Martin, P. (2025). "Stranded asset" | Thyssenkrupp's green steel plant not viable if supply of cheap renewable hydrogen never arrives. *Hydrogen Insight*.https://www.hydrogeninsight.com/industrial/stranded-asset-thyssenkrupps-green-steel-plant-not-viable-if-supply-of-cheap-renewable-hydrogen-never-arrives/2-1-1795325

Maurya, S., Shavkidinova, D., Shrivastava, V., & Subrahmanyam, S. (2025). Effects of Green Supply Chain Management Practices on Environmental and Firm Sustainability Performance. *ACTA INNOVATIONS*, 55, 13–22. https://www.actainnovations.com/index.php/pub/article/view/401

Mazzi, F., & Floridi, L. (Eds.). (2023). *The ethics of artificial intelligence for the Sustainable Development Goals*. Springer. DOI: 10.1007/978-3-031-21147-8

McNown, R., Sam, C. Y., & Goh, S. K. (2018). Bootstrap ARDL bounds testing approach: Replication and extension. *Energy Economics*, *69*, 1–16. DOI: 10.1016/j.eneco.2017.10.001

Medrano, V. C. (2021). Metaheuristic and matheuristic approaches for multi-objective optimization problems in process engineering: application to the hydrogen supply chain design. Doctoral dissertation, Institut National Polytechnique de Toulouse-INPT.

Mehrabi, N., Morstatter, F., Saxena, N., Lerman, K., & Galstyan, A. (2021). A survey on bias and fairness in machine learning. *ACM Computing Surveys*, *54*(6), 1–35. DOI: 10.1145/3457607

Mele, M., Magazzino, C., Schneider, N., Gurrieri, A. R., & Golpira, H. (2022). Innovation, income, and waste disposal operations in Korea: Evidence from a spectral granger causality analysis and artificial neural networks experiments. *Economics and Politics*, *39*(2), 427–459.

Microsoft. (2021). *AI for Earth: Sustainability program.* https://www.microsoft.com/ai-for-earth

Miller, J., & Smith, T. (2019). AI in Hiring: An End to Bias? *Technology in Human Resources*, *34*(2), 77–89.

Miller, T., Durlik, I., Kostecka, E., Kozlovska, P., Łobodzińska, A., Sokołowska, S., & Nowy, A. (2025). Integrating Artificial Intelligence Agents with the Internet of Things for Enhanced Environmental Monitoring: Applications in Water Quality and Climate Data. *Electronics (Basel)*, *14*(4), 696. DOI: 10.3390/electronics14040696

Ministry of New and Renewable Energy. India. (2023). https://mnre.gov.in/en/hydrogen-overview/

Mitchell, M.(1998). An introduction to genetic algorithms. MIT Press. (DOI:) ISBN electronic:9780262280013DOI: 10.7551/mit-press/3927.001.0001

Mitić, P., Fedajev, A., Radulescu, M., Hudea, O. S., & Streimikiene, D. (2024). Fostering green transition in Central and Eastern Europe: Carbon dioxide emissions, industrialization, financial development, and electricity nexus. *Technological and Economic Development of Economy*, *30*(4), 1009–1036. DOI: 10.3846/tede.2024.20630

Mohammad, B. T. (2020). The Future of Culinary Tourism: An Emerging Dimension for the Tourism Industry of Bangladesh. I-Manager's. *Journal of Marketing*, *15*(1), 27. DOI: 10.26634/jmgt.15.1.17181

Mohammad, B. T. (2021). An assessment of the roles of the social network in developing the Tourism Industry in Bangladesh. *International Journal of Business, Law, and Education*, *2*(3), 85–93. DOI: 10.56442/ijble.v2i3.21

Mohammad, B. T. (2024). Implementing Artificial Intelligence and Virtual Experiences in Hospitality. In Manohar, S., Mittal, A., Raju, S., & Nair, A. J. (Eds.), *Advances in Hospitality, Tourism, and the Services Industry* (pp. 145–160). IGI Global., DOI: 10.4018/979-8-3693-2019-8.ch009

Mohammad, B. T. (2025). Maximizing Impact: The Role of Influencer Marketing in Contemporary Tourism Marketing. In Özsungur, F. (Ed.), *Navigating Organizational Behavior in the Digital Age with AI* (pp. 277–304). IGI Global Scientific Publishing., DOI: 10.4018/979-8-3693-8442-8.ch011

Mosweunyane, M. (2019). The economic contribution of mining to Botswana's economy. *Resources Policy*, *62*, 44–51. DOI: 10.1016/j.resourpol.2019.03.002

Mukhtarov, S. (2024). Do renewable energy and total factor productivity eliminate CO_2 emissions in Turkey? *Environmental Economics and Policy Studies*, *26*(2), 307–324. DOI: 10.1007/s10018-023-00377-x

Murshed, M., Apergis, N., Alam, M. S., Khan, U., & Mahmud, S. (2022). The impacts of renewable energy, financial inclusivity, globalization, economic growth, and urbanization on carbon productivity: Evidence from net moderation and mediation effects of energy efficiency gains. *Renewable Energy*, *196*, 824–838. DOI: 10.1016/j.renene.2022.07.012

Narayanan, S., & Antoniou, C. (2023). Shared mobility services towards Mobility as a Service (MaaS): What, who, and when? *Transportation Research Part A, Policy and Practice*, *168*, 103581. DOI: 10.1016/j.tra.2023.103581

Năstasă, A., & Dumitra, T.-C. (2024). Artificial intelligence and sustainable development during the pandemic: An overview of the scientific debates. *Heliyon*, *10*(1), e030412. DOI: 10.1016/j.heliyon.2023.e030412

Natarajan, S. K., Shanmurthy, P., Arockiam, D., Balusamy, B., & Selvarajan, S. (2024). Optimized machine learning model for air quality index prediction in major cities in India. *Scientific Reports*, *14*(1), 6795. DOI: 10.1038/s41598-024-54807-1

National Green Hydrogen Mission. (2023). Ministry of New and Renewable Energy, Government of India.

Nishant, R., Kennedy, M., & Corbett, J. (2020). Artificial intelligence for sustainability: Challenges, opportunities, and a research agenda. *International Journal of Information Management*, *53*, 102104. DOI: 10.1016/j.ijinfomgt.2020.102104

Nivedita, V., Begum, S. S., Aldehim, G., Alashjaee, A. M., Arasi, M. A., Sikkandar, M. Y., Jayasankar, T., & Vivek, S. (2024). Plastic debris detection along coastal waters using Sentinel-2 satellite data and machine learning techniques. *Marine Pollution Bulletin*, 209 (Part A), 117106.DOI: 10.1016/j.marpolbul.2024.117106

Norges Bank Investment Management. (2022). *Annual report 2022*. Oslo: Norges Bank. https://www.nbim.no/en/publications/

Obaideen, K., Yousef, B. A. A., AlMallahi, M. N., Tan, Y. C., Mahmoud, M., Jaber, H., & Ramadan, M. (2022). An overview of smart irrigation systems using IoT. *Energy Nexus*, *7*, 100124. DOI: 10.1016/j.nexus.2022.100124

OECD. (2011). *Towards green growth*. OECD Publishing., DOI: 10.1787/9789264111318-

OECD. (2018). *OECD science, technology and innovation outlook 2018: Adapting to technological and societal disruptions*. OECD Publishing., DOI: 10.1787/sti_in_outlook-2018-

Ofori-Sasu, D., Abor, J. Y., Agyekum Donkor, G. N., & Otchere, I. (2023). Renewable energy consumption and carbon emissions in developing countries: The role of capital markets. *International Journal of Sustainable Energy*, *42*(1), 1407–1429. DOI: 10.1080/14786451.2023.2268857

Olawade, D. B., Fapohunda, O., Wada, O. Z., Usman, S. O., Ige, A. O., Ajisafe, O., & Oladapo, B. I. (2024a). Smart waste management: A paradigm shift enabled by artificial intelligence. *Waste Management Bulletin*, *2*(2), 244–263. DOI: 10.1016/j.wmb.2024.05.001

Olawade, D. B., Wada, O. Z., David-Olawade, A. C., Fapohunda, O., Ige, A. O., & Ling, J. (2024b). Artificial intelligence potential for net-zero sustainability: Current evidence and prospects. *Next Sustainability*, *4*, 100041. DOI: 10.1016/j.nxsust.2024.100041

Olawade, D. B., Wada, O. Z., Ige, A. O., Egbewole, B. I., Olojo, A., & Oladapo, B. I. (2024c). Artificial intelligence in environmental monitoring: Advancements, challenges, and future directions. *Hygiene and Environmental Health Advances*, *12*, 100114. DOI: 10.1016/j.heha.2024.100114

Organisation for Economic Co-operation and Development. (2024). OECD principles on artificial intelligence. https://oecd.ai

Orssatto, J. (2001). Environmental challenges in organizations. In Smelser, N. J., & Baltes, P. B. (Eds.), *International Encyclopedia of the Social & Behavioral Sciences* (pp. 4590–4592). Pergamon., DOI: 10.1016/B0-08-043076-7/04244-3

Ospanova, A. K., & Zakirova, D. I. (2020). Conditions and prospects of employment in the renewable energy sector. *Вестникуниверситета. Туран*, (2), 112–116.

Pandey, A., & Majumdar, R. (2023). Assessing End-of-Life Room Air Conditioner Recycling Potential for Sustainable Resource Utilization in India: A Case Study for Reducing Environmental Burden. In *Anthropogenic Environmental Hazards: Compensation and Mitigation* (pp. 41-69). Cham: Springer Nature Switzerland.(DOI:) ISBN 978-3-031-41012-3DOI: 10.1007/978-3-031-41013-0_3

Pandey, A., & Majumdar, R. (2025). Energy Efficiency and Circularity: Insights from Adoption Trends of Washing Machines, Critical Materials Demand and Responsible Use Strategies. In Osabohien, R. (Ed.), *Energy Efficiency in Critical Times: Security, Economics and Transition* (pp. 3–18). Elsevier., DOI: 10.1016/B978-0-443-28949-1.00001-1

Pandey, V., Sircar, A., Bist, N., Solanki, K., & Yadav, K. (2023). Accelerating the renewable energy sector through Industry 4.0: Optimization opportunities in the digital revolution. *International Journal of Innovation Studies*, *7*(2), 171–188. DOI: 10.1016/j.ijis.2023.03.003

Pappas, I. O., Mikalef, P., Krogstie, J., & Giannakos, M. (2021). Big data and business analytics ecosystems: Paving the way towards digital transformation and sustainable societies. *Information Systems and e-Business Management*, *19*(4), 1355–1355. DOI: 10.1007/s10257-021-00538-z

Park, J. Y. (1992). Canonical cointegrating regressions. *Econometrica*, *60*(1), 119–143. DOI: 10.2307/2951679

Pascual, C., & Zambetakis, E. (2010). The geopolitics of energy. *Energy security: Economics, politics, strategies, and implications*, 9-35.

Patidar, R., Yadav, D., & Mallya, H. (2024). *How can Hydrogen Electrolysers be Made in India? A Bottom-up Cost Assessment to Quantify the Indigenisation Potential*. Council of Energy, Environment and Water.

Pavot, D. (2021). Le Fonds monétaire international. Revue québécoise de droit international, 283–302.

Pelkki, J., & Sherman, H. (2020). Measuring the economic contribution of tourism in the Nordic countries. *Tourism Economics*, *26*(7), 1155–1173. DOI: 10.1177/1354816620921649

Pérez-Beltrán, C. H., Robles, A. D., Rodriguez, N. A., Ortega-Gavilán, F., & Jiménez-Carvelo, A. M. (2024). Artificial intelligence and water quality: From drinking water to wastewater. *Trends in Analytical Chemistry*, *172*, 117597. DOI: 10.1016/j.trac.2024.117597

Pesaran, M. H., Shin, Y., & Smith, R. J. (1996). *Testing for the'Existence of a Long-run Relationship'* (No. 9622). Faculty of Economics, University of Cambridge.

Pesaran, M. H., & Shin, Y. (1995). *An autoregressive distributed lag modelling approach to cointegration analysis* (Vol. 9514). Department of Applied Economics, University of Cambridge.

Pesaran, M. H., Shin, Y., & Smith, R. J. (2001). Bounds testing approaches to the analysis of level relationships. *Journal of Applied Econometrics*, *16*(3), 289–326. DOI: 10.1002/jae.616

Phillips, P. C. B., & Hansen, B. E. (1990). Statistical inference in instrumental variables regression with I(1) processes. *The Review of Economic Studies*, *57*(1), 99–125. DOI: 10.2307/2297545

Popescu, S. M., Mansoor, S., Wani, O. A., Kumar, S. S., Sharma, V., Sharma, A., Arya, V. M., Kirkham, M. B., Hou, D., Bolan, N., & Chung, Y. S. (2024, February 20). Artificial intelligence and IoT-driven technologies for environmental pollution monitoring and management. *Frontiers in Environmental Science*, *12*, 1336088. Advance online publication. DOI: 10.3389/fenvs.2024.1336088

Popp, D. (2002). Induced innovation and energy prices. *The American Economic Review*, *92*(1), 160–180. DOI: 10.1257/000282802760015658

Purcel, A. A. (2020). *Economic development and environmental quality nexus in developing and transition economies* (Doctoral dissertation, Université Clermont Auvergne [2017-2020]; Universitatea Babe -Bolyai (Cluj-Napoca, Roumanie; 1945-....)).

Purvis, B., Mao, Y., & Robinson, D. (2019). Three pillars of sustainability: In search of conceptual origins. *Sustainability Science*, *14*(3), 681–695. DOI: 10.1007/s11625-018-0627-5

Pushpalatha, V., Mallikarjuna, P. B., Mahendra, H. N., Subramoniam, S. R., & Mallikarjunaswamy, S. (2025). Land use and land cover classification for change detection studies using a convolutional neural network. *Applied Computing and Geosciences*, *25*, 100227. DOI: 10.1016/j.acags.2025.100227

Raghavan, M., Barocas, S., Kleinberg, J., & Levy, K. (2021). Mitigating bias in algorithmic hiring: Evaluating claims and practices. *Proceedings of the 2021 ACM Conference on Fairness, Accountability, and Transparency*, 469-481. DOI: 10.1145/3442188.3445923

Rahwan, I., Cebrian, M., Obradovich, N., Bongard, J., Bonnefon, J. F., Breazeal, C., Crandall, J. W., Christakis, N. A., Couzin, I. D., Jackson, M. O., Jennings, N. R., Kamar, E., Kloumann, I. M., Larochelle, H., Lazer, D., McElreath, R., Mislove, A., Parkes, D. C., Pentland, A. S., & Wellman, M. (2019). Machine behaviour. *Nature*, *568*(7753), 477–486. DOI: 10.1038/s41586-019-1138-y PMID: 31019318

Raihan, A. (2024). A review of the potential opportunities and challenges of the digital economy for sustainability. *Innovation and Green Development*, *3*(4), 100174. DOI: 10.1016/j.igd.2024.100174

Rajasekhar, N., Radhakrishnan, T. K., & Samsudeen, N. (2025). Exploring reinforcement learning in process control: A comprehensive survey. *International Journal of Systems Science*, *56*(14), 1–30. DOI: 10.1080/00207721.2025.2469821

Ramadan, M. N. A., Ali, M. A. H., Khoo, S. Y., Alkhedher, M., & Alherbawi, M. (2024). Real-time IoT-powered AI system for monitoring and forecasting air pollution in an industrial environment. *Ecotoxicology and Environmental Safety*, *283*, 116856. DOI: 10.1016/j.ecoenv.2024.116856

Ranpara, R. (2025). Energy-efficient green AI architectures for circular economies through multi-layered sustainable resource optimization framework. *Discover Sustainability*, *6*(1), 1031. DOI: 10.1007/s43621-025-01846-x

Rashid, A. B., & Kausik, M. A. K. (2024). AI revolutionizing industries worldwide: A comprehensive overview of its diverse applications. *Hybrid Advances*, *7*, 100277. DOI: 10.1016/j.hybadv.2024.100277

Ravikumar, S., Vellingiri, G., Sellaperumal, P., Pandian, K., Sivasankar, A., & Sangchul, H. (2024). Real-time nitrogen monitoring and management to augment N use efficiency and ecosystem sustainability–A review. *Journal of Hazardous Materials Advances*, *16*, 100466. DOI: 10.1016/j.hazadv.2024.100466

Regona, M., Yigitcanlar, T., Hon, C., & Teo, M. (2024). Artificial intelligence and sustainable development goals: Systematic literature review of the construction industry. *Sustainable Cities and Society*, *108*, 105499. DOI: 10.1016/j.scs.2024.105499

Reynolds, S. A., Beery, S., Burgess, N., Burgman, M., Butchart, S. H. M., Cooke, S. J., Coomes, D., Danielsen, F., Di Minin, E., Durán, A. P., Gassert, F., Hinsley, A., Jaffer, S., Jones, J. P. G., Li, B. V., Mac Aodha, O., Madhavapeddy, A., O'Donnell, S. A. L., Oxbury, W. M., & Sutherland, W. J. (2025). The potential for AI to revolutionize conservation: A horizon scan. *Trends in Ecology & Evolution*, *40*(2), 191–207. DOI: 10.1016/j.tree.2024.11.013

Rockström, J., Steffen, W., Noone, K., Persson, Å., Chapin, F. S.III, Lambin, E. F., Lenton, T. M., Scheffer, M., Folke, C., Schellnhuber, H. J., Nykvist, B., De Wit, C. A., Hughes, T., van der Leeuw, S., Rodhe, H., Sörlin, S., Snyder, P. K., Costanza, R., Svedin, U., & Foley, J. A. (2009). A safe operating space for humanity. *Nature*, *461*(7263), 472–475. DOI: 10.1038/461472a

Rolnick, D., Donti, P. L., Kaack, L. H., Kochanski, K., Lacoste, A., Sankaran, K., Ross, A. S., Milojevic-Dupont, N., Jaques, N., Waldman-Brown, A., Luccioni, A. S., Maharaj, T., Sherwin, E. D., Mukkavilli, S. K., Kording, K. P., Gomes, C. P., Ng, A. Y., Hassabis, D., Platt, J. C., & Bengio, Y. (2022). Tackling climate change with machine learning. *ACM Computing Surveys*, 55(2). *ACM Computing Surveys*, *42*(2), 1–96. DOI: 10.1145/3485128

Saberi, S., Kouhizadeh, M., Sarkis, J., & Shen, L. (2018). Blockchain technology and its relationships to sustainable supply chain management. *International Journal of Production Research*, *57*(3), 2117–2135. DOI: 10.1080/00207543.2018.1533261

Sachithra, V., & Subhashini, L. D. C. S. (2023). How artificial intelligence is used to achieve agricultural sustainability: A systematic review. *Artificial Intelligence in Agriculture*, *8*, 46–59. DOI: 10.1016/j.aiia.2023.04.002

Sadorsky, P. (2009). Renewable energy consumption and income in emerging economies. *Energy Policy*, *37*(10), 4021–4028. DOI: 10.1016/j.enpol.2009.05.003

Sahoo, S., Singha, C., Govind, A., & Moghimi, A. (2025). Review of climate-resilient agriculture for ensuring food security: Sustainability opportunities and challenges of India. *Environmental and Sustainability Indicators*, *25*, 100544. DOI: 10.1016/j.indic.2024.100544

Saiz-Rubio, V., & Rovira-Más, F. (2020). From smart farming towards agriculture 5.0: A review on crop data management. *Agronomy (Basel)*, *10*(2), 207. DOI: 10.3390/agronomy10020207

Salmi, A., Quarshie, A. M., Scott-Kennel, J., & Kähkönen, A.-K. (2023). Biodiversity management: A supply chain practice view. *Journal of Purchasing and Supply Management*, *29*(4), 100865. DOI: 10.1016/j.pursup.2023.100865

Salomon, R. (1997, April). Raising theoretical questions about the utility of genetic algorithms. *International Conference on Evolutionary Programming* (pp. 275-284). Berlin, Heidelberg: Springer Berlin Heidelberg. DOI: 10.1007/BFb0014818

Sam, C. Y., McNown, R., & Goh, S. K. (2018). An augmented autoregressive distributed lag bounds test for cointegration. *Economic Modelling*, *70*, 418–426. DOI: 10.1016/j.econmod.2017.11.021

Saurabh, K., & Majumdar, R. (2022). Fuels for sustainable transport in India. In *Clean fuels for mobility* (pp. 27–55). Springer Singapore. DOI: 10.1007/978-981-16-8747-1_3

Saurabh, K., & Majumdar, R. (2023). Functional use-based positioning of conventional vehicles in conjunction with alternate low-emission fuels. In *Renewable fuels for sustainable mobility* (pp. 97–159). Springer Nature Singapore. DOI: 10.1007/978-981-99-1392-3_5

Saxena, S., & Khandelwal, P. (2020). AI-enabled personalized service and human touch in hospitality: A study of guest experiences. *Tourism and Hospitality Study*, *20*(3), 300–315. DOI: 10.1177/1467358419869432

Saxena, S., & Khandelwal, P. (2020). Diversity and Inclusion in Hospitality: A Comprehensive Overview. *Hospitality & Society*, *10*(2), 153–170. DOI: 10.1386/hosp_00023_7

Schmager, S., Pappas, I. O., & Vassilakopoulou, P. (2025). Understanding human-centered AI: A review of its defining elements and a research agenda. *Behaviour & Information Technology*, *44*(15), 1–40. DOI: 10.1080/0144929X.2024.2448719

Schoormann, T., Strobel, G., Möller, F., Petrik, D., & Zschech, P. (2023). Artificial intelligence for sustainability: A systematic review of information systems literature. *Communications of the Association for Information Systems*, *52*(1), 199–237. DOI: 10.17705/1CAIS.05209

Schütze, P. (2024). The problem of sustainable AI: A critical assessment of an emerging phenomenon. *Weizenbaum Journal of the Digital Society*, *4*(1), 1–21.

Schwartz, R., Dodge, J., Smith, N. A., & Etzioni, O. (2020). Green AI. *Communications of the ACM*, *63*(12), 54–63. DOI: 10.1145/3381831

Shahbaz, M., Zakaria, M., Shahzad, S. J. H., & Mahalik, M. K. (2018). The energy consumption and economic growth nexus in top ten energy-consuming countries: Fresh evidence from using the quantile-on-quantile approach. *Energy Economics*, *71*, 282–301. DOI: 10.1016/j.eneco.2018.02.023

Shah, H., Hellegers, P., & Siderius, C. (2021). Climate risk to agriculture: A synthesis to define different types of critical moments. *Climate Risk Management*, *34*, 100378. DOI: 10.1016/j.crm.2021.100378

Shahzad, U. (2012). The need for renewable energy sources. *ITEE Journal.* 2(1), ISSN:2306-708X

Shakti Sustainable Energy Foundation. (2023). Energy Dialogues: Annual Report 2023. Shakti Foundation. https://shaktifoundation.in/wp-content/uploads/2024/05/shakti-annual-report-2023.pdf

Sharif, A., Saqib, N., Dong, K., & Khan, S. A. R. (2022). Nexus between green technology innovation, green financing, and CO2 emissions in the G7 countries: The moderating role of social globalisation. *Sustainable Development (Bradford), 30*(6), 1934–1946. DOI: 10.1002/sd.2360

Sharma, I., & Birman, S. (2024). Biodiversity loss, ecosystem services, and their role in promoting sustainable health. In Singh, P., & Yadav, N. (Eds.), *The climate-health-sustainability nexus*. Springer. DOI: 10.1007/978-3-031-56564-9_7

Sharma, R., Shahbaz, M., Kautish, P., & Vo, X. V. (2021). Analyzing the impact of export diversification and technological innovation on renewable energy consumption: Evidences from BRICS nations. *Renewable Energy, 178*, 1034–1045. DOI: 10.1016/j.renene.2021.06.125

Shetty, S. S., Deepthi, D., Harshitha, S., Sonkusare, S., Naik, P. B., Kumari, S. N., & Madhyastha, H. (2023). Environmental pollutants and their effects on human health. *Heliyon, 9*(9), e19496. DOI: 10.1016/j.heliyon.2023.e19496

Shivanna, K. R. (2022). Climate change and its impact on biodiversity and human welfare. *Proceedings of the Indian National Science Academy. Part A, Physical Sciences, 88*(2), 160–171. DOI: 10.1007/s43538-022-00073-6

Shobanke, M., Bhatt, M., & Shittu, E. (2025). Advancements and future outlook of artificial intelligence in energy and climate change modeling. *Advances in Applied Energy, 17*, 100211. DOI: 10.1016/j.adapen.2025.100211

Siau, K., & Wang, W. (2020). Ethical and Legal Implications of AI: Ensuring Fairness and Accountability in AI Systems. *Journal of Artificial Intelligence Study, 69*(1), 229–248.

Singh, R.. (2021). The Role of Inclusive Culture in Enhancing Employee and Customer Experience in the Hospitality Industry. *International Journal of Hospitality Management*, *95*, 102887. DOI: 10.1016/j.ijhm.2021.102887

Solarin, S. A., Bello, M. O., & Tiwari, A. K. (2022). The impact of technological innovation on renewable energy production: Accounting for the roles of economic and environmental factors using a method of moments quantile regression. *Heliyon*, *8*(7), e09913. DOI: 10.1016/j.heliyon.2022.e09913 PMID: 35855992

Soleimani, R., Soleimani-Babakamali, M. H., Meng, S., Avci, O., & Taciroglu, E. (2024). Computer vision tools for early post-disaster assessment: Enhancing generalizability. Engineering *Applications of Artificial Intelligence,* 136(Part A), 108855.DOI: 10.1016/j.engappai.2024.108855

Solow, R. M. (1956). A contribution to the theory of economic growth. *The Quarterly Journal of Economics*, *70*(1), 65–94. DOI: 10.2307/1884513

Soytas, U., Sari, R., & Ewing, B. T. (2007). Energy consumption, income, and carbon emissions in the United States. *Ecological Economics*, *62*(3-4), 482–489. DOI: 10.1016/j.ecolecon.2006.07.009

Stamatakis, E., Zoulias, E., Tzamalis, G., Massina, Z., Analytis, V., Christodoulou, C., & Stubos, A. (2018). Metal hydride hydrogen compressors: Current developments & early markets. *Renewable Energy*, *127*, 850–862. DOI: 10.1016/j.renene.2018.04.073

Stern, D. I. (2004). The rise and fall of the Environmental Kuznets Curve. *World Development*, *32*(8), 1419–1439. DOI: 10.1016/j.worlddev.2004.03.004

Stock, J. H., & Watson, M. W. (1993). A simple estimator of cointegrating vectors in higher order integrated systems. *Econometrica*, *61*(4), 783–820. DOI: 10.2307/2951763

Strubell, E., Ganesh, A., & McCallum, A. (2019). Energy and policy considerations for deep learning in NLP. *Proceedings of the 57th Annual Meeting of the Association for Computational Linguistics*, 3645–3650. DOI: 10.18653/v1/P19-1355

Strubell, E., Ganesh, A., & McCallum, A. (2020). Energy and policy considerations for deep learning in NLP. In *Proceedings of the 58th Annual Meeting of the Association for Computational Linguistics (ACL)* (pp. 3645–3650). ACL. DOI: 10.18653/v1/2020.acl-main.345

Subeesh, A., & Mehta, C. R. (2021). Automation and digitization of agriculture using artificial intelligence and the Internet of Things. *Artificial Intelligence in Agriculture*, *5*, 278–291. DOI: 10.1016/j.aiia.2021.11.004

Subrahmanyam, S. (2025). Emerging Technologies and Shift in Employment in the Transportation Sector. In Olga Titovna, E., Elango, D., Kumar, P., Mehra, P., & Verma, R. (Eds.), *Integrating Sustainability and Autonomous Transportation for Enhanced Urban Mobility* (pp. 149–178). IGI Global Scientific Publishing., DOI: 10.4018/979-8-3373-0882-1.ch006

Subrahmanyam, S. (2025). Integrating AI and AR Into Teaching and Scholarly Communication. In Vrba, J., & Huynh, T. (Eds.), *Revolutionizing Academic Research With AI and Augmented Reality* (pp. 179–212). IGI Global Scientific Publishing., DOI: 10.4018/979-8-3373-1414-3.ch006

Subrahmanyam, S. (2025). Leveraging Data for Climate Action: Smart Governance in the Digital Age. In Uğur, Ö., & Doğan, K. (Eds.), *Designing Effective Public Policies to Address Global Warming* (pp. 285–316). IGI Global Scientific Publishing., DOI: 10.4018/979-8-3373-1310-8.ch012

Subrahmanyam, S. (2025). Smart Cities and E-Government: How Startups Are Transforming Urban Life. In Mishra, D., Kumar, R., & Abdul Hamid, A. (Eds.), *Startup-Driven E-Government: Digital Innovation for Sustainable Ecosystems* (pp. 465–490). IGI Global Scientific Publishing., DOI: 10.4018/979-8-3373-0817-3.ch018

Subrahmanyam, S., Khalife, D., & El-Chaarani, H. (2024). Towards Sustainable Future: Exploring Renewable Energy Solutions and Environmental Impacts. *ACTA INNOVATIONS*, *51*(1), 15–24. DOI: 10.62441/ActaInnovations.51.3

Subrahmanyam, S., & Sri, G. S. (2025). Challenges and Opportunities for Tech Entrepreneurs in Agriculture. In Whig, P., & Elngar, A. (Eds.), *Precision and Intelligence in Agriculture: Advanced Technologies for Sustainable Farming* (pp. 1–28). IGI Global Scientific Publishing., DOI: 10.4018/979-8-3373-5283-1.ch001

Su, C. W., Khan, K., Umar, M., & Zhang, W. (2021). Does renewable energy redefine geopolitical risks? *Energy Policy*, *158*, 112566. DOI: 10.1016/j.enpol.2021.112566

Sun, Y., Li, M., Zhang, M., Khan, H. S. U. D., Li, J., Li, Z., Sun, H., Zhu, Y., & Anaba, O. A. (2021). A study on China's economic growth, green energy technology, and carbon emissions based on the Kuznets curve (EKC). *Environmental Science and Pollution Research International*, *28*(6), 7200–7211. DOI: 10.1007/s11356-020-11019-0

Supriyono, W., Wibawa, A. P., Suyono, , & Kurniawan, F. (2024). Advancements in natural language processing: Implications, challenges, and future directions. *Telematics and Informatics Reports*, *16*, 100173. DOI: 10.1016/j.teler.2024.100173

Taddeo, M. (2023). Artificial Intelligence in the Colonial Matrix of Power. *Philosophy & Technology*, *36*(1), 1–18. DOI: 10.1007/s13347-023-00687-8

Talukder, M. B. (2025). Revolutionizing Hospitality: Leveraging Mobile Apps and Cutting-Edge Room Technologies in the Hotel Industry. In B. Varghese & S. H. (Eds.), *Advancing Smart Tourism Through Analytics* (pp. 315-332). IGI Global Scientific Publishing. DOI: 10.4018/979-8-3693-3715-8.ch017

Talukder, M. B., Kabir, F., Kaiser, F., & Hoque, M. (2025). Perspectives for the Potential and Future of Marine Tourism in Bangladesh. In Alkier, R., Catenazzo, G., Milojica, V., & Zając, A. (Eds.), *Cases on Effective Destination Management* (pp. 83–104). IGI Global Scientific Publishing., DOI: 10.4018/979-8-3693-1548-4.ch004

Talukder, M. B., & Kumar, S. (2024). The Development of ChatGPT and Its Implications for the Future of Customer Service in the Hospitality Industry. In Derbali, A. M. S. (Ed.), (pp. 100–126). Advances in Information Security, Privacy, and Ethics. IGI Global., DOI: 10.4018/979-8-3693-1511-8.ch005

Talukder, M. B., Kumar, S., & Das Tonny, O. (2025). Innovative Solutions for Employee Well-Being in the Digital Hospitality Era. In Ahmad, B., Abrar, M., & Saeed, M. (Eds.), *Marketing Technology-Infused Hospitality: Upskilling Frontline Employees for Competitiveness* (pp. 231–258). IGI Global Scientific Publishing., DOI: 10.4018/979-8-3693-7127-5.ch009

Talukder, M. B., Kumar, S., Sood, K., & Grima, S. (2023). Information Technology, Food Service Quality, and Restaurant Revisit Intention. *International Journal of Sustainable Development and Planning*, *18*(1), 295–303. DOI: 10.18280/ijsdp.180131

Talukder, M. B., Kumar, S., & Tyagi, P. K. (Eds.). (2024). *Impact of AI and Tech-Driven Solutions in Hospitality and Tourism*. IGI Global., DOI: 10.4018/979-8-3693-6755-1

Tang, D. Y., & Zhang, Y. (2020). Do shareholders benefit from green bonds? *Journal of Corporate Finance*, *61*, 101427. DOI: 10.1016/j.jcorpfin.2018.12.001

Truby, J. (2020). Governing Artificial Intelligence to benefit the UN Sustainable Development Goals. *Sustainable Development (Bradford)*, *28*(4), 946–959. DOI: 10.1002/sd.2048

UCDP. (n.d.). *Uppsala Conflict Data Program*.https://ucdp.uu.se/

UNESCO. (2021). *Recommendation on the Ethics of Artificial Intelligence*. UNESCO. https://unesdoc.unesco.org/ark:/48223/pf0000380455

United Nations World Tourism Organization (UNWTO). (2019). Inclusive growth and the future of tourism: A United Nations perspective. Retrieved from https://www.unwto.org

United Nations. (2015). *Transforming our world: The 2030 Agenda for Sustainable Development*. New York: UN. https://sdgs.un.org/2030agenda

United Nations. (2023). *The Sustainable Development Goals Report 2023: Special Edition*. United Nations. https://unstats.un.org/sdgs/report/2023/

Van de Graaf, T., Overland, I., Scholten, D., & Westphal, K. (2020). The new oil? The geopolitics and international governance of hydrogen. *Energy Research & Social Science*, *70*, 101667. DOI: 10.1016/j.erss.2020.101667 PMID: 32835007

van der Sluijs, J. P., & Vaage, N. S. (2016). Pollinators and global food security: The need for holistic global stewardship. *Food Ethics*, *1*(1), 75–91. DOI: 10.1007/s41055-016-0003-z

Van Wynsberghe, A. (2021). Sustainable AI: AI for sustainability and the sustainability of AI. *AI and Ethics*, *1*(3), 213–218. DOI: 10.1007/s43681-021-00043-6

van Wynsberghe, A., Vandemeulebroucke, T., Bolte, L., & Nachid, J. (2022). Towards the sustainability of AI: Multi-disciplinary approaches to investigate the hidden costs of AI [Editorial]. *Sustainability (Basel)*, *14*(24), 16352. DOI: 10.3390/su142416352

Verdecchia, R., Sallou, J., & Cruz, L. (2023). A systematic review of Green AI. *Wiley Interdisciplinary Reviews. Data Mining and Knowledge Discovery*, *13*(1), e1507. DOI: 10.1002/widm.1507

Vinuesa, R., & Sirmacek, B. (2021). Interpretable deep-learning models to help achieve the Sustainable Development Goals. *Nature Machine Intelligence*, *3*(11), 926. Advance online publication. DOI: 10.1038/s42256-021-00414-y

Wang, Y. (2024). Application of Artificial Intelligence Technology in the Agricultural Field. *Transactions on Computer Science and Intelligent Systems Research*, *5*, 457–463. DOI: 10.62051/aeay9r82

Wang, Y., Li, C., & Zhang, H. (2022). AI-driven personalization in hospitality: Balancing efficiency and guest privacy. *Journal of Hospitality Marketing & Management, 31*(6), 671–690.

Wang, Z., Wang, T., Zhang, X., Wang, J., Yang, Y., Sun, Y., Guo, X., Wu, Q., Nepovimova, E., Watson, A. E., & Kuca, K. (2024). Biodiversity conservation in the context of climate change: Facing challenges and management strategies. *The Science of the Total Environment, 937*, 173377. DOI: 10.1016/j.scitotenv.2024.173377

Waqas, M., Humphries, U. W., Chueasa, B., & Wangwongchai, A. (2024). Artificial intelligence and numerical weather prediction models: A technical survey. *Natural Hazards Research*. (Advance online publication). DOI: 10.1016/j.nhres.2024.11.004

Weiskopf, S. R., Rubenstein, M. A., Crozier, L. G., Gaichas, S., Griffis, R., Halofsky, J. E., Hyde, K. J. W., Morelli, T. L., Morisette, J. T., Muñoz, R. C., Pershing, A. J., Peterson, D. L., Poudel, R., Staudinger, M. D., Sutton-Grier, A. E., Thompson, L., Vose, J., Weltzin, J. F., & Whyte, K. P. (2020). Climate change affects biodiversity, ecosystems, ecosystem services, and natural resource management in the United States— *cience of The Total Environment,* 733, 137782..DOI: 10.1016/j.scitotenv.2020.137782

Wijaya, C. Y. (2024). Python's itertools for memory-efficient iteration – NBD Lite #23. *Non-Brand Data*. https://www.nb-data.com/p/pythons-itertools-for-memory-efficient

Wilson, C., & van der Velden, M. (2022). Sustainable AI: An integrated model to guide public sector decision-making. *Technology in Society, 68*, 101926. DOI: 10.1016/j.techsoc.2022.101926

World Bank. (2022). [Washington, DC: World Bank. https://databank.worldbank.org/source/world-development-indicators]. *World Development Indicators, 2022,* •••.

World Bank. (2025). *Devising a Strategic Approach to Artificial Intelligence: A Handbook for Policy Makers*. World Bank Group. https://openknowledge.worldbank.org/entities/publication/7bf93f96-1ed1-4407-a008-906ae80f3fd8

World Intellectual Property Organization (WIPO). (2021). *World Intellectual Property Indicators 2021*. Geneva: WIPO. https://www.wipo.int/publications/en/details.jsp?id=4526

Wu, C., Yang, Y., Zhang, Y., Xu, H., He, X., Wu, X., & Chou, S. (2024). Hard carbon for sodium-ion batteries: Progress, strategies and future perspective. *Chemical Science (Cambridge)*, *15*(17), 6244–6268. DOI: 10.1039/D4SC00734D PMID: 38699270

Xu, A., Zhu, Y., & Wang, W. (2023). Micro green technology innovation effects of green finance pilot policy—From the perspectives of action points and green value. *Journal of Business Research*, *159*, 113724. DOI: 10.1016/j.jbusres.2023.113724

Xu, Y., Liu, X., Cao, X., Huang, C., Liu, E., Qian, S., Liu, X., Wu, Y., Dong, F., Qiu, C.-W., Qiu, J., Hua, K., Su, W., Wu, J., Xu, H., Han, Y., Fu, C., Yin, Z., Liu, M., & Zhang, J. (2021). A*rtificial intelligence: A powerful paradigm for scientific research. Innovation (Cambridge (Mass.))*, *2*(4), 100179. DOI: 10.1016/j.xinn.2021.100179

Xu, Y., Tian, Y., Cai, X., Wu, C., & Mian, Z. (2025). Air quality forecasting and rating based on machine learning algorithm and cumulative logit model: An empirical study for Lanzhou city of China. *Environment, Development and Sustainability*. Advance online publication. DOI: 10.1007/s10668-024-05792-y

Yang, M., Hunger, R., Berrettoni, S., Sprecher, B., & Wang, B. (2023). A review of hydrogen storage and transport technologies. *Clean Energy*, *7*(1), 190–216. DOI: 10.1093/ce/zkad021

Yang, Q., Liu, Y., Chen, T., & Tong, Y. (2019). Federated machine learning: Concept and applications. *ACM Transactions on Intelligent Systems and Technology*, *10*(2), 1–19. DOI: 10.1145/3298981

Yilanci, V., & Pata, U. K. (2020). Investigating the EKC hypothesis for China: The role of economic complexity on ecological footprint. *Environmental Science and Pollution Research International*, *27*(26), 32683–32694. DOI: 10.1007/s11356-020-09434-4

Yu, P., Wei, Y., Ma, L., Wang, B., Yung, E. H. K., & Chen, Y. (2024). rbanization and the urban critical zone. *arth Critical Zone,* 1(1), 100011. DOI: 10.1016/j.ecz.2024.100011

Yu, X., Fan, L., & Yu, Y. (2025). Analysis based on corporate efficiency and external environment. *Sustainability (Basel), 17*(9), 3819. DOI: 10.3390/su17093819

Zakaria, Z., & Kamarudin, S. K. (2021). A review of alkaline solid polymer membrane in the application of AEM electrolyzer: Materials and characterization. *International Journal of Energy Research, 45*(13), 18337–18354. DOI: 10.1002/er.6983

Zhang, D., Zheng, M., Feng, G. F., & Chang, C. P. (2022). Does an environmental policy bring green innovation in renewable energy? *Renewable Energy, 195*, 1113–1124. DOI: 10.1016/j.renene.2022.06.074

Zhang, Y., Carballo, A., Yang, H., & Takeda, K. (2023). Perception and sensing for autonomous vehicles under adverse weather conditions: A survey. *ISPRS Journal of Photogrammetry and Remote Sensing, 196*, 146–177. DOI: 10.1016/j.isprsjprs.2022.12.021

Zhao, A. P., Li, S., Cao, Z., Hu, P. J.-H., Wang, J., Xiang, Y., Xie, D., & Lu, X. (2024). I for science: Predicting infectious diseases. *ournal of Safety Science and Resilience,* 5(2), 130–146. DOI: 10.1038/s41467-019-14108-y

Zhao, Q., Su, C. W., & Guo, J. M. (2024). Does technological innovation promote renewable energy investment? *SAGE Open, 14*(1), 21582440241227760. DOI: 10.1177/21582440241227760

Zhou, Y., & Gu, B. (2024). The impacts of human activities on Earth's Critical Zone. *arth Critical Zone,* 1(1), 100004. DOI: 10.1016/j.ecz.2024.100004

Zhou, M., Zhang, X., & Li, Y. (2022). Can green patents reduce carbon emission intensity? *Frontiers in Environmental Science, 29*(45), 68000–68012. DOI: 10.3389/fenvs.2022.1084977

Zhou, W., Zhang, Y., & Li, X. (2024). Artificial intelligence, green technological progress, energy conservation, and carbon emission reduction in China: An examination based on dynamic spatial Durbin modeling. *Journal of Cleaner Production, 446*, 141142. DOI: 10.1016/j.jclepro.2024.141142

Zhou, Y., Li, R., Lv, Z., Liu, J., Zhou, H., & Xu, C. (2022). Green hydrogen: A promising way to a carbon-free society. *Chinese Journal of Chemical Engineering, 43*, 2–13. Advance online publication. DOI: 10.1016/j.cjche.2022.02.001

Zivot, E., & Andrews, D. W. K. (1992). Further evidence on the great crash, the oil price shock, and the unit root hypothesis. *Journal of Business & Economic Statistics, 10*(3), 251–270. DOI: 10.1080/07350015.1992.10509904

About the Contributors

Amal Jmaii is an Assistant Professor in Quantitative Economics at the Department of Quantitative Methods, Faculty of Economic Sciences and Management, University of Tunis, Tunisia. His research interests primarily focus on applied econometrics, development economics, and climate change policy. Dr. Jmaii is also an active reviewer for several prestigious academic journals, including the African Development Review and Climate Policy. He is a member of the Arab Council for Social Sciences and the Laboratory for Research in Quantitative Development Economics., which focus on advancing research in economics. With extensive expertise in both theoretical and empirical methods, Dr. Jmaii has made significant contributions to understanding economic dynamics, particularly in the context of environmental challenges. His work is especially focused on the African and Mediterranean regions, aiming to bridge the gap between quantitative analysis and real-world economic issues. His academic endeavors emphasize sustainable development and the impact of climate change on economic outcomes, with a particular interest in how these challenges intersect with broader development goals.

***

Mohammad Al-Khaldy is an Assistant professor of Business Intelligence and Data Analytics at University of Petra, Jordan. He completed his PhD in Artificial Intelligence and Data Science for the University of Hull -United Kingdom - 2017. Alkhaldy's research interests include data analytics, machine learning, predictive analytics, NLP, and decision support systems. His research has been published extensively in academic journals and conferences. Alkhaldy taught a variety of courses in Artificial intelligence and business intelligence, including Data Mining, Business Analytics, Computer Programming, Intelligent business systems, Data Visualization, and machine learning. Alkhaldy is a member of Jordan Computers Society, and Arab Robotics & AI Association. He also a reviewer for several other academic conferences and journals.

Mohammad Alauthman is an Associate Professor in the Information Security Department at the Faculty of Information Technology, University of Petra, Amman, Jordan. His research interests include network security, intrusion detection systems, and applying AI techniques—such as machine learning and deep learning—for botnet and DDoS detection, spam filtering, IoT security, and network traffic classification. He earned his Ph.D. in Computer Science from Northumbria University, UK, in 2016. Dr. Alauthman has received multiple research grants supporting advanced AI-driven intrusion detection systems and international collaboration. He is also actively involved in Erasmus+ projects, including BITTCOIN-JO (technology transfer), RL4Eng (remote engineering labs), Pro-GREEN LABs (green competences in education), and COMMO (mobility and cooperation across Mediterranean and Balkan institutions), contributing to innovation, sustainability, and cross-border academic development.

Amjad Aldweesh is a computer associate professor interested in the Blockchain and Smart contracts technology as well as cyber security. Amjad has a Bachelor degree in computer science. He has a MSc degree in advanced computer science and security from the University of Manchester with distinction. Amjad is the second in the UK and the first in the middle east to have a PhD in the Blockchain and Smart contracts technology from Newcastle University.

Ammar Almomani is a seasoned academic, researcher, and consultant with 20+ years of experience in cybersecurity, AI, and computer science. He holds a Ph.D. in Advanced Internet Security from Universiti Sains Malaysia and has taught over 45 specialized courses. He serves in the IT departments at Al-Balqa Applied University (Jordan) and Higher Colleges of Technology (UAE), contributing to research, curriculum design, and program accreditation (ABET, AACSB). He holds 10 patents (Germany and India) and has published 165+ articles (104 in Scopus), earning global recognition, a UAE Golden Visa, and ranking among the Top 2% of Global Researchers (Stanford & Scopus, 2023–2024). Prof. Almomani also supervises MSc/Ph.D. students internationally, chairs conferences, and engages in industry collaborations. With 113,000+ ResearchGate readers.Prof. Almomani continues to make a significant impact in the fields of cybersecurity,AI and higher education fostering innovation .

Nishtha Chhabra is a research scholar, whose research interests are Clean and Sustainable Energy, Tactile Mathematics, and Algorithm Bias.

Manjunatha Reddy G. R. is an accomplished botanist, academic leader, and researcher with over two decades of experience in teaching, research, and institutional development. He earned his M.Sc. and Ph.D. in Botany from Bangalore University and an M.Phil. in Biotechnology from Bharathidasan University, Tamil Nadu. His doctoral research focused on in vitro regeneration and the influence of Arbuscular mycorrhizal (AM) fungi on micropropagated Withania somnifera (Indian ginseng), reflecting his expertise in plant biotechnology, mycorrhizal biology, and conservation science. Dr. Reddy began his academic career in 2004 as a Lecturer at AMC American College, Bangalore, and subsequently served in teaching and research roles at SRN Adarsh College, Bangalore University, and Dayanand Sagar institutions. His leadership journey includes serving as Principal at Anjanadri PU College (2014–2017) and Rathnagiri PU College under the RVS Group of Institutions (2017–2024). Currently, he serves as a Guest Faculty in the Department of Botany at Bangalore University, while also undertaking visiting faculty assignments for interdisciplinary programs. As a researcher, Dr. Reddy has published extensively in peer-reviewed international journals and authored multiple book chapters with leading publishers, including Springer, IGI Global, CRC Press, Cambridge Scholars, Apple Academic Press, and Integrated Publications (indexed in Scopus & WoS). His work spans plant–microbe interactions, plant breeding, omics technologies, nanotechnology in food sciences, and the application of artificial intelligence for biodiversity conservation and sustainability. He also contributes as a reviewer for IGI Global and regularly presents his research at national and international scientific conferences, workshops, and symposia. In recognition of his commitment to teaching and mentoring, Dr. Reddy received the Star Teacher Award (2012). He also serves as a Scientist Mentor with Planting Science (USA), a program sponsored by the Botanical Society of America and the National Science Foundation, where he guides school and undergraduate students in plant biology research. Beyond research and teaching, Dr. Reddy has been actively involved in institution-building, academic quality assurance (NAAC, IQAC), curriculum design, and organizing scientific seminars and outreach activities. He has also contributed to biodiversity awareness and conservation initiatives, including seed ball distribution and public science engagement programs. Dr. Reddy's career reflects a deep commitment to advancing plant sciences, environmental sustainability, and innovative pedagogy. His vision is to integrate modern technologies such as AI, omics, and remote sensing with traditional plant biology to address pressing challenges in agriculture, biodiversity conservation, and climate change resilience, while continuing to inspire the next generation of scientists and students.

Tapasi Ghosh is an Associate Professor and Head, Department of Data Sciences and Analytics, Ramaiah University of Applied Sciences, India. Her PhD degree is in Physics in the area of Pattern Recognition and Data Analysis techniques. Her present research interest lies in the intersection of Machine Learning, Deep Learning and experimental nuclear physics, along with the uncertainty quantification of Language Models and Retrieval Augmented Generation. She has been part of several international high-energy experiments and has published research articles in journals. She has also secured grants from various Federal Government agencies, including the Ministry of Science, Technology, and Innovation in Brazil and the Department of Science and Technology in India, as Principal Investigator. She is equally excited about exploring the algorithmic innovation and optimisation techniques in the green hydrogen sector.

Sanjeev Kumar Is a Professor in Lovely Professional University Punjab India. He received Undergraduate in Hotel Management from Osmania University, Postgraduate in Tourism Management from Madurai Kamaraj University. He completed Doctor of Philosophy in Hospitality

Management in 2019 from Amity University Jaipur India. His research areas lies in food Service Industry, his research focuses on Alcoholic beverages, Event management and Sustainable Management Practices, Metaverse, AI Machine Learning and Artificial Intelligence. He published more than 60 research papers, articles and chapters in Scopus Indexed, UGC Approved and peer reviewed Journals and books. Dr. Sanjeev Kumar participated and acted as resource person in various National and International conferences, seminars, session chair, research workshops and industry talks and his work has been widely cited. Dr. Sanjeev also edited more than 12 books with various International Publishers such as IGI Global, Cambridge Scholars, Emerald, CABI, Bentham Science, Taylor & Francis. Dr Sanjeev is an active researcher and has published numerous research articles in prestigious national and international journals and books.

Rudrodip Majumdar is currently an Associate Professor in the Energy, Environment, and Climate Change Programme at NIAS w.e.f. 01 July 2025. Previously, he served as an Assistant Professor at the institute from August 2019 to June 2025. He has a PhD in Nuclear Engineering from North Carolina State University in the USA and an M.Tech. in Nuclear Engineering from IIT Kanpur. Before joining NIAS, Rudrodip worked as an Institute Postdoctoral Fellow at IIT Bombay and as a Postdoctoral Research Assistant at North Carolina State University. Rudrodip's professional research interests centre around Sustainability, encompassing Renewable and Clean Energy, Nuclear and Plasma Fusion Energy, Industrial Applications of Plasma, and Analyses of Energy-efficient Sustainable Systems. To date, Rudrodip has published 36 research articles in reputed International Journals, 12 Chapters in Edited Volumes (Monographs) of Repute, and 21 papers in International Conference Proceedings. His recent work on the evaluation of energy transition-readiness in low-to-medium-income households in Bengaluru has been highly appreciated by the Office of the Principal Scientific Advisor to the Government of India. By nomination, Rudrodip has been selected as a Review Editor of the Energy Storage section in Frontiers in Energy Research Journal.

Kuldeep Singh currently serves as an Assistant Professor in Amity School of Hospitality, Amity University, Haryana, India. He completed his Ph.D. in tourism from Maharshi Dayanand University (Rohtak) India in 2021. He is also a UGC (Net- JRF qualified). Dr. Singh has also served the tourism industry for a couple of years and more than three years in academics. Dr. Singh has so far published more than 40 research articles in both international and national referred journals as well as in edited books in the field of Tourism. Currently, He is serving as an editor of book series in various reputed publications (Emerald, IIP series). Dr. Singh is passionate about the academic areas of Service Quality Management, Rural tourism, Ecotourism, and Sustainable tourism. He also won an aspiring researchers welcome award from Indian Hospitality Congress. His credentials may be verified on various research platforms like Google Scholar, SSRN, LinkedIn, Academia, and Research Gate.

Subramanyam T is a highly distinguished member of the Faculty of Mathematical and Physical Sciences, RUAS. He brings in 16 plus years of academic experience as a Guest Faculty, Assistant Professor, Associate Professor at various esteemed institutions such as Sri Venkateswara University, Pondicherry University (A Central University), CHRIST (Deemed to be University) and AIMS Institute for Higher Education, Bangalore. He is vastly experienced in administration as Director for the Research Centre, Department Head, Departmental Level Advisory and Planning Committee member, and a member of BOS, the Academic Council, University level Audit and Admissions panel. He took the opportunity to study best practices in world-class universities by visiting universities in Hong Kong as part of a leadership exposure visit and interacting with top administrative professionals. In addition, he has 3 years of industrial experience as a Senior Statistical Analyst. Besides being Master of Science and Master of Philosophy, Dr Subramanyam is a full-time research scholar with a PhD in Statistics from Sri Venkateswara University, Tirupati. 26 of his papers have appeared in national and international journals, been indexed in international databases (Scopus, EBSCO, Google Scholar) and UGC approved. He has presented more than 15 research papers at national/international seminars and conferences. He has conducted and attended workshops, symposia, quality improvement programs and faculty development programs. On several occasions, he has been invited to deliver lectures relating to management, social and health sciences.

Mohammad Badruddoza Talukder is an Associate Professor, College of Tourism and Hospitality Management, IUBAT - International University of Business Agriculture and Technology, Dhaka, Bangladesh. He holds PhD in Hotel Management from Lovely Professional University, India. He has been teaching various courses in the Department of Tourism and Hospitality at various universities in Bangladesh since 2008. His research areas include tourism management, hotel management, hospitality management, food & beverage management, and accommodation management, where he has published research papers in well-known journals in Bangladesh and abroad. Mr. Talukder is one of the executive members of the Tourism Educators Association of Bangladesh. He has led training and consulting for a wide range of hospitality organizations in Bangladesh. He just became an honorary facilitator at the Bangladesh Tourism Board's Bangabandhu international tourism and hospitality training institution.

Index

A

Affordable Energy 156, 186, 187
AI-Powered Recruitment 23, 26
and Resource Management 56, 122
Artificial Intelligence 1, 3, 4, 5, 6, 7, 8, 9, 10, 11, 12, 13, 15, 18, 20, 21, 22, 23, 24, 26, 27, 29, 59, 60, 61, 62, 63, 64, 66, 67, 68, 69, 70, 71, 113, 114, 116, 117, 118, 120, 121, 122, 124, 129, 133, 134, 138, 139, 140, 142, 145, 146, 147, 148, 149, 151, 152, 153, 171, 194, 195, 197, 220, 221, 222, 223, 225, 226, 231, 235, 236, 239, 240, 241, 242, 243, 244, 246, 247, 248, 250

B

Biodiversity Conservation 29, 30, 70, 116, 120

C

Carbon Emissions 32, 37, 92, 96, 100, 103, 105, 106, 108, 109, 118, 126, 130, 141, 198, 199, 200, 202, 212, 213, 225, 228, 229, 230, 231, 235, 238, 239, 240, 241, 244, 249
Climate Change 29, 30, 31, 32, 33, 38, 42, 44, 45, 48, 56, 59, 61, 62, 63, 69, 70, 71, 74, 104, 110, 111, 113, 114, 116, 117, 118, 120, 122, 125, 132, 134, 138, 139, 145, 150, 157, 189, 196, 220, 221, 222, 226, 228, 247
Climate Change Mitigation 44, 116, 120, 221
CO2 Emissions 73, 74, 75, 76, 77, 79, 80, 83, 85, 86, 87, 92, 93, 94, 95, 96, 97, 100, 101, 102, 107, 110, 235, 236, 238, 239, 241, 242, 243, 246, 248
Cultural Sensitivity 14, 23, 26, 27

D

Data Governance 129, 130, 131, 132, 139, 142, 153, 198, 200, 211
Diversity and Inclusion 1, 2, 3, 4, 6, 8, 9, 13, 15, 16, 17, 19, 20, 24, 27

E

Economic Growth 73, 74, 76, 77, 78, 79, 80, 92, 93, 94, 95, 96, 97, 100, 101, 102, 106, 108, 109, 111, 114, 154, 156, 160, 230, 232, 235, 238, 239, 240, 241, 246, 248
Energy Efficiency 49, 50, 77, 78, 79, 83, 101, 105, 118, 119, 122, 126, 133, 141, 142, 192, 200, 226, 228, 232, 238, 242, 243, 248
Energy Security 156, 157, 158, 160, 161, 162, 163, 164, 183, 185, 187, 192
Environmental Conservation 113
Environmental Impact 47, 48, 50, 51, 53, 56, 63, 93, 96, 130, 139, 145, 154, 156, 159, 168, 198, 202
Environmental Sustainability 29, 30, 35, 36, 37, 40, 52, 54, 56, 60, 63, 97, 102, 111, 121, 124, 129, 208, 225, 226, 229, 236, 239, 241, 244
Ethical AI 3, 6, 10, 139, 140, 144, 146, 153, 217

F

Fiscal Incentives 102, 158, 225
Fourier-Augmented ARDL 73, 95, 102, 110

G

Global Sustainability 39, 56, 113, 114, 116, 119, 120, 124, 132, 133, 134, 135, 136, 137, 140, 145, 146
Green Hydrogen 156, 159, 160, 161, 162, 163, 164, 165, 166, 167, 168, 170, 171, 172, 173, 174, 175, 176, 177, 178, 183, 184, 185, 186, 187, 188, 189, 190, 191, 194, 195

H

Hospitality 1, 2, 3, 4, 5, 6, 8, 9, 10, 11, 12, 13, 14, 15, 16, 18, 19, 20, 21, 22, 23, 24, 25, 26, 27

I

Inclusive Hospitality Practices 26

M

Machine Learning 4, 7, 8, 10, 29, 34, 37, 38, 46, 59, 62, 66, 114, 117, 118, 120, 121, 125, 126, 127, 139, 140, 149, 150, 152, 194, 203, 211, 212, 217, 218, 221, 222, 228, 246

N

Norway 73, 74, 75, 76, 77, 78, 79, 80, 83, 84, 87, 92, 93, 95, 96, 97, 100, 101, 102, 104, 105, 107, 110

O

OECD 100, 101, 102, 104, 107, 108, 111, 137, 138, 143, 146, 149, 225, 239, 240, 241, 242, 243, 244, 246

P

Panel ARDL 225, 236, 237, 241
Policy Frameworks 79, 104, 185, 198

R

Regulatory Frameworks 119, 130, 146, 208, 219, 225, 243
Renewable Energy 32, 35, 49, 50, 56, 60, 65, 73, 74, 75, 76, 77, 78, 79, 80, 83, 84, 86, 92, 93, 94, 95, 96, 97, 100, 101, 102, 103, 105, 106, 107, 108, 110, 111, 113, 114, 116, 117, 118, 119, 120, 121, 122, 124, 126, 130, 133, 134, 139, 140, 141, 142, 143, 144, 145, 146, 151, 154, 157, 158, 159, 161, 163, 164, 168, 185, 186, 190, 191, 192, 193, 195, 196, 201, 202, 203, 205, 212, 217, 219, 229, 231, 238, 241, 247, 248, 249
Renewable Energy Optimization 113, 119, 121, 145, 154
Resource Availability 194
Resource Efficiency 113, 119, 122, 140, 153, 218

S

Supply Chain Vulnerabilities 161
Sustainable AI 66, 70, 130, 136, 143, 145, 197, 198, 199, 200, 201, 203, 204, 206, 208, 209, 210, 211, 213, 215, 216, 218, 219, 220, 221, 222, 223
Sustainable Development Goals 18, 35, 68, 113, 116, 126, 131, 134, 138, 139, 144, 146, 152, 154, 187, 200, 221, 223, 227, 239, 243, 245
Sustainable Finance 122, 147, 225, 227, 229, 230, 231, 235, 236, 238, 239, 240, 241, 242, 243, 244, 245, 248

T

Technological Innovation 73, 76, 77, 78, 79, 80, 84, 92, 94, 95, 96, 97, 100, 102, 106, 107, 110, 111, 135, 242, 247, 249

www.ingramcontent.com/pod-product-compliance
Lightning Source LLC
LaVergne TN
LVHW080858300926
849162LV00003B/464